The Acid Alkaline Balance Diet

The Acid Alkaline Balance Diet

*An Innovative Program
for Ridding Your Body
of Acidic Wastes*

Felicia Drury Kliment

Contemporary Books

Chicago New York San Francisco Lisbon London Madrid Mexico City
Milan New Delhi San Juan Seoul Singapore Sydney Toronto

Library of Congress Cataloging-in-Publication Data

Kliment, Felicia Drury.
    The acid-alkaline balance diet : an innovative program for ridding your body
of acidic wastes / Felicia Drury Kliment.
        p.   cm.
    Includes bibliographical references and index.
    ISBN 0-658-01695-4
    1. Acid-base imbalances—Diet therapy.   2. Acid-base imbalances—
Complications.   I. Title.

RC630.K565   2002
616.3'992—dc21   2002019076

Contemporary Books
A Division of The McGraw·Hill Companies

10 11 12 13 14 15 DOC/DOC 0 9 8 7 6 5

ISBN 0-658-01695-4

This book was set in Janson
Printed and bound by R. R. Donnelley—Crawfordsville

Cover design by Scott Rattray
Interior design by Hespenheide Design

McGraw-Hill books are available at special quantity discounts to use as premiums and
sales promotions, or for use in corporate training programs. For more information, please
write to the Director of Special Sales, Professional Publishing, McGraw-Hill, Two Penn
Plaza, New York, NY 10121-2298. Or contact your local bookstore.

The information in this book is not intended to be a substitute for the medical advice of
physicians. The reader should consult with his or her doctor in all matters relating to
health. Although every effort has been made to ensure that information is presented
accurately in this book, the ultimate responsibility for proper medical treatment rests with
the physician. Neither the author nor the publisher can be held responsible for errors or
for any consequences arising from the use of information contained here.

This book is printed on acid-free paper.

To Stephen

Pamela and Steve   Jennifer and Sean

Katie and Matthew

The Greatest Family on Earth

To my mother for preparing me for life's challenges, and to my brother Felix for his sense of humor, wit, and style.

CONTENTS

ACKNOWLEDGMENTS

I would like to thank Ray Peat, Ph.D., a pioneer in the field of endocrinology, for his invaluable research and analysis of hormones, and Sang Whang, for his knowledge of the use of far infrared energy in Japan as applied to the treatment of degenerative disease. I am also grateful to Professor Joseph Jiggetts for bringing me into the special education program at City College of the City University of New York and for the research and writing we did together in the field of nutrition.

This book would not have come about without the encouragement of Susan Davis and Claudia McCowan. Claudia's careful and exacting job of editing also contributed to the book. Kathy Keil, my editor at Contemporary Books/McGraw-Hill, was supportive, patient, and, above all, willing to make last-minute, time-consuming changes for the sake of the book's quality. Thanks, too, to Katherine Hinkebein for her diligence in seeing the book through production.

INTRODUCTION

It took me twenty years of researching, writing, and consulting in the field of alternative health before I found the common denominator in all degenerative diseases: acidic wastes. These wastes are largely the by-products of the food we eat. Wherever these wastes accumulate in the body, they cause nearby organs to malfunction and degenerate.

Before I ever became aware that acidic wastes could cause serious health problems, I was devising simple strategies to reduce the acid levels in my body. After a stressful day at work, I would climb into a tub of hot water—unusual for me, as I am a confirmed shower taker—or drink some hot milk. I later learned that hot baths and hot milk reduce excess acidity in the urine, which has a calming effect on the nerves. Another effective remedy I'd use was an ice pack on my upset stomach, which gave me relief within seconds. I read later in the medical journal *Lancet* that cold temperatures stimulate the production of antihistamines, which in turn destroy the histamines that trigger the production of stomach acids.

Yet if you had asked me at the time if high acid levels in the body were dangerous to health, I would have denied it. As well-versed as I was in alternative medicine, my knowledge of hyperacidity was limited to the antacid digestive tablets advertised on television commercials. After all, my mother has had acid indigestion all her life, and she was healthy and vigorous past her eighties. Now I think I know why my mother is still in good shape at ninety-four, living by herself and driving a car. Whenever she has a stomach upset, she uses an old folk remedy handed down from her mother: one-eighth teaspoon each of bicarbonate of soda, spirits of ammonia, and essence of peppermint. The alkalinity of the ammonia and bicarbonate of soda neutralizes the acidic residues in the stomach—the by-products of foods not adequately broken down.

While I was successfully (if unknowingly) treating my own symptoms of acidity, those who had come to me for advice on how to alleviate their health problems were not all so lucky. Some felt no better after they had taken my advice than before. An abundance of health foods, herbs, and vitamins had passed through their bodies and, it seemed, left them untouched. Something was missing.

A Chinese acupuncturist friend gave me an early clue. Aware of the ancient Chinese belief that all living and nonliving things were predominantly yin or yang, I asked her what these opposites actually meant. She answered, "Yin is acid; yang is alkaline." This was exactly what I had learned in chemistry, namely, that all earthly elements were made up of different combinations of acid particles (positively charged protons) and alkaline particles (negatively charged electrons). It is the magnetic attractions and repulsions between these particles that cause atoms to form molecules, molecular chains, and ionic compounds, the building blocks of the body's tissues and fluids. It follows that normal body function depends upon the correct balance of acid and alkaline particles in the blood, lymph, enzymes, urine, and other body fluids. This was the factor that I had overlooked in the health problems of my patients.

I knew that the Chinese treated illness by using yin and yang herbs and acupuncture needles to bring about a balance in the body between these two opposing principles. I had a hunch that I could get even better results in restoring acid-alkaline balance in the body using diet and alkaline particles to rid the body of acidic wastes.

While acid and alkaline substances are both vital to life, acid favors the decomposition of living things, while alkali prevents it. An example of this are the corpses buried in the fourteenth century under the cathedral of Venzone in Italy. Some corpses have remained intact, while others have become skeletons. The dead bodies interred where the underground water contains a high concentration of alkaline-forming lime have become mummified, whereas the flesh of the bodies buried in places where the water is highly acidic has been eaten away by bacteria.[1]

Once I came to understand the destruction that elevated acidic levels in the body could cause, I made the removal of acidic wastes my first priority in restoring health. The client of mine who perhaps benefited most from my new approach to healing was José, a sixteen-year-old student at one of New York City's most competitive academic high schools who had had pains in his abdomen for some time. The doctors couldn't decide whether the pain came from an infected appendix or stones in the gallbladder, so to "play safe," they had both organs surgically removed. Shortly after, José developed systemic lupus erythematosus (SLE), usually referred to as lupus, an autoimmune disease in which the internal organs are destroyed by the body's own immune system. The disease used to be fatal, usually within three years of onset. Now a combination of prednisone and chemotherapy keeps patients alive for a considerable period of time—unless the immune system is strong enough to overcome the toxicity of the chemotherapy and attacks the kidneys.

This is what had happened to José. His immune cells had eaten holes in his kidneys. As a result, his kidneys leaked protein, which pooled in the lower part of the body and in the urine, causing his ankles and feet to swell and turning his urine brown.

José had lost fifty pounds. The doctor could not promise that he would ever be able to return to school, and a foundation that sponsors free trips anywhere in the United States for children with chronic life-threatening diseases paid for a one-week trip to Disney World for José and his family. Because it was obvious to José's mother that he was losing his battle to stay alive, she asked me for help.

Although José had given up all soft drinks on orders from his doctor when he became ill, his lupus indicated that he was suffering the aftereffects of having drunk six to eight bottles of cola a day, starting at the age of seven. Soft drinks, particularly colas, are so acidic that José would have had to drink thirty-two glasses of water to neutralize a single glass of Coke! I started José out on five glasses of alkaline water (see Resources) a day to clear out the acidic wastes that must have accumulated in his body from his soft drink addiction.

After only one week on alkaline water, José began to show signs of improvement. At this point, I recommended two to eight pints daily of freshly squeezed carrot and beet juice to assist the alkaline water in cleaning out his liver. Since the Coumadin (a drug also used as a rat poison) that the doctor had prescribed for a large blood clot in his leg had not dissolved the clot, I had José start taking 200 units of vitamin E a day, gradually increasing the dose to 1,600 units.

Three weeks after his treatment began, José's kidneys stopped leaking, the swelling in his feet and ankles was down, and his blood clot disappeared. José's lupus is now in remission.

José was the first of many individuals I advised who regained their health when the toxic acids that had injured their bodies were removed. The successful outcome of this treatment in the vast majority of cases has led me to believe that the removal of acidic wastes is the prime factor in restoring health to the body.

"Science is built up of facts, as a house is built of stones; but an accumulation of facts is no more a science than a heap of stones is a house."

—*Jules-Henri Poincaré*
    French mathematician, physicist, and philosopher, 1854–1912

PART I

ACIDIC WASTES: THE REAL CULPRIT BEHIND DEGENERATIVE DISEASE

CHAPTER 1

HOW ACIDIC WASTES CAUSE DISEASE

Detoxification is even more important to longevity than good nutrition. French physiologist Alexia Carrell kept pieces of chicken heart tissue alive in a solution containing the same mineral levels found in chicken blood plasma for twenty-eight years.[1] The cells in the tissue stopped dividing and died out when he stopped changing the solution, although he continued to place minerals in the solution in the same amount. The chicken's heart cells, although provided with the necessary raw materials, could not carry on their metabolic activities because the fluid in which they were placed had become filled with acidic wastes.

Scientists have conducted similar experimental research studies with live human cells in the last twenty years. But, unlike Carrell, they have not provided a solution that would keep the cells alive indefinitely. The fluids in which these cells were contained were changed so rarely that one scientist who did a chemical analysis described them as "fetid swamps." Not surprisingly, the human cells divided to form new cells a limited number of times before they died out. This has led researchers to conclude that living cells contain a "death" gene or a hormone secreted from the pituitary gland that triggers the death of the cell after it undergoes a specific number of cell divisions. The conclusion that a death-wielding chemical in the body causes the death of cells by putting an end to their ability to divide and generate new cells implies that there is nothing we can do to prolong life. Carrell's more meticulous experiment gives the lie to this fatalistic attitude, and inspires the hope that human life can be extended well beyond its current limits.

The environment of the human body is not as easily detoxified as the test-tube environment of Carrell's chicken heart tissue. Even so, our bodies do have a built-in detoxifying mechanism in the liver, as well as filtering systems in the kidneys, lymph nodes, and lungs. The liver evolved to handle naturally occurring toxic by-products of foods—for example, the sulfuric and phosphoric acid by-products of sulfur and phosphorus in grains—not artificial chemicals such as flavor enhancers, chemical preservatives, and pesticides. These the liver can't dispose of, so the acidic toxic wastes remain in the body, causing organs to malfunction wherever they settle.

The body, however, does try to place these acids out of harm's way. Keichi Morishita, in his book *The Hidden Truth of Cancer*, writes that when the blood is in danger of becoming too acidic, the acid binds with calcium, an alkaline mineral, and is deposited as far away from the circulating blood as possible.[2] This fact gave me a hint as to why my teeth began growing in middle age. I looked in the mirror one day and noticed that my four upper front teeth, the incisors, had grown—and unevenly. They had also become so sensitive that I couldn't brush them. I had been having acid indigestion with increasing frequency during the same period of time that my teeth grew. Could the acids in my stomach have been encapsulated in the bonelike substance in my front teeth, where they weren't in any danger of acidifying the blood? From then on, I avoided foods that gave me acid indigestion and my teeth soon lost their sensitivity and stopped "growing."

We live in a society where it is almost impossible to avoid altogether eating some chemicalized, processed foods that leave acidic residues. As we age, inevitably, these wastes are calcified and deposited on bone joints and other areas of the skeletal system. By the time most people reach the age of fifty, they have acquired a few enlarged knuckles and calcium spurs in the heel, on the vertebrae, or in muscle tissue. These calcium deposits can be painful, but are not life-threatening.

Acidity and Cardiovascular Disease

Acidic wastes, however, are not always rendered less harmful by being safely entombed in calcium deposits. When the body's acidic load becomes too large, some acid particles remain in the blood. They trigger the onset of cardiovascular disease by making scratches and bumps on the inside walls of arteries and veins. These injuries are "bandaged" over with cholesterol, triglycerides, calcium, and other wastes. Of course, the higher the cholesterol and triglyceride levels, the thicker the "bandage" and the narrower the arteries.

Still, a high cholesterol level is not the underlying cause of hardening of the arteries. Cholesterol and other thick, sticky substances cannot adhere to vessel walls that are smooth. Only after the arterial vessel walls become pitted and scratched by acid particles are fatty plaques able to stick to them.

Narrowed arteries are dangerous for two reasons. Not only can fatty plaques become detached from the walls and travel through the bloodstream to the brain where they cause strokes, they also raise blood pressure. This in turn increases the likelihood of a heart attack. That the injury of arterial walls by acid particles is the major cause of high blood pressure is strongly indicated by the clinical studies of Dr. Kancho Kuninaha, who successfully lowered the blood pressure of many of his patients with alkaline water.[3] (See Resources for information on how to obtain alkaline water.) Normalized blood pressure readings indicated that the arteries had opened up, and the alkaline particles in the water had removed the fatty plaques and acidic wastes from the arterial walls.

Acidity and Cancer

While the health of the cardiovascular system is threatened most by injuries inflicted by acid particles in arteries, the other organs of the body—the liver, pancreas, lungs, and so on—are most likely to degenerate when acidic wastes accumulate in the nearby capillaries that feed them. The acidic wastes thicken the blood, and the coagulated blood cannot carry the quantity of nutrients and oxygen the organs need to function efficiently.

When we refer to the malfunction of organs, we really mean the abnormal functions of the millions of cells that make up the organ. These cells depend, among other things, upon oxygen to manufacture energy and upon amino acids for their repair and regeneration. When the cell is deprived of these substances, it either dies and turns into acidic waste or adapts to the new oxygen- and nutrient-deprived environment by becoming malignant. The cancer cell can live in such an environment for two reasons. First, it obtains its energy from fermentation, a process that is carried on without oxygen. Second, multiplying continually, it grabs the few available nutrients. Normal cells, deprived of nutrients gobbled up by the rapidly multiplying cancer cells, stop dividing and die.

Clearly, the prevention of cancer should begin with removing from the body acidic wastes that turn normal cells into cancerous ones. If an individual is being treated for cancer, the removal of acidic wastes generated by the toxic chemotherapy could prevent a recurrence.

My friend Maureen and I were having lunch together for the first time in three years. I was struck by how healthy and youthful she looked at the age of sixty-five. I asked her to what she attributed her survival from breast cancer surgery some fifteen years before, even though she had been told after the mastectomy of her left breast that her cancer had spread to her lymph glands. She answered, "During the five years I was on chemotherapy, I never took an antinausea pill. Instead, I let myself throw up whenever I needed to." In so doing, Maureen had deprived her cancer cells of the acidic environment in which they thrive.

Acidity and Alcoholism

On the surface, there does not seem to be a connection between cancer and alcoholism—yet the purging of acidic wastes is effective in both cases. In his book *A Monk Swimming: A Memoir*, Malachy McCourt wrote that at the age of seventy-two, after a lifetime of nightly intoxication, he was still healthy thanks to the fact that he "knelt down in the bathroom" after he came home from his nightly binges.[4] By throwing up the acids generated in his digestive tract, McCourt spared his liver the damage it would have sustained from acid aldehyde, the highly toxic by-product of alcohol.

CHAPTER 2

RIDDING YOUR BODY OF ACIDIC WASTES

Some twenty years ago, my husband and I spent a week on the island of Nevis, known to its inhabitants as "the pearl of the Caribbean." It was at that time entirely unspoiled. Hiking along a coastal road that circled the island, we came across a village woman said to be 106 years old. She sat in front of the open door of her hut; before her was a grill. A bubbling sound came from a big frying pan placed on top of it in which she was boiling soft-shell crabs. These crabs and the other seafood she ate daily came directly from the ocean no more than fifty yards from her hut. The rest of her food supplies were even closer at hand. As we looked around at the sloping sides of the valley in which her hut was situated, we noticed rows of squash and other vegetables wedged between tangles of tropical foliage.

The key to her longevity, we suspected, was that she lived her life in accordance with the cycles of nature. The nutrient loss in the foods she ate was minimal, since the fish and plants were alive only minutes before she prepared and ate them. She got her seafood from the fishermen just returned from their early morning fishing expeditions, as they tied their boats to the dock. By raising vegetables in her own "backyard," she satisfied two basic tenets of good health: she ate food that was locally grown and in season. Since the tropical weather enabled her to grow her vegetable garden all year long, she never had to resort to canned or frozen food, thus avoiding the chemical preservatives and nutrient loss characteristic of processed food.

The chance encounter with this ancient but vigorous lady and her organically grown garden in the midst of natural surroundings illustrates the benefits to health achieved by following one's traditional diet and of eating foods plucked fresh from earth and sea. It also points up the contrast to our own lives, which have been damaged by modern agriculture and food preservation methods, as well as a scientific theory that doesn't take into account the detrimental effects of processing and chemical additives in assessing the nutritional value of food.

Acidic and Alkaline Foods

Dr. R. A. Wiley, a physicist, described in his book *Bio Balance* the diets he recommended to individuals with mental disorders, which were composed of either predominantly alkaline or acidic foods, depending on the blood pH of the individual.[1] On the surface, it would seem that such a diet would be helpful in reducing acidic wastes in the body. There are, however, several factors that would indicate otherwise. First, there is a difference of opinion as to which foods are acid forming and which alkaline forming. For example, bananas, avocados, asparagus, artichokes, and spinach are considered by Zen Buddhists to be acid producing, while Western scientists believe them to be alkaline because, when burned, they leave mostly alkaline mineral ashes. Second, the fact is that many acid-forming vegetables are very effective cleansers of the body's acidic wastes. The juice of carrots and beets, with their high percentage of acid-forming sulphur and phosphorus, effectively clean out the acidic wastes from the liver, kidneys, and bladder. The juice of cabbage, high in acidic chlorine and sulfur, cleanses the acid wastes adhering to the mucous membranes of the stomach and intestinal tract. An excellent remedy for gum disease and infections in general is the highly acidic vitamin C. Alkaline minerals are also effective cleansers. Potassium, calcium, sodium, and magnesium in dandelions, endive, and lettuce reduce hyperacidity in all the organs of the body. Indeed, acid and alkaline minerals act together to cleanse the body, just as a combined solution of vinegar (acid) and bicarbonate of soda (alkaline) makes an excellent household cleaner.

It is necessary then to make a distinction between acids that are toxic and cause the body's organs to degenerate and those that rid the body of acidic wastes and, by doing so, prevent degenerative disease. We cannot just assume that foods high in acid-forming minerals will add to the store of acidic wastes in the body and therefore must be avoided.

Proof that an acidic diet does not threaten the blood's pH factor nor cause degenerative disease is that several populations known for their longevity have predominantly acidic diets. One example is the macrobiotic diet developed by Dr. Sagen Ishizuka in the latter half of the nineteenth century to cure his kidney disease, which Western medicine had failed to do. Although it is based on the concept of balancing opposites—yin (acid) and yang (alkaline)—the dietary staple of the macrobiotic diet is brown rice, which contains a high level of acid-forming phosphorus.

Dr. Weston Price, an American dentist, traveled during the 1930s in Africa, the outback of Australia, and the Arctic, and studied the relationship between diet and health in the tribes in these regions, which still followed the traditional diets of their forefathers.[2] He found these people to be in robust health, free of cardiovascular disease and cancer, even though their diets were higher in acidic particles than alkaline ones.

Thus it seems that an alkaline diet is not necessary either for the maintenance of health or for a normal 7.4 alkaline pH blood plasma. Normalizing acid-alkaline balance in the blood should not be the basis for working out a diet for two more reasons: First, clusters of acidic, toxic wastes in various parts of the body don't necessarily raise acid blood levels. It is therefore doubtful that balancing the acid-alkaline blood pH through diet would make any inroads into concentrations of acidic wastes located in the intercellular fluids or in blood capillaries far from major blood supplies. Second, the amount of enzymes, bile, hydrochloric acid, and other metabolites the body manufactures for the breakdown of nutrients is not determined by the acid-alkaline blood pH, but by the particular foods that sustained the individual's ancestors for thousands of years.

The Ancestral Diet

The best way to present the digestive system with the kinds of food molecules it is capable of breaking down is for each person to eat the same kind of dietary staple as his or her ancestors. Individuals whose ancestors were primarily meat eaters should make meat the staple of their diet. Those whose ancestors ate a lot of fish as well as meat should eat fish two or three times a week, while individuals of Asian descent benefit from following the grain-eating traditions of their cultures. The fact is that nutrients not part of a person's cultural heritage are incompatible with that individual's biochemistry. Indeed, Solomon Katz of the University of Pennsylvania has proved in his research that people's genetic makeup is shaped by their food practices.[3] A case in point are the U.S. immigrants from India who have experienced a sharp increase in heart disease because they eat meat instead of grains, the mainstay of the diet in India.[4] Not all individuals, however, have the same metabolism as their ancestors. Many people are of mixed descent, and there are variations in individual metabolisms within any given population cluster. Fortunately, a simple, self-administered test (given later in this chapter) can determine whether you have a grain-eating or meat-eating metabolism or whether your digestive apparatus can handle both dietary staples.

During the earlier part of the twentieth century in the United States, the general public viewed health in relation to nutrition either in terms of providing food for the hungry or, for those who had enough to eat, the balanced meal. This was a meal in which the three food groups— protein, carbohydrates, and fats—were represented. Textbooks typically described food according to food type, weight in grams, and calories. The implication was that the processing of foods and chemical additives did not affect nutritional quality. In the 1960s on the wall of my doctor's office was a poster featuring the ideal dinner plate—a lamb chop, mashed potatoes swimming in butter, some corn (canned), a slice of white bread with a pat of butter, a glass of milk, and canned fruit and a cookie for dessert.

The sacred aura surrounding the balanced meal dimmed somewhat when mainstream medicine began to take notice of statistical research studies done in the 1950s that showed that during World War II, Europeans, deprived of butter and fatty meat, were less apt to develop cardiovascular disease than before the war—in fact subsequent studies showed they died of such infectious diseases as tuberculosis before they were old enough to develop hardened arteries. A healthy diet was now considered to be one in which polyunsaturated oils replaced animal and dairy fats—even though studies had long linked polyunsaturates with cancer.[5]

By the 1980s the medical establishment began advocating fruits and vegetables because studies showed they prevented degenerative disease. The research studies were undertaken largely in response to the public's interest in the subject and its huge expenditures on organically grown produce and whole grains.

While Dr. Weston Price equated good health with natural foods such as raw milk and butter, fresh produce, and whole grain flour, Dr. Roger J. Williams, a biochemist who did his research studies around the middle of the twentieth century, viewed nutrition in terms of the nutrients that make up food: amino acids, vitamins, and minerals. But breaking up food into its component parts is the only similarity between Williams and the mainstream medical establishment. Williams was revolutionary in his assertions that cellular malnutrition, rather than bacteria and viruses, was the major cause of disease. He backed up his theory with his research on yeast cells, which showed that the efficiency with which a cell carried out its metabolic activities is determined by the nourishment it receives.[6] He found further that cells die off not only because they don't get everything they need, but also because they are poisoned by chemical additives.

Williams not only brought to light the error in the thinking of doctors and nutritionists that good nutrition as a disease preventative meant eating adequate amounts of protein, carbohydrates, fats, and sugar without regard to vitamin and mineral content; he also pointed up individual differences in the size and shape of organs, even the microscopic organs (organelles) within the body's cells. He concluded that these structural differences were inherited, and along with diet had a profound effect on physical and mental health. Williams, then, recognized two biological truths that continue to be given short shrift by the medical establishment: the needs of the body's metabolic machinery for quantities of vitamins, minerals, and amino acids that cannot be obtained from processed foods, and the connection between variability in organ structure and function and the individual's state of health. He also came to the conclusion that individuals who are susceptible to disease have, because of their biochemical individuality, distinctive patterns of nutritional needs.

Williams, however, did not explore this issue further. He simply hypothesized that the nutritional requirements of individuals were determined by either susceptibility or resistance to disease. When Williams conducted his research (the 1940s through the 1960s), little information was available on individual differences in metabolism and how they determine dietary requirements. As a result Williams viewed diet only from the perspective of disease prevention and treatment. For example, he recommended the I. M. Stillman diet for anyone who was overweight (lean meat, poultry, fish, seafood, cottage cheese, low dessert, and almost no carbohydrates and fat) without regard to individual differences in body structure and biochemistry.

Dr. Max Gerson, an immigrant from Nazi Germany, used diet and detoxification in the 1940s and 1950s to heal advanced cancers. In his book *A Cancer Therapy*, Gerson described fifty "terminal" cancer cases that he cured.[7] Like Williams, he recommended a single diet for the cure and prevention of illness. He stated that 75 percent of the diet should consist of fresh raw, juiced, or stewed fruits and vegetables that "contain all the necessary nutritional substances in their proper quantity, mixture, and composition." (Gerson's daughter, Charlotte Gerson Straus, founded the Gerson Institute in 1978 to ensure continuing research in the Gerson therapy treatment.)

In the 1970s Dr. William Donald Kelley, a dentist, and his associate, William L. Wolcott, formulated the theory that individual variation in autonomic nervous system function created different food metabolisms. The nerves of the autonomic nervous system, which extend from the brain through the spinal cord, and from there to the organs, are composed of two branches, the parasympathetic and sympathetic, each regulating a different set of organ systems. The parasympathetic nerves ensure the survival of the internal body environment by accelerating the processes of digestion and assimilation of food, and the repair and rebuilding of body cells. The sympathetic nerves, on the other hand, protect the body from danger in the environment outside the body by speeding up the flow of hormones from the thyroid, adrenals, and pituitary. This makes the heart beat faster, the blood circulate more rapidly, and more oxygen to flow into the lungs, actions that speed up the thought processes and supply the body with bursts of energy needed in earlier times for fighting, hunting, and outmaneuvering enemies. The sympathetic and parasympathetic, however, not only speed up the functions of the organs over which each has control, but act as a brake on the other half of the autonomic nervous system by slowing its actions.

One reason why these two halves of the autonomic nervous system act in opposite ways is because their acid-alkaline ratios are different. The parasympathetic nerves are predominantly alkaline while the sympathetic nerves are more acidic. When the acid-alkaline balance between these two nerve branches is normal it keeps the metabolic functions in balance. But when it is out of kilter, one of the halves of the autonomic nervous system exerts too much control over the other half. As a result, some organs function at too great a speed while others function too slowly. In a few individuals, however, the parasympathetic and sympathetic nerves regulate organ function at about the same rate. This variation in autonomic nervous system function creates three different metabolic types: the balanced metabolism, the parasympathetic dominant, and the sympathetic dominant, each with its own nutritional needs.

Kelley's theory on metabolic food typing was built primarily on the research of Emanuel Revici, M.D., and George Watson, Ph.D., both of whom held that the imbalance of certain cellular functions was the cause of disease. Revici believed that in some individuals the regeneration (anabolism) and breakdown (catabolism) of cells don't proceed at the same rate. When this disparity occurs, according to Revici, cellular membranes deteriorate, making it possible for cancer and AIDS viruses to enter cells through tears and holes in cellular membranes. He uses injections of fatty acid molecular chains to heal damaged cell membranes and to bring about an equilibrium between anabolic/catabolic function. Revici's intervention has cured an impressive number of cancer and AIDS cases. Watson based his metabolic classification on the rate at which cells oxidize (burn food for energy). He believed that in some people the cells burn food too fast while in others cells oxidize food too slowly and that either imbalance, if too pronounced, can cause mental disorders. He used diet and nutritional supplements to normalize oxidation in order to heal such mental illnesses as chronic depression, bipolar disorder, hyperactivity, and obsessive compulsive disorders.

Watson's and Revici's theories on the relationship between imbalances in cellular metabolism and disease fit neatly into Kelley's metabolic typing theory based on the imbalance of the autonomic nervous system. To take one example, an individual who is parasympathetic dominant is usually also overactive in terms of generating new cells (according to Revici) and burning up fuel (according to Watson). Thus a diet designed to bring about a better balance between the parasympathetic and sympathetic nerve branches also normalizes the speed of oxidation and the regeneration and death (anabolism/catabolism) of cells. In other words, balancing the autonomic nervous system takes care of both the cellular malfunctions that Revici and Watson contend are the underlying cause of disease.

The Metabolic-Type Diet

Kelley reversed the course of many chronic diseases, including cancer, by lessening the disparity between the rate at which the parasympathetic and sympathetic nerves use up fuel. His choice of diets and nutritional supplements were made on this basis. Since parasympathetic dominant individuals are fast oxidizers, Kelley says they should eat foods such as beef, lamb, pork, and venison because the body burns them up slowly, forcing the parasympathetic nerves to slow the rate at which they normally use up energy. The result is a better balance between the oxidation rate of the parasympathetic and sympathetic halves of the autonomic nervous system—and by extension the rate at which organs controlled by the parasympathetic and sympathetic nerve branches function.

For those who are slow oxidizers, that is, sympathetic dominant, Kelley recommends grains as the dietary staple, because they are broken down fast, forcing the parasympathetic nerves to accelerate their slow oxidation rate (expenditure of energy). Those individuals whose parasympathetic and sympathetic nerve branches are balanced can eat either meat or grain. There is some variation within each of the three metabolic types.

Another method for individualizing diet is based on blood type. Dr. Peter J. D'Adamo, N.D., and his father, also a naturopath, postulated that blood type O, the oldest blood type, developed in response to the meat diet of the hunter/gatherer before the cultivation of grains began in various parts of the world between nine thousand and eleven thousand years ago. Type O individuals, like their meat-eating ancestors, according to D'Adamo, need large amounts of meat and small quantities of carbohydrates. In fact, type O individuals with their high levels of stomach acids needed for breaking down meat, tendency toward an underactive thyroid, and need for vigorous exercise fit the profile of Kelly's parasympathetic dominant metabolic type. (Kelley, however, recommends meat, fat, and butter for the parasympathetic dominant, whereas D'Adamo suggests lean meat for individuals with blood type O.)

Blood type A, according to D'Adamo, represents an adaptation to the cultivation of grains. Blood type A's need for grains and light exercise, and its slow oxidation rate, fit the profile of the sympathetic dominant. Blood type B, D'Adamo states, evolved as a result of the migration of tribes to colder climates. It would also seem to have come about as a result of an adaptation to dairy products and could explain why so many Asian Indians who have a long history of drinking cow's milk have blood type B.

THE METABOLIC-TYPE TEST

Kelley determined metabolic type by having his patients answer hundreds of questions in a bound book, but he also used a simpler test that works just as well:

➤ Swallow fifty milligrams of niacin on an empty stomach. If, within a half-hour, your skin turns red and you feel very, very hot and itchy, you have a meat-eating metabolism. If you feel warmer and have a better color in your face, then you have a balanced metabolism. If you don't feel anything, then you have a grain-eating metabolism.

> ➤ If you want to confirm the first test, take eight grams of vitamin C a day for three days in a row. If you feel depressed, lethargic, exhausted, and irritable, or if you are a woman and experience vaginal irritation, then you have a meat-eating metabolism. If you don't notice any change at all, you have a balanced metabolism. But if you feel an improvement—more energy, better quality of sleep—then you have a grain-eating metabolism.

Source: Adapted from *Healthview* newsletter, November 1977.

Just as the victorious army in a battle is usually the one with the most ammunition and foot soldiers, so the dominant half of the autonomic nervous system tends to have the greater supply of nutrients. By accommodating your diet to your metabolic type (parasympathetic or sympathetic dominant), you can reduce the excessive nutrient levels of the dominant nerves in your autonomic nervous system and at the same time build up a supply of nutrients that will speed up the underactive half. A better balanced autonomic nervous system will reduce the acidic wastes that sluggish organ function leaves behind.

Nutrition for the Meat Eater

If you are parasympathetic dominant and therefore a fast oxidizer, you have large quantities of acid for the digestion of meat. In that case you should limit your intake of such acidic nutrients as vitamin C, lemon juice, and vinegar so as not to speed up your already too rapid digestion of protein. You also have high levels of potassium in relation to calcium and so should eat very little fruit and limit the amount of green leafy vegetables in your diet since these foods have high potassium levels. Generous amounts of calcium will also help bring potassium levels into better balance. Vitamins that use up fuel quickly, thereby speeding up the meat eater's already too rapid oxidation rate are B_1, B_2, B_3 in the form of niacin, and B_6, so limit the intake of these vitamins to fifty milligrams each daily.

Nutritional supplements and foods that are slow oxidizers are beneficial because they slow down your fast oxidation rate. This includes peas, green beans, cauliflower, and root vegetables with the exception of potatoes, which are digested quickly, as well as the nutrients phosphorus, B_3 in the form of niacinamide, inositol, choline, pantothenic acid, and B_{15}.

Nutrition for the Grain Eater

If you are a grain eater (sympathetic dominant), and therefore a slow oxidizer, you should eat sparingly of the foods recommended for the parasympathetic dominant, since these will slow down your oxidation rate even more. On the other hand, eat generous portions of the foods that the parasympathetic dominant should eat very little of. Besides grains, the sympathetic dominant does well on fowl and fish. Generous amounts of potassium will help balance the high calcium levels of the sympathetic dominant and speed up the burning of fuels; as will the fast oxidizing nutrients niacin, magnesium, folic acid, and vitamin C. Unlike the parasympathetic dominant, the sympathetic dominant can eat generous amounts of green leafy vegetables, fruit, broccoli, potatoes, and onions. Slow oxidizing nutrients recommended for the parasympathetic dominant such as choline and B_{15} should be taken in limited amounts by the sympathetic dominant individual.

By balancing the two halves of the autonomic nervous system, sluggish organs pick up speed and are thereby able to eliminate acidic waste accumulations, the underlying cause of autonomic nervous system imbalance.

Food Allergies

Finding your metabolic type and following up with an appropriate diet doesn't always do away with health problems because it's possible to be allergic to foods even though they're suited to your metabolic type. For example, I'm allergic to calcium and most of the B vitamins, as well as carrot juice, all food items recommended for the parasympathetic dominant nervous system.

THE PULSE TEST

Find out the normal range of your pulse rate by taking your pulse for one week before rising (while lying down), just before each meal, and again before going to bed. To take your pulse, place the first two fingers of the right hand on the wrist. Use a watch or clock with a second hand. Wait until the second hand reaches sixty, then count the beats until the second hand has returned to sixty (one minute). If you have any problems taking your pulse, use a blood pressure device that also measures pulse rate. If your highest pulse count every day for a week is not over eighty-four and if it is the same each day, you probably don't have any allergies.

When you are ready to test for allergies, test one food at a time—for example a banana, oatmeal, or a plain slice of bread. Take your pulse just before eating, one-half hour after eating, and one hour after that. Don't eat anything the night before you begin testing for foods. If you are a smoker, don't smoke while you are testing your pulse for allergies.

Coca is vague about the number of beats above the normal rate that indicates an allergy. I have found that if your pulse one-half hour after eating a single food is four to five beats higher than before eating, you're having an allergic reaction to that particular food.

From my experience, blood pressure readings in individuals over fifty are just as accurate a test for allergies as the pulse test and easier to measure, especially if you take your blood pressure with an electrical device. (Don't use a battery-run blood pressure machine, however, because it gives inaccurate readings when the battery is running down.) A blood pressure reading taken one-half hour after eating that is over 135/85 is a good indication of a food allergy. The higher the blood pressure reading—like the more accelerated the pulse rate—the more allergic you are to the food you are testing.

One method for detecting allergies is the pulse test. Dr. Arthur Coca discovered that food allergies increase the pulse when he noticed that whenever his wife ate certain foods she had an angina attack and her pulse raced. His wife's heart problems disappeared after she eliminated those foods that increased her pulse rate.

In the course of using the pulse test to uncover food allergies, Coca discovered that a whole range of illnesses including migraine headaches, epilepsy, obesity, ulcers, emotional problems, hypertension, asthma, and diabetes could be caused by food allergies because, after eliminating allergy-causing foods, these health problems usually disappeared.

One of the most impressive cures through food allergy prevention was that of a multiple sclerosis (MS) patient of Dr. Milo G. Meyer of Michigan City, Indiana.[8] This MS victim, a young man, smoked non-stop all day. He was already badly crippled; he was not able to negotiate the stairs or hold up a baseball bat. After smoking, his pulse rate zoomed upward from sixty-eight to ninety-two beats per minute. This convinced him to give up smoking. Five days after he had done so, he could play baseball with his son and go up and down the stairs without holding the banister. This man's complete recovery from MS—four years later he was still free of the disease—is not an isolated success story. A report by Coca and Meyer describes the elimination of MS in fourteen of fifteen cases by an antiallergy program.

Even if you haven't been diagnosed with a health problem but have such "minor" symptoms as fatigue, sleeplessness, mild indigestion, dry eyes, constipation, headaches, or restlessness, you should test yourself for food allergies, particularly those foods that you eat most often since these are the ones you are most likely to have developed a reaction to.

The Four-Day Rotation Diet

While an increased pulse rate after eating reveals what foods your immune system reacts against, it doesn't indicate maladaptive food reactions due to deficiencies in digestive juices: enzymes, hydrochloric acid, bile, and/or juices produced by the intestinal flora. For such individuals, Theron Randolph's four-day rotation diet works well, because, with no single food eaten more than once every five days, digestive enzymes involved in the breakdown of a particular food have a chance to build up. In the rotation diet even fats and oils are rotated. For example, butter on day one, olive oil on day two, the third day coconut oil, and on the fourth, grapeseed oil. On the fifth day the cycle starts all over again. You go back to butter as well as all the other food items listed for day one.

Before you start the four-day rotation diet, give up caffeine, alcohol, and cigarettes, and for the first three months avoid those foods you eat twice or more a week since they can be assumed to cause an allergic reaction. Dr. William Philpott, a neurologist who specializes in magnets, is so enthusiastic about the four-day rotation diet that when people call him to order magnets, before he takes their order he urges them to go on this diet. Philpott himself is one of its beneficiaries. According to his wife he is healthier at age eighty-five than he was at fifty—before he went on the rotation diet that cured him of Type II diabetes and arthritis.

The Randolph diet is especially effective in reversing the course of Type II diabetes because it usually strikes people fifty or older who are deficient in digestive juices. In such individuals, digestion slows down, leaving undigested food particles that turn into acidic waste. These find their way into the blood and lymph vessels that feed the insulin-producing glands—the islet of Langerhans—in the pancreas. As these vessels become clogged with waste, they block the transport of insulin from the pancreas to the blood. Lack of insulin in the blood means that sugar doesn't get burned up, so that blood sugar levels become elevated and produce diabetic symptoms. In a diet like Theron Randolph's, in which a food is eaten only once every five days, it is speedily digested, leaving very little acidic waste to cause mischief, because there are enough digestive juices to effect the complete breakdown of the food.

The four-day rotation diet works best for individuals who build up acidic wastes because of digestive juice deficiencies. However, it is less effective in cases where degenerative disease is caused by allergic reactions. Multiple sclerosis, the deterioration of the myelin sheathing on the nerve cells, is an example of a disease in which maladaptive reaction to foods is nearly always caused by allergies. That's because it usually strikes individuals in their thirties—at an age when most individuals still have sufficient food enzyme levels. Thus the first step in the program to reverse the course of MS should be allergy testing. If this doesn't work the four-day rotation diet should be tried.

Not everyone is able to solve a health problem by avoiding foods they don't digest properly or by going on the four-day rotation diet. The Greeks believed in the rejuvenating effects of purging; the type of evacuation depending on the season. Hippocrates, the most celebrated physician of ancient Greece, extolled the health benefits of regurgitation. He wrote, "If what must be cleansed from the body is the kind that may be evacuated by voluntary bowel movements and vomiting, it is beneficial and easy to endure." Hippocrates recommended colonics during the summer because the heat made the body bilious, causing heaviness in the lumbar region and knees. During the six winter months, however, he believed that vomiting should be used to rid the body of phlegm lodged in the upper part of the body.

Enzymes

Even before Dr. Kelley devised individual diet plans according to metabolic type, like Max Gerson he had accomplished a significant number of cancer cures by putting all his patients on the same diet—I knew two of his patients whom he had successfully treated with a standard diet: an elderly lady, considered terminally ill with lung cancer, and an airline pilot who had a recurrence of liver cancer. The success of Kelley's and Gerson's diets is due to their providing the maximum possible amount of enzymes. Gerson and Kelley not only prescribed lots of pancreatic enzyme supplements with meals, they made solid and juiced vegetables and fruit eaten raw to preserve their enzyme content the cornerstone of their diet regimen. In doing so, they revived a practice based on the discovery of a nineteenth-century Scottish embryologist, Dr. John Beard, who developed the theory based on his research studies that pancreatic enzymes could destroy cancer cells. Dr. Nicholas

Gonzalez, M.D., in an interview in the March–April 2000 issue of *New Life* magazine, stated that in the 1920s a number of physicians in the United States and Europe successfully used enzyme treatment for cancer.[9] With the discovery of radiation, however, Beard's enzyme protocol was forgotten.

The emphasis on raw fruit and vegetables worked to the advantage of Kelley's and Gerson's cancer patients for several reasons. First, by supplying the digestive system with food enzymes, the enzyme manufacturing apparatus in the pancreas was free to produce the kinds of enzymes needed to kill off cancer cells. Second, large quantities of low-calorie fruit and vegetables must be eaten to satisfy hunger. This results in the intake of large quantities of nutrients. Third, solid fruit and fruit and vegetable juice detoxify the liver and neutralize the acidic-waste filled fluid that cancer cells feed on.

But fruit and vegetables are low in calories and so they have correspondingly low enzyme levels. They are nevertheless the best source of enzymes for cancer patients who can't eat large quantities of raw meat, dairy products, and raw, unfiltered honey, which are rich in enzymes. Individuals with other chronic diseases, however, can benefit from them.

When my maternal grandfather was an engineering student at the University of Berlin, he developed indigestion. He undertook a cure by eating nothing but raw beef (steak tartare) for several months and had no more stomach problems afterwards. Until the end of his life, my grandfather made what he referred to as scraped meat once a week. He used round steak because of its low fat content, and scraped the meat from the fiber with his hunting knife. He then added the yolk of a raw egg to the mixture and spread it on buttered brown bread topped with raw onions. The raw beef cured my grandfather's indigestion by supplying his digestive system with the food-digesting enzymes that the overworked, malfunctioning enzyme-production machinery in his pancreas was not producing in sufficient quantities. The raw beef cure was not my grandfather's idea. At the time he was a young man living in Germany, physicians understood that raw foods had healing properties and used them as therapeutic agents to cure disease.

In 1930, the German government passed legislation to the effect that honey was not to be sold for table use unless it contained the starch-digesting enzyme amylase. The Netherlands passed a similar law in 1925. In the United States there has never been a law prohibiting the removal of amylase from honey. One might expect brands of honey sold in health food stores to contain amylase, but most of this honey is clear, an indication that the pollen in which amylase is found has been filtered out. An exception is a brand of honey called Really Raw. Its thick, opaque quality substantiates the ingredients it lists on the label: pollen as well as propolis (the glue the worker bees use to repair the hive) and royal jelly, which the worker bees feed to the queen bee to extend her life span from a few weeks—the life span of the other female bees—to as long as ten years.

While honey is the best source of the starch-digesting enzyme amylase, the raw cow's milk cheese sold in many health food stores is a rich source of the fat-digesting enzyme lipase and protease, a protein-digesting enzyme. Organic Valley is one such brand. The high fat content of cheese, however, makes it wise to follow the old folk adage of the cheese-loving Dutch: "At breakfast, cheese is gold, at lunch it is silver, and at dinner it is lead." Eating this high-fat dairy product in the morning and at noon, but not in the evening, agrees with the digestive process. In the daytime the body digests and absorbs food quickly, but in the evening and at night these processes slow down. Blood flows more slowly, so the fat particles in the blood are more likely to remain undigested and turn into acidic waste.

It is very difficult to find raw butter, but the same company that makes raw milk cheese, Organic Valley, makes the next best thing—unsalted, cultured butter. Live cultures are added to the churning cream and allowed to ferment for a minimum of sixteen hours.

It was common for physicians in the early part of the twentieth century to use raw milk and butter made from raw milk for therapeutic purposes. Raw milk has a cortisone-like factor that prevents stiffness in the joints.[10] It was also used by physicians to alleviate the symptoms of diabetes until insulin came into use. Federal and state laws requiring pasteurization of dairy products, however, make raw milk almost impossible to come by. But one organic milk farm at least avoids pasteurizing its milk at high heat. Louis Pasteur discovered that milk heated to 140 degrees for one-half hour was enough to kill bacteria. Port Madison Goat's milk farm in the Seattle area follows this procedure to preserve some of the enzymes in the milk. Their baby goats thrive on goat's milk heated at 140 degrees but get sick if the milk is heated to 160 degrees. Given the deterioration in health of newborn goats who are fed milk just 20 degrees hotter than Pasteur's infection preventive 140 degrees, how healthy could it be for human babies to be fed milk steam heated at the boiling temperature of 212 degrees? This is the temperature at which the agribusiness dairies heat their milk.

At this temperature practically all the nutrients in the milk are destroyed as well as the acidity needed to break down the calcium. The purpose of boiling the milk at 212 degrees is not to keep the public safe from bacteria that causes disease but to extend the shelf life of the product. The law, which requires pasteurization of milk to kill off disease-causing bacteria, should prohibit the heating of milk for purposes that have nothing to do with the prevention of infectious disease. I buy a brand of organic milk called Organic Life because it hasn't been heated to such a high temperature that all the enzymes have been destroyed. I know this because if I don't use it up in two days it spoils. A brand of milk that seems to last forever in the refrigerator, even if it is labeled organic, should be avoided.

Fats and Oils

Most doctors recommend that only 10 to 15 percent of the diet consist of fat because they believe it to be a major contributing factor in the development of degenerative diseases, including colon and rectal cancer, the second leading causes of cancer-related deaths in the United States. It was therefore a shock to the medical community when two studies involving thousands of individuals indicated that a low-fat, high-fiber diet did not reduce the incidence of colon cancer.[11]

These studies assumed that a low-fat diet, like a high-fiber one, is a colon and rectal cancer preventative—based on the erroneous assumption that a high-fat diet is conducive to the development of cancer. A study found that women on a low-fat diet had the same rate of breast cancer as women who consumed large quantities of fat.[12] What isn't considered is the fact that soluble fibers cannot neutralize carcinogens unless they are first absorbed by fat present in the colon. It seems likely therefore that the low-fat, high-fiber diet didn't reduce colon cancer because there was not enough fat to absorb the carcinogenic substances in the intestines.

High-fat diets have also been linked to cardiovascular disease because it is assumed that the fat the body doesn't need sticks to the walls of arteries and hardens them. In fact, fatty cholesterol adheres to arterial walls because these walls have already sustained injuries. The layering of fat over inflamed, scratched, and bruised vessel walls in the arteries is simply a response mechanism, designed to protect the arteries from further damage.

One of the more likely causes of artery deterioration was revealed in a study done in 1972 at the University of Hawaii with pigs as subjects. Eighty-five percent of the pigs fed high levels of sugar developed heart disease, while the pigs fed a diet in which 10 percent of the sugar was replaced by coconut oil or beef tallow retained normal heart function. It seems that the small percentage of fat fed to the pigs actually protected their arteries from the sharp, acidic crystals of sugar.

Fat is one of the basic food types, along with carbohydrates and protein, that the body requires to sustain itself. The body itself has a high fat content. Aside from water, there is more fat in the body than any other substance. Cellular membranes that surround the cytoplasm of each cell are made up almost entirely of fatty acid (the form of fat into which the fat we eat is broken down), and the brain is more than 60 percent fatty acid. Moreover, fatty acids, along with protein (in the form of amino acids) play a vital role in the manufacture of energy. Transportation of oxygen by the red blood cells would not be possible without the fatty acid and protein membrane of the red blood cell through which oxygen gains entry into the cell.

There is evidence that too little fat is harmful to the body. When Max Gerson began using nutrition to treat cancer, the diet he recommended contained only fats and oils that were intrinsic to the food.

Later on he included fat and oil supplements and got a better rate of recovery. Mental as well as physical health is dependent upon the consumption of enough fats and oils. This is shown in studies in which children with emotional disorders who were put on a low-fat diet became more aggressive and violent.[13]

Given the role of fat in the production of cellular energy, in blood clotting, in the production of hormones and bile, and in immune system function, a more realistic ratio of fat in relation to the other food types in the diet is 25 to 30 percent. Establishing the minimum daily fat requirement leads to the next problem, namely, the kinds of fat the body needs. Cellular membranes contain saturated, monounsaturated, and polyunsaturated fats; while the brain structure is made up of a mix of saturated and polyunsaturated fats of the omega-3, docosahexaenoic acid (DHA), and omega-6, arachidonic acid (AA) families.

Not only does the wide range of fatty acids in the body point out the variety of fats we should eat to satisfy the body's fat requirements, the fatty acid requirements of the brain—one part omega-3 oils (found in saltwater fish, green leafy vegetables, and eggs) to four parts omega-6 fats (found in meat and polyunsaturated oils such as corn and safflower oil)—indicate the types and quantities of fat and oil with which the brain should be supplied.

In the last seventy-five years, however, people have been eating far more meat, margarine, and omega-6 oils like corn, safflower, and cottonseed oil than they have fish and green leafy vegetables which contain omega-3 oils. These dietary changes have thrown the four-to-one ratio of omega-6 and omega-3 oils in the brain out of kilter. Given this drastic change, scientists estimate that the brain is now made up of thirty times more omega-6 than omega-3 oils.

Fats and Oils for the Meat Eater

Do deficiencies in omega-3 oils due to the overeating of meat fat and corn, safflower, and cottonseed oils indicate that everyone should eat large quantities of green, leafy vegetables and saltwater fish and also curb their consumption of meat and polyunsaturated oils? It depends on your metabolic type. If you have a meat-eating metabolism, a diet heavy in meat is healthy, unless the meat you buy is from agribusiness livestock. As a meat eater, you are limited in the amount of green leafy vegetables (omega-3) you can eat. But you can eat saltwater fish and avoid corn, safflower, and cottonseed oils so as not to raise omega-6 fatty acid levels in the brain.

Fats and Oils for the Grain Eater

It's easier for the grain-eating metabolic type to balance omega-6 and omega-3 fatty acids, since grain eaters thrive on large amounts of green, leafy vegetables. Fish is also particularly compatible with the grain eater's metabolism. Like the meat eater, the grain eater should avoid corn, safflower, and cottonseed oils not only because of the omega-6 overload in the brain, but also because they give off toxic lipid peroxides. Studies show an increase in the rate of cancer among heavy users of these polyunsaturated vegetable oils. Long-chain oils were less of a problem before grains were refined because the vitamin E in whole grains helps neutralize the toxins generated by polyunsaturated oils as the body breaks them down into fatty acids.

Margarine and mayonnaise should be avoided because they are made of oils that have been hydrogenated. During the process of hydrogenation all the nutrients are removed from the oil. As a result, the digestive system must rob the body of its own store of nutrients to break down the empty calories in the hydrogenated fat. Hydrogenation also leaves in the oils trace amounts of aluminum and nickel, which may find their way into the brain and contribute to the development of Alzheimer's disease.

Rancid fats and oils are another major problem. Hamburgers, french fries, and doughnuts sold in fast food restaurants and stores are cooked at temperatures so high that the structure of their fat molecules is altered. They become rigid and elongated. These misshapen molecules, when eaten and absorbed into the body's cellular membranes (the walls of cells), stiffen them. Some scientists believe this could give rise to emotional problems and learning disabilities in children because rigid cell membranes could interfere with the transmission of thoughts between brain cells.

Trans fats, which come about when hydrogenation alters the molecular structure of fatty acid into the trans fat configuration, and rancid fats should clearly be avoided. But as far as other fats and oils are concerned, it's not so easy to label them either good or bad. For example, if you take vitamin E supplements when you eat polyunsaturated vegetable oils, they lose most of their toxicity. Another example of a very healthy oil that under certain conditions can become toxic is the oil in fish. To make fish oil available to the body and to prevent it from becoming toxic, short-chain fat molecules are needed to break up its long molecular chains. Short-chained fats and oils act like scissors, cutting up the long chains of fat molecules in fish oil into pieces that are small enough to be absorbed through cell membranes. Butter is good for this purpose because it contains short chains of butyric fatty acid. The short molecular chains in butter are also beneficial because they are burned up rather than stored as fat.

The medium molecular chains in coconut oil can also break up the long-chained molecules in fish oil. It's because of these medium chains that coconut oil is burned up, which makes it good for weight loss as well as a source of energy. Coconut oil also keeps the energy-producing factories in the cells—the mitochondria—in good repair and can be heated to a very high temperature without becoming toxic. According to the chemist Ray Peat, Ph.D., coconut oil is a very effective cancer preventive. People have a hard time believing that coconut oil has so many health benefits when it is supersaturated. But a saturated fat with single bonds that bind atoms together doesn't break down and become toxic when it is subjected to heat the way the double- and triple-bonded polyunsaturated oils do.

Meat fat is also stable because it contains saturated and monounsaturated fatty acids. I knew a healthy woman in her late nineties who ate fatty meat and cream sauce made with butter every day. She claimed the meat was more easily digested if eaten with butter. Her intuition was correct because short-chained fatty acids in butter break apart the long-chained saturated fats in the meat, making them available to the body.

It's probably wise, however, to avoid eating large quantities of meat fat because the enzyme lipase used to break down fat is destroyed when meat is cooked. Individuals who write on alternative medicine and nutrition topics wax enthusiastic about the cardiovascular health of the traditional Eskimos who ate whale and seal fat as if it were candy. But the Eskimos ate their fat raw. Raw fat leaves behind practically no acetone or other acidic waste, the toxic by-products of cooked fat that can cause degeneration of the heart and arteries.

In the winter my husband and I often eat roast duck at a Hungarian restaurant on the upper east side of Manhattan. We felt we were damaging our arteries, eating what was essentially nine-tenths crispy skin and saturated fat and one-tenth meat, until I read that in the Gascony region of France where people are known for their longevity, duck and goose fat make up almost all the fat in the diet. People in this region cook everything in duck fat, snack on fried duck skin, spread goose or duck fat on bread, and eat liver pâté (foie gras), which is 87 percent duck or goose fat. Despite this high intake of cooked, saturated fat that contains no fat-digesting lipase, out of 100,000 middle-aged Frenchmen in this region, only 80 die of heart attacks yearly, whereas in the rest of France the number is 145. In the United States, 315 out of 100,000 middle-aged men die of heart attacks each year.[14] Further proof that the longevity of people in this region—ninety-five-year-olds are common—is due to their consumption of duck and goose fat is the fact that in a part of the region where people eat the most fat—they have foie gras three or four times weekly—they live longer than in areas where foie gras is eaten only once a week. Scientists speculate that the health benefits of duck and goose fat could be due to the similarity of their molecular structure to that of olive oil.

The low death rates from heart disease of duck and goose fat–eating people, however, could also be due to their custom of drinking one or two glasses of red or white wine, an equal amount of mineral water, and a salad whenever they eat duck or goose.

Olive oil has received a great deal of favorable publicity in recent years. Some people refer to it as the miracle oil because of the longevity of the inhabitants of the islands off the coasts of Italy, Greece, and Spain who consume huge amounts of olive oil. In Sardinia where cancer and heart disease are rare, the inhabitants drink olive oil by the glassful.

It's doubtful, however, that we could obtain the same healthy arteries by increasing our intake of olive oil. The oil drunk on these islands is greenish, opaque, and thick—whereas even the olive oil labeled unfiltered in supermarkets and health food stores is yellow and clear, an indication that enough nutrients have been filtered out to give the oil a "pure" look.

SOME HEALTHY FATS AND OILS

➤ Coconut oil. This supersaturated oil does not increase cholesterol levels because it is burned up. It is an excellent cooking oil because it can be heated to a very high temperature without being denatured and becoming carcinogenic. Spectrum coconut oil is sold in health food stores. (The organic version has a jar with a green lid.)

➤ Ghee (the liquid part of butter). This is good for cooking because it doesn't break down. It was used in Ayurvedic medicine, the ancient Indian form of healing, because it was thought to be good for the *ojas* (soul). It's sold in health food stores.

➤ Goose and duck fat. This fat is healthy for the cardiovascular system. Save the fat given off by the roasting duck or goose. Refrigerate and use as a spread on bread.

➤ Extra virgin olive oil. Two Spanish brands, Columela Picual and Nunez de Prado, are greenish and opaque and therefore contain more nutrients than clear, yellow olive oil. Unfiltered olive oil prevents artery damage and cancer. Order through the Whole Foods Market website: wholefoodsmarket.com.

➤ Freeze-dried vegetables. The green powder in a jar sold in health food stores is a great source of omega-3 fatty acid because its made up mostly of green leafy vegetables. Two or three spoonfuls in apple juice daily is a good substitute for those who don't like green leafy vegetables.

➤ Butter. Cultured, unsalted butter (Organic Valley) is available in health-food stores.

Fiber

Fiber-rich foods help prevent many degenerative diseases. In the intestines, fibers bind with bile acids, so they can't damage the lining of the intestinal walls, and when fiber is broken down, its short-chain fatty acids neutralize carcinogenic substances in the colon. Fibers also help control Type II diabetes and heart disease. According to a study published in May 2000 in *The New England Journal of Medicine*, the Type II diabetics on a diet with twice the fiber consumed by those in another group of diabetics had more nearly normal levels of blood sugar and insulin as well as lower cholesterol and triglyceride levels.[15]

The individual's choice of fiber, however, must conform to his or her metabolic type. The grain eater is fortunate because grain provides fiber in far more bulk than the raw fruits and vegetables from which the meat-eating metabolic types must obtain the bulk of their fiber needs.

How Fiber Cured Angela's Digestive Problems

Angela, although only in her early twenties, had suffered painful muscle spasms in her stomach for a year. At the recommendation of a nutritionist she took pancreatic enzymes, and when these didn't help she went to an herbalist. The herbalist prescribed a formula made up of fennel seed, chamomile flowers, dandelion, gentian, and ginger roots. The herbal digestive aid didn't work either.

Had these alternative health-care specialists questioned Angela about her eating habits and considered her ethnic background, they might have discovered the cause of her stomach problems. Before Angela moved to the Seattle area she lived in the desert country west of Tucson with other members of her tribal group, the Seri Indians. When she left the desert, she took with her the craving for hot sauce that Indians living in hot climates seem to develop. However, lacking the special hot peppers she needed to make this hot sauce, Angela ate chili dogs and tortilla chips with salsa. She also ate white rice and white bread in place of the cholla cactus buds, tepary beans, and mesquite that she and the other Indians living in the desert ate.

Her new diet lacked the soluble fibers of her traditional diet, which had speeded the transit of hot sauce through her digestive tract, not giving it a chance to irritate her stomach tissues. As it was, her fiber-deficient diet slowed her digestion, leaving in her digestive tract spicy, acidic food residues that inflamed her stomach muscles and caused them to go into spasms.

Angela began eating oatmeal, seven-grain bread, and sprouted wheat bread for its enzyme content. The fibers, along with the enzyme supplements she was taking, broke down her foods at a faster pace and the hot, spicy foods moved more quickly through her digestive tract. This gave her inflamed stomach tissues a chance to heal. Soon after, her stomach spasms went away.

Obtaining Environmentally Sound Meat and Seafood

Most meat sold in supermarkets should be avoided because it comes from animals that have been fed grain containing pesticides, hormones, and subtherapeutic antibiotics, and who have lived out their bleak existence in cubicles so small they can barely turn around. Once butchered, the meat is injected with glutamate and chlorinated water, sprayed with phosphates to avoid E. coli, and wrapped in plastic.

My client Ann was addicted to meat when she lived in the United States, but when she moved to Mexico where the cattle graze strictly on grass she lost her craving. Ann weighed thirty pounds more when she ate the meat from hormone-fed United States–raised steer than she does now on a diet of hormone-free beef. Her experience is an example of the accelerating effect of hormones on appetite and the increase in weight that results from it.

There are small farms scattered throughout the United States that raise free-range livestock that are fed pesticide- and hormone-free feed, and who have their own processing plants so that they retain quality control of their meat products at every stage. One such operation is the Niman Ranch in the San Francisco Bay area. Niman buys its calves and lambs from neighboring ranches, where they are raised according to Niman's own specifications, and rears them to maturity on a wide variety of feed: corn, wheat, soy meal, sugar beet pulp, cane molasses, and hay. The animals are allowed to choose their own feed and the meat is processed in Niman's own facilities in San Francisco.

Niman Ranch lamb, like Niman beef, is raised on small ranches. It is fed on grasses and grain that are organically grown. Lambs graze on rain-irrigated grain in late winter and spring, move to clover fields in early and mid-summer, then to fields of corn and alfalfa in late summer and fall. After harvest, crops are rotated, ensuring nutrient-rich feed. You can order Niman beef and lamb by phone: 510-808-0330.

In Iowa, there are also a handful of farmers who raise their livestock without the aid of hormones and pesticides. One of these farms, owned by Kelly and Nina Biensen, has organized a marketing group called Eden Farms that raises Berkshire pigs, a breed known for its flavor and well-marbled meat.[16] The Biensens let their hogs move around "in and out of shelter" even in cold weather, and feeds them soybean meal, ground corn, vitamins, and minerals, but no animal parts. This regimen yields a meat strong in flavor and juiciness quite unlike the dry, cardboard quality of supermarket pork. The Biensens and thirty-six other farms in Iowa sell their pork to Niman Ranch. It can be ordered by phone at the Niman telephone number: 510-808-0330.

The Jamison Farm rears lamb according to a method developed by the French scientist Andre Voisin called intensive rotational grazing.[17] For approximately nine months of the year they eat nothing but grass. Border collies move the lamb every couple of days from one enclosed field of grass to another. In each field they nibble the grass and clover down to the nub, which releases the nitrogen from the clover into the soil already enriched by sheep droppings. This results in an incredibly fertile soil which grows another field of grass in just three weeks. This method of growing grass and clover makes sheep raising viable economically and eliminates the need for pesticides, hormones, and antibiotics. The Jamisons have their own processing plant. You can order their meat by calling 800-237-5262.

Conservation beef ranches raise free-range beef cattle that are fed on grasses and raised without antibiotics and hormones. The meat is dry-aged a minimum of twenty-one days (the old-fashioned way), and each package is stamped with the watershed or ecosystem of origin. Call 877-749-7177 or order from their website: www.conservationbeef.org/ guide.html.

The Wild Salmon Supermarket, a store in Seattle, takes mail orders for fresh, line-caught salmon, halibut, red snapper, ling cod, and black cod, as well as Dungeness crabs. The fish is packed in ice and shipped overnight. Call 1-888-222-3474. The website is www.wildsalmonsea food.com. (In troll-caught fish a net catches hundreds of fish at a time, so the fish on the bottom of the pile become bruised. For this reason, line-caught fish is superior.)

Obtaining the Freshest Vegetables

In an arrangement called Community Supported Agriculture (CSA), the public provides the seed money to farmers and is reimbursed with baskets of vegetables throughout the summer as they are harvested. The farms that take part in CSA are small and usually raise their produce organically. To find out if there are such farms in your vicinity, buy the book *Farms of Tomorrow Revisited*, which lists nearly a thousand CSAs. It can be ordered by credit card or phone from Chelsea Green, Inc., 800-639-4099.

Cooking to Preserve the Nutrient Value of Foods

Some people say that the best way to become healthy is to throw away the kitchen stove. Raw vegetables should be eaten with every meal, but some cooked vegetables are essential for good health, because cooking makes beta carotene, two other carotene pigments, and lycopene avail- able to the body. The carotene pigments are converted in the body to vitamin A, and lycopene helps prevent prostate and pancreatic cancer. Nevertheless, cooking destroys enzymes and some vitamins unless cer- tain guidelines are followed:

- To cook vegetables place a fireproof pad under a saucepan. Cook without water unless you drink it after the vegetables are cooked. Or cook in tomatoes or soup stock. Cook under low heat for one and a half to two hours.[18]
- Cook all root vegetables in their jackets.
- Bake potatoes until done at 500 degrees, since quick cooking at very high heat, like slow cooking at very low heat, preserves some nutrients.
- Place vegetables in a little water in a saucepan and cook at low heat, leaving the center of the vegetables hard.
- Roast meat without adding water at 400 to 500 degrees until done. This prevents glutamate from being freed up. The glutamate that is detached from other amino acids in the process of simmering meat is just as likely to cause an allergic reaction as the MSG flavoring in processed food. (A useful book on this subject is *Battling the MSG Myth* by Debby Anglesey. See Bibliography.)
- When roasting, broiling, or pan frying organically raised beef, lamb, and pork, leave the center of the roast raw and bloody to preserve some of the enzymes.
- Use ceramic or glass pots and pans since all metal, including stainless steel, when scratched, leaches metal into food.

Devices to Detoxify the Body

Long before the advent of modern medicine, cultures developed ways to detoxify the body, some of which are still in use today. Indians in the Western hemisphere used sweat lodges; one reservation in North Dakota has begun using them again. The Japanese still use hot baths, as do the Greeks, who in ancient times purged themselves seasonally with colonics and regurgitation. While the Scandinavians developed saunas similar to the Indian sweat lodges, the central Europeans used highly mineralized waters and clay wraps to draw the toxins out of the body. Spas are still popular. In Germany everyone past sixty-five gets two six-week vacations at a spa paid for by the government.

Modern technology has made possible the invention of devices for ridding the body of toxins that are far more convenient than many traditional practices because they can be used in the course of the day while sleeping, working, and so on. One such device is the far infrared mattress pad invented by Japanese scientists. The safe, direct current in the pad (converted from the universal AC) flows through carbon-impregnated sheets, radiating heat waves which penetrate the innermost recesses of the body and dissolve and remove acid wastes—like the sun's red light waves which ripen vegetation by lifting out the acid. Of all the heat waves that radiate from the sun, infrared is the safest and most healthy. Alkaline water also rids the body of acidic waste. A water ionizer can separate out the positively charged acidic particles from the negatively charged alkaline particles, thereby creating alkaline water for drinking and cooking, and acidic water for washing since the skin is acidic.[19]

While far infrared energy rids the body of waste through its deep, penetrating heat, negatively charged magnetic mattress pads do so through polar force. When you sleep on a magnetic pad or place a magnet anywhere on your body, the positively charged ions in the iron in the blood are attracted to the negatively charged ions emitted by the magnet. This increases the blood supply in the area, and this increased blood flow oxygenates the tissues, reducing acid wastes and the inflammation they cause. Dr. Philpott says that he has normalized high blood pressure in individuals with magnetic sleeping pads, which lower blood pressure by removing the fatty plaque buildup on artery walls.

Just as negatively and positively charged particles occur in the earth and in water, they are also found in the air. In the purest atmosphere— in the mountains, forests, and along the seashore—there are four negatively charged particles for every three positively charged ones. The ionizing air cleaner I own generates negatively and positively charged ions in the same ratio of four to three as the earth's atmosphere, but it is the negatively charged particles that clean the air. They stick to the positively charged dust particles and other contaminants, and the combined weight causes them to drop to the floor. My air cleaner also generates ozone (O_3), which oxidizes (burns up) molds, mildew, and airborne bacteria such as the tuberculosis bacillus.

Pure air is invigorating because with the acidic, toxic pollutants removed, it carries more oxygen. This additional oxygen is transported by the blood to the cells, where it is converted by the process of respiration into energy. Increasing the body's energy level not only promotes a sense of well-being but also enables the metabolic processes within the body to work efficiently in eliminating the acidic wastes that lay the groundwork for degenerative diseases. Only after purging these wastes is it possible to stabilize the body's internal environment.

After carefully evaluating the results of my advice to hundreds of individuals, I'm convinced that toxicity in the form of acidic waste is the primary cause of degenerative disease. Unfortunately the national obsession with nutritional supplements obscures the vital role played by the excretion of acidic toxins in normalizing organ function. Nutritional supplements are usually necessary to heal the injured organ(s), but it is difficult to heal an organ system until the acidic wastes that caused the injury are first removed.

A diet tailored to the individual's metabolism helps reduce acidic waste levels in the body. With the information contained in this chapter you should be able to find the diet that is right for you. Food items as well as nutritional supplements beneficial for particular health problems are discussed in Part II.

ACHIEVING PH BALANCE TO TREAT SPECIFIC AILMENTS

CHAPTER 3

DIGESTIVE AILMENTS

Acidic wastes are the by-products of all body functions and are removed in sweat, urine, and stool. It's only when acidic debris from undigested food raises acid waste levels excessively that the body is unable to dispose of it. The most common sign of hyperacidity is acid indigestion, usually referred to as acid reflux.

Acid Reflux

Acid reflux, a burning in the throat and chest, occurs when the acidic waste contents of the stomach flow into the esophagus (throat). Unlike the stomach, the esophagus doesn't have a thick mucous lining to protect it from the damaging effects of acidic debris. If acid reflux is chronic, it causes swelling and redness in the esophageal and stomach tissues. This can lead to the destruction of the mucous lining in the stomach as well as stomach, esophageal, and duodenal ulcers (the duodenum, the uppermost part of the small intestine, is attached to the bottom of the stomach).

Symptoms of acid indigestion can be a lifesaver because they provide evidence that acidic waste in the digestive tract is reaching dangerous levels and therefore accumulating in other parts of the body as well. Sooner or later excessive acidic waste levels give rise to degenerative disease. Many individuals, however, develop debilitating illness without having any symptoms of acid indigestion; so they don't see the link between acidic waste and degenerative disease. Even those with acid reflux, gastritis (inflammation of the stomach), nausea, bloating, gallstones, and ulcers, where diet is an obvious culprit, find it hard to believe that foods that cause digestive problems can also injure organs outside the digestive tract. Yet every ache and pain in the body that isn't the result of physical injury is triggered by the acidic waste-products of inappropriate and/or nutrient-deficient food.

Unhappily for their patients, mainstream doctors view symptoms of illness as signs of disease rather than as reactions to metabolically inappropriate foods. Julie was a victim of this approach. Six years ago on her way home from a party, her heart started racing, her hands trembled, and minutes later she had a seizure. Because tests came out negative, the doctor concluded that she had the flu. But instead of getting over the "flu," she developed shivering fits, felt tremendous pressure in her head, and could hardly hold herself up. After she had seven seizures in one week, the doctor conducted more extensive tests. An EEG (electroencephalogram), performed while she slept, showed that her brain waves were off the charts: 1:2 is normal; hers had slowed to 1:600. A blood workup revealed that she had an adrenal insufficiency and her antibodies were so elevated that they were a strong indication of an autoimmune disorder. The doctor suspected lupus. Julie was already taking antiseizure medication and was now told that she should take prednisone, a steroid hormone, and undergo cytotoxin chemotherapy. She decided that these drugs were the proverbial straws that would break the camel's back, so she took matters into her own hands and went to a naturopathic physician. The first thing that Dr. Eileen Stretch, the naturopath, did was to test for allergies. The tests indicated that Julie was allergic to wheat, sugar, dairy, caffeine, alcohol, bananas, and potatoes. Julie went on an allergy-free diet and in a few days her symptoms melted away. She regained her sense of well-being, alertness, and ability to concentrate two to three weeks later. The nightmare was over. Thinking back on her illness, what frightens Julie most is the fact that as sick as she was, she had no symptoms of indigestion from her food allergies and therefore no clue as to why she was so ill. Julie's experience demonstrates that the role of diet in initiating an illness should be given first consideration even when the patient has no symptoms of indigestion.

I would probably have missed this connection myself if years ago when I began having symptoms of acid indigestion I hadn't been teaching the basic 101 course in chemistry—a course I had never before taught. The timing was fortuitous. Along with my students, I learned that a balance of acidic particles (positively charged protons) and alkaline particles (negatively charged electrons) make up the basic structure of the elements—principally, carbon, nitrogen, oxygen, and hydrogen—out of which all the molecules in the fluids and tissues in our bodies are made. (Neutrons in the nucleus of atoms are neutral not only in the sense that they are nonreactive but also because they have no distinguishing characteristics.) When a compound contains more electrons (hydroxyl ions, OH-) than protons (hydrogen ions, H+), it is referred to as alkaline forming; when the ratio is in reverse, it's said to be acid forming. This made me realize the full implications of having acid indigestion. If acid-alkaline particles in a particular ratio characterized the blood, lymph, bile, urine, gastric juices, and other fluids in the body, hyperacidity could inflict damage on the organ systems by upsetting this balance.

The Real Cause of Acid Reflux

Doctors have tried to cure acid reflux by surgically repairing the valve between the stomach and esophagus to keep it from opening up and letting stomach acids pour into the esophagus. In view of the fact that the results of this operation have been disappointing, there has to be another explanation for acid reflux. The most likely one is that acidic waste gas molecules in the stomach open the valve that closes off the stomach from the esophagus by causing it to go into a spasm. (This valve should remain closed when the individual is not eating.) The acidic waste then flows into the esophagus. Since this acid is the waste product from improperly digested food, the only way to get rid of acid reflux is to find foods that the digestive metabolism breaks down completely so that minimal acidic waste is left over.

Efficient digestion depends on the alternating actions of acid and alkaline digestive juices that split up the food molecules. The alkaline enzyme ptyalin in the mouth breaks down starch; acidic gastric juices, such as pepsin, break up protein in the stomach; alkaline pancreatic enzymes digest protein and alkaline bile emulsifies fats and oils in the small intestine, while acidic flora complete the digestion of protein there. Acid reflux can disrupt this acid-alkaline sequence by changing the pH factor in the stomach and small intestine.

How this happens is revealed by the typical contents of the vomit heartburn sufferers throw up in an effort to get rid of the burning sensation in the throat and chest. After a highly acidic liquid is expelled, alkaline-forming bile often comes up, indicating that the bile has flowed from the small intestine into the stomach, where it doesn't belong. This occurs when the valve between the stomach and small intestine opens up, most likely because of an acidic waste–induced spasm. The alkaline-forming bile in the stomach alkalinizes the acidic gastric juices, interfering with their breakdown of protein. As a result not only does the undigested protein turn into acidic waste, the alternating acid-alkaline balance in the digestive tract is disrupted.

The Healing Value of Raw Potatoes

Once I understood how foods that the digestive system can't handle disrupt the acid-alkaline balance by acidifying the digestive tract, I eliminated those foods that gave me acid reflux: tea; coffee; sharp-tasting vegetables such as radishes, onions, and garlic; herbs and spices; and oils. The food that I digested best was potatoes. I made them my breakfast and lunch staple—cooking them in a frying pan along with some vegetables in a little water, which I drank—only because they didn't give me acid indigestion. I never anticipated the miraculous effect they would have. At the beginning, I cooked the potatoes until they were soft because I couldn't digest raw vegetables. Eventually, to preserve some of the vitamins and enzymes, I began leaving a small spot in the center of the potatoes raw. As my digestive tract started to heal, I was able to leave more of the potato raw, until finally I cooked only the outermost part of the potato. After I had been on this nearly raw potato diet for a year, I went to a dinner party where the hostess served a highly spiced paella. I ate it and, for the first time in years after eating a spicy dish, had no acid indigestion. A few weeks later I had a pizza with garlic with the same benign effect. My digestive problems gradually became a thing of the past. The occasional stomach upset goes away when I eat a piece of raw potato. It also acts as an appetite suppressant, absorbing the acidic wastes in the stomach that can create artificial hunger.

The alkaline-forming starch in the potatoes had healed my indigestion in part by absorbing and neutralizing the acidic waste in my stomach and intestines. I discovered that there was another component in potatoes involved in this healing when I read a reprint of a paper that Francis M. Pottenger Jr., M.D., gave at the thirty-eighth Annual Meeting of the American Therapeutic Society, in Atlantic City, June 4, 1937.[1] In it he discussed the importance of the gluelike mucilage in raw foods in helping the enzymes in the stomach break down the food mass. This brought to mind that when I ran my fingers along the inside surface of the pan in which I had cooked potatoes, I felt a slippery, gluelike coating. This was clearly the mucilage or mucin that is found in raw foods and that the heat from cooking had separated out from the rest of the potatoes. Mucilage is most abundant in okra and raw meat and, as I discovered, is also plentiful in potatoes.

The nearly raw potatoes I'd been eating supplied two substances that improved my digestion: water, which enables the food mass in the stomach to absorb the digestive enzyme juices, and sticky mucilage, which by coating the food mass prevents the water from seeping out. Given the vital role played by water and mucilage in the absorption of enzymes in the stomach, how could a diet of totally cooked food, which has very little of either, be digested efficiently? It can't. Unlike a food mass containing some raw foods which is thoroughly mixed together and forms a gluey lump in the stomach, a cooked food mass in the stomach forms distinct layers: cooked meat, the heaviest, on the bottom; bread or cake next; then a layer of vegetables, and mashed potatoes interspersed through the three layers. A chemical analysis of cooked food masses showed that a layer of water on top of it was acidic (not from hydrochloric acid), an indication that the food was beginning to ferment. Rapid digestion that leaves little or no food debris can't take place unless enzymes are able to penetrate the food mass, and this isn't possible unless some raw foods, with their abundant supply of water and mucilage, are eaten at every meal. Mucilage also heals the lining of the stomach and builds up the layer of mucus that covers it. In my case, it was the thickening of this mucous layer from the mucilage in potatoes that made my stomach impervious to the irritating effects of spicy and acid tasting foods. It makes sense that potatoes—as well as bananas (discussed later on in this chapter)—can heal the surface tissue lining the stomach, since they have long been used by nonindustrial cultures to heal skin irritations and wounds. The American Indians placed a slice of raw potato on the eyelid to heal pinkeye, and in West Africa herbalists covered the incisions they made—for example, when they cut a circular-shaped piece out of the skull in order to drain fluid from the brain—with banana peels.

The nearly raw potato diet can take anywhere from two months to a year and a half to work. How long it takes depends, first, on the extent of the acidic waste buildup in the digestive tract and, second, on how much of the potato you leave raw. You can sometimes speed up the healing process by drinking a glass of raw potato juice a day. Although potatoes are digested quickly, even those who digest their foods too fast (the parasympathetic dominant) can eat potatoes if they're barely cooked, in which case they're broken down slowly enough that they don't speed up digestion. Raw potatoes, like gelatin, not only improve digestion by reducing acidity, they also heal stomach injuries—ulcers, lesions, and inflammation (gastritis)—by building up the protective mucous lining of the stomach.

Potatoes are not only good medicine, they have enormous nutritional value. This was proved when this protein-rich carbohydrate almost singlehandedly kept the Irish alive for a 150-year period. Potatoes became the dietary staple of the Irish with the final takeover of northern Ireland by the British in 1690 in the Battle of the Boyne. The most fertile land was given to the officers of the victorious British army, and Irish farmers were forced to plant potatoes, the only crop that would grow on the barren soil left to them. The potato blight of 1843 put an end to the consumption of potatoes for many years by destroying every potato crop in Ireland.

An Important Side Benefit to the Potato Diet: The Loss of the Desire to Binge

The raw potato diet had another benefit for myself and fifteen others who went on it and had the same eating disorder as I did. It eliminated our intense craving for food. The potato diet also brought to light what caused my feeding frenzies in the first place. My food binges began in childhood, at the age of ten. Before that, ear, throat, and stomach infections and three bouts of scarlet fever had killed my appetite, causing such a severe calcium deficiency that I got rickets. The day my childhood illnesses came to an end my appetite switched on. Ten years of continual infections had left behind an enormous amount of acidic waste from the toxins produced by the waste matter from live bacteria as well as from their dead bodies. This is what had overstimulated my appetite as soon as I stopped getting ear infections.

Gelatin Supplies Needed Mucilage

Pottenger mentioned powdered okra and beet juice as effective hydrophilic colloids (sticky substances that have an affinity for water) but believed the most practical and effective musilagenous substance was gelatin taken with each meal, either sprinkled on food or added to liquid. (Gelatin, however, should be avoided by anyone who is allergic to monosodium glutamate. Gelatin contains the amino acids arginine and glycine, which, separated from other amino acids when the chicken bones used to make the gelatin are simmered in water, overstimulate the brain cells of anyone sensitive to them.) For an individual with alcoholic-related gastritis, gelatin with its enormous mucilage content is often the only remedy that will counteract the corrosive effect of alcohol on the lining of the stomach and small intestine. Gelatin also has great nutritive value, an added benefit for alcoholics who have lost interest in food, and Edgar Cayce in one of his readings stated that gelatin aids in the absorption of vitamins and minerals. Dr. Bernard Jensen in *Foods That Heal* writes that because the calcium in gelatin (45 percent of gelatin consists of calcium) is derived from chicken bones, it's the most easily assimilable form of that mineral.[2]

Ulcers

The ground was laid for my mother's gallbladder attacks and ulcers at birth. She was given cow's milk as a baby and continued to drink it until, at the age of five, the chronic rash on her face and arms was diagnosed as an allergic reaction to milk. From the time my mother was in her early thirties, she suffered from gallbladder attacks. She relieved her painful gallbladder with a hot water bottle and drank a mixture of peppermint, spirits of ammonia, and sodium bicarbonate in water to lessen the nausea that accompanied these attacks. A surgeon who was a friend of the family talked her into having her gallbladder removed by assuring her that, because the gallbladder's only function was storing bile, it was expendable. (In fact the gallbladder has other functions besides that of storage as the next case history shows.) During the operation he did some exploratory surgery and discovered that every square inch of the lining of her stomach was covered with ulcers. The surgeon, Dr. Hoffmeyer, later told my mother that he regretted having taken out her gallbladder because the diet for ulcers (at the time) emphasized milk, butter, and cream. Without the gallbladder to release bile into the small intestine as needed for the breakdown of the fat in these dairy products, the liver, not built for this task, has to take over. Dr. Hoffmeyer, in blithely assuring my mother that one gallbladder less made no difference, hadn't foreseen the one condition where it did.

The Healing Quality of Raw Cabbage Juice

My mother's "gallbladder" attacks became more frequent and increased in severity after her gallbladder was removed. Still, it wasn't until she was in her eighties that I was able to convince her to try raw cabbage juice, an extraordinarily effective treatment for ulcers. She drank two pints of it daily, sometimes adding carrots, and in only two weeks began having fewer stomach upsets. Two months later she stopped having them altogether. Only when she doesn't drink a pint of cabbage juice for four days running does she have a recurrence of the pain and nausea that she used to have almost daily.

The effectiveness of raw cabbage juice in healing ulcers is evidence that acid-forming foods can reduce acidity in the digestive tract.

Despite the fact that patients with gastric ulcers practically always have elevated acid levels in the stomach, the acid-forming minerals in cabbage—sulphur, chlorine, and iodine—clean out the acidic waste in the stomach, allowing the ulcers to heal and the mucous membrane to rebuild itself. The beneficial action of acid-forming minerals comes from the fact that, unlike acidic waste which is pure acid and therefore highly caustic, there are alkaline components in acid-forming minerals that dilute the acid.

The Preventive Role of Whole Grains

Many studies show that whole grains are also an effective remedy for an ulcerated stomach. Where unrefined wheat is the dietary staple, for example, in northern India and China and in parts of Africa, ulcers are rare. On the other hand, in Japan, where white rice has replaced the traditional brown rice as a dietary staple, peptic ulcers, once almost unheard-of, have become common.[4] No one knows just what fiber does to heal ulcers. One theory is that it reduces gastric enzymes, which are considered to be the cause of acid reflux as well as ulcers. If this were the case, ulcers would worsen because gastric enzymes speed up digestion so there isn't any leftover acidic food debris to make holes in the stomach lining or cause ulcers. The theory that fiber toughens up the stomach lining has more merit since the rough texture of fiber acts as a broom, sweeping away the irritating acidic debris particles lodged in the lining of the stomach. However, according to Frank I. Tovey, M.D., a surgeon and ulcer researcher at the University of London, the fact that ulcers have skyrocketed everywhere in the world since 1900—along with the rise in coronary heart disease—when the removal of the husk covering the grain became widespread, suggests that some of the benefits of fiber come from its nutrients, particularly vitamins E and B, in addition to the fact that it moves waste matter along the intestinal tract.[5]

One of the most effective organic whole wheat breads in healing ulcers is Manna bread because it's made of sprouted grain, an excellent source of digestive enzymes as well as vitamin E and the B complex. Because meat eaters (parasympathetic dominant) don't digest grains well, they have to derive most of their fiber needs from raw fruits and vegetables, which don't have the quantity of B and E vitamins that grains have. This makes vitamin E and B-complex supplements a necessity for those with a meat-eating metabolism who suffer acid indigestion and ulcers.

Healing Mucilage in Bananas, Plantains, and Cabbage Juice

Bananas and plantains—especially green plantains—and raw cabbage juice heal ulcers by thickening the mucous lining of the stomach. Dr. Ralph Best, a British pharmacist at the University of Aston in Birmingham, observed in autopsies of animals fed banana powder a thickening of the stomach wall. Dr. Garnett Cheney, a researcher at Stanford University, wrote in *California Medicine* in 1949 of his treatment of twenty-six ulcer patients with cabbage juice, twenty-four of whom made a complete recovery in three to four weeks.[6] Of the nineteen patients in the control group who were treated with conventional medicines, only six recovered. Dr. E. M. Vermel in a Russian medical journal, *Clinical Medicine*, published in 1960, stated that many independent investigations confirmed Dr. Cheney's research, and that stomach ulcers disappeared in 85 percent of the 500 subjects in these studies.[7] Vermel believed that vitamin U, about which nothing is known, supplies a nutrient needed for the formation of mucus. The mucilage in bananas and cabbage, being gluelike and slippery like mucus, is the more likely supplier of the elements that rebuild the mucous lining of the stomach.

Despite all the documentation showing the healing effect of cabbage juice and banana powder on ulcers, the treatment of choice for ulcers in recent years has become antibiotics. This is due to the discovery by two Australian medical researchers, Doctors Barry Marshall and Robin Warren, of *H. pylori* bacteria as the cause of ulcers. This discovery made antibiotics appear to be a cure for ulcers and so obscured the need to find out why the bacteria settled in the stomach in the first place. In fact, bacteria thrive on acidic waste; they settle wherever acid levels are high, and wherever this is the case the tissue is already inflamed. Inflamed tissue in the stomach and duodenum (uppermost part of the small intestine) is also apt to be ulcerated. As bacteria die and the remains turn into acidic waste, inflammation becomes more severe, increasing the likelihood that more ulcers will form. By killing off the

H. pylori bacteria, antibiotics reduce the inflammation, but they can't eliminate the redness and swelling caused by dietary acidic waste. Only after the foods that triggered the inflammation are given up can inflamed and ulcerated tissues be completely and permanently healed.

SUGGESTIONS FOR ULCERS

➤ Potatoes—preferably Idaho potatoes, but red potatoes are good too. Buy medium to large potatoes, barely cook if possible, once or twice daily, accompanied by lightly cooked vegetables. The Irish who lived on a diet of potatoes and little else left the skins on their potatoes when they boiled them and used the water as a base for soup.

➤ Gelatin—one-half to one ounce in liquid or sprinkled on food. (See Resources.) An excellent source of mucilage.

➤ Raw vegetables with every meal to provide the mucilage and water needed for complete digestion.

➤ Raw cabbage juice—two glasses a day or as much as needed.

➤ Bananas or plantains—daily, as many as you can comfortably eat.

➤ Vitamin E—400 to 1,600 units daily. Researchers Jon A. Kangas, Ph.D., K. Michael Schmidt, Ph.D., and George F. Solomon, M.D., reported in *Clinical Nutrition* in September 1972 that of two groups of mice subjected to stress, the group given 100 units of vitamin E daily had far fewer and less severe ulcers than the control group.[8]

➤ Vitamin A—25,000 to 50,000 units daily. Experiments conducted and written up by T. L. Harris in the *Society for Experimental Biology and Medicine*, March 1947, show that rats given vitamin A as well as vitamin E were shown by autopsies to have no ulcers.[9] Vitamin A helps build mucous membranes.

➤ Vitamin C—500 milligrams. In building up collagen, the "glue" that holds the epithelial cells together on the surface of organs, vitamin C helps ensure the integrity of the digestive tract lining.

Gallstones

Although bile crystallizes into stone when the gallbladder becomes supersaturated with cholesterol, a cholesterol-rich saturated fat diet helps prevent gallstones. Two siblings, John and Margaret, illustrate this point. Their mother gave them plenty of vegetables, salads, and fruit, but being cholesterol conscious, served only lean meat and no butter. Margaret's and John's only source of fatty acids was olive oil in the salads they had every night with their dinner. Both suffered from constipation.

When John graduated from college and moved to his own apartment, he ate out every night at fast food restaurants where he invariably ordered a cheeseburger and french fries. Nevertheless, from the day he left home his constipation vanished. John was now eating saturated fats and this change in diet, despite the nutritional deficiencies, had solved his elimination problems. His younger sister Margaret, however, continued to be constipated after she moved away from home. Like her mother, she avoided butter and trimmed the fat off meat. She also took birth control pills. Five years later she stopped taking them long enough to become pregnant and give birth to a healthy boy. About a year after she had gone back on birth control pills, she woke up in agony. Pain from a spot under her right rib cage, where the gallbladder is located, radiated into her chest and down her left arm. Afraid that she was having a heart attack, her husband rushed her to the hospital where an MRI revealed that she had gallstones. One of them, half an inch in diameter, was blocking her gallbladder duct. The bile, trapped in her gallbladder by the obstruction, had been diverted into the bloodstream, giving her skin and the whites of her eyes a yellowish tint. Because the gallbladder was badly inflamed, the doctors removed it.

Margaret met three of the criteria that have been linked to gallstones. She had been on a low-cholesterol diet for years, had been constipated for the same period of time, and had been taking birth control pills. A low-cholesterol diet, by causing constipation, can pave the way for gallstones. Cholesterol is one of the raw materials out of which the salts and acids in bile are made. Bile salts stimulate peristalsis, the alternate contraction and relaxation of the muscles in the digestive tract that move food and waste matter along. Thus a diet low in cholesterol can result in a deficiency of bile salts that slows the movement of the muscles in the colon, making elimination of stool more difficult.

Constipation increases the likelihood of gallstones by causing the waste matter in the colon to putrefy and give off toxins. The toxins are carried by the blood from the colon to the liver to be detoxified, but when the liver is too overworked to neutralize it, the toxins flow back into general circulation and are carried to the kidneys for excretion. When the kidneys are too congested to filter it out of the blood, the blood carries it back to the liver which incorporates it in bile and releases it into the gallbladder. There, it bonds with cholesterol and hardens into stone. A case control study by F. Pixley, published in *Gut*, titled "Dietary Factors in the Etiology of Gallstones," showed a relationship between stone formation and supersaturated quantities of cholesterol in the bladder.[10] Gallstones can also form when the liver and kidneys are too congested to process the fatty acids altered by excessive blood levels of estrogen.

Few people who have gallstones realize that they are a sign that the overaccumulation of toxic acidic waste in the body has damaged their liver and kidneys to the point where they can no longer eliminate it from the body. Gallstones thus represent the last-ditch effort of the liver to remove acidic waste from the blood so that it doesn't lower (acidify) the blood pH factor.

Thus whether or not gallstone sufferers have had their gallbladders removed, to prevent the further accumulation of acidic wastes in the body it is necessary to remove from the diet whatever it is that caused gallstones to form. In Lydia's case it meant giving up birth control pills and polyunsaturated oils, eating butter, saturated meat fat, and soybeans for their lecithin content. (Lecithin in powdered form should be avoided because it turns rancid when exposed to air or heat.) She also increased the amount of olive oil she put in salads because, like lecithin, it breaks up fat molecules, and ate as many grapes as she could stand to improve elimination. Because the white spots and ridges on her nails indicated a mineral deficiency, she took a mineral complex (four 225-milligram capsules of silica). Before long, her nails lost their ridgy quality, her elimination improved, and her complexion cleared up, three signs that she was beginning to detoxify.

Vegetables and fruit are a higher quality source of minerals than mineral supplements since plants convert the inorganic minerals in rain and groundwater to an organic form. Nevertheless, many long-lived peoples around the world use inorganic minerals even when fruits and vegetables are plentiful. The Abkasians, an enclave of people living in the foothills of the Caucasus mountains where centenarians are common, break off stalactites from ceilings in caves, soak them in bowls of water placed in the sun, and drink the mineral-rich water; and the tribes living near Lake Victoria in Uganda, Africa, collect the now-inorganic remains of large winged insects that accumulate along the shores of the lake, dry them, and use them in puddings. The value of these and other inorganic mineral supplements is that they are available in far larger quantities than the organic minerals in raw plant food.

SUGGESTIONS FOR GALLSTONES

➤ Grapes, beets, and endive. These detoxify the liver, kidneys, and gallbladder and improve digestion and elimination.

➤ Ice pack—relieves pain during a gallbladder attack by reducing inflammation.

➤ Whole grains (if you have a grain-eating metabolism), for their roughage and vitamin B and E content. Manna bread, made with sprouted seeds, provides food enzymes in addition to the nutrients found in whole grain bread.

➤ Thyroid medication. (See Resources.) An underactive thyroid can reduce the secretion of gastric juice in the stomach, and has been linked to gallbladder disease.

➤ Cayenne pepper—stimulates good digestion, including the breakdown of fats, which helps prevent gallstones without irritating the stomach. It's also a good overall body tonic. The West Indian population in Jamaica, where the cayenne plant grows in profusion on the sides of mountains, tell me they nibble on a cayenne leaf whenever they feel sick because its healing properties work for all illnesses.

➤ Ox bile. This comes in a loose powder. Place it in capsules and take two capsules with meals. When there isn't enough bile because some of it has crystallized into gallstones, ox bile is a good substitute.

➤ Lipase. Two capsules with each meal helps bile emulsify fats.

➤ Olive oil. Take three to four tablespoons a day to increase the flow of bile.

➤ The gallbladder flush. Drink as much apple juice as possible for three or four days. (The malic acid in apples helps dissolve gallstones.) On the fifth, sixth, and seventh day, use a castor oil pack on the liver for one hour. (See Resources for castor oil pack paraphernalia.) On the eighth day, take two teaspoons of Epsom salts after lunch and two hours later take two more teaspoons of Epsom salts. On day nine eat only a grapefruit for dinner and at bedtime drink four ounces of extra virgin olive oil. Sleep on your right side. The next morning one hour before breakfast, take two teaspoons of Epsom salts.

➤ Vitamins. See the supplement suggestions at the end of the section on ulcers.

➤ Ground psyllium husks and clay suspended in water mixed in juice are good colon cleansers. You can get these items from Sonne.

Colitis, Ileitis, and Other Inflammatory Intestinal Disorders

Bess, age sixty-six, had had colitis (inflammation of the colon) and ileitis (inflammation of the last section of the small intestine) since her mid-twenties. Like many individuals with an inflammatory intestinal condition, she had mental problems. It was an attribute she had inherited; many members of her family suffered from depression, several had committed suicide, and three of her grandparents had died of Alzheimer's. Bess's anxiety led to feelings of depression so severe that they clouded over the sunny disposition she had had as a child. She came to hate herself, not just who she was but the way she looked. For twenty years she had avoided looking at herself in the mirror. The little self-esteem she possessed went into her nails, which she kept beautifully manicured. Despite all her insecurities, she charmed everyone she met and was extremely well informed on almost any topic that came up in a conversation; her knowledge of medical terminology, for example, was extensive.

Bess had been something of a child prodigy. She learned to read at the age of eighteen months and was reading a newspaper at the age of two. She had a talent similar to those of idiot savants and one that she can still perform today. Without looking, she can write at the same time with both hands, her left hand writing from left to right and her right hand from right to left until her hands meet. Having grown up during the late 1930s and early 1940s when child prodigies were in vogue, she had become a regular panel member on the "The Quiz Kids," a radio show on which child "geniuses" were asked questions too difficult for most adults to answer.

The most recent of Bess's colitis and ileitis attacks had occurred when she removed books from the built-in bookshelves in her living room so that they could be painted. Looking at the empty bookshelves triggered painful cramps, bloating, and diarrhea. After they had been painted and the books replaced on the shelves, she had an even worse attack of cramps and diarrhea. Bess had had so many bouts of diarrhea over the years that she had developed ulcerated colitis. Her bouts of inflammatory bowel disorder were synchronized with her attacks of anxiety.

Of course many individuals with inflammatory intestinal problems don't experience the same severe stress levels as Bess, but it's hard to find anyone with an inflammatory bowel disorder who doesn't insist that his or her attacks are triggered by stress. The stress might be the result of a major upheaval in their lives such as being fired from a job or the death of a close relative, but more likely arises from taking on a responsibility that isn't part of the daily routine: redoing a kitchen, planning a wedding, job hunting, making preparations for a trip, working overtime, and so on.

Why Anxiety and Stress Affect the Intestines

The following anecdote about Foster, a teenager, points up the connection between intestinal problems and nervous disorders. Maria, his mother, tells the story of standing in the doorway of his bedroom one morning, when, before she had a chance to wake him, he sat up, looked at her, and remarked that she had just cleaned her teeth. He said that he could smell the mint flavor of her toothpaste—despite the fact that his bed was on the far wall opposite the door and Maria hadn't had a chance to open her mouth to say anything. Foster had developed this abnormally acute sense of smell after he and his family moved into a house that harbored toxic mold. The mold not only damaged Foster's nervous system—indicated by the fact that he developed some behavioral problems—it caused his stool to turn yellow, an indication that his intestinal yeast cell infection had become more severe.

Emotional stress initiates intestinal infections and inflammatory disorders because it acidifies the blood. Hyperacidity is taken by the body as a sign of imminent danger, so the adrenal hormones divert the blood flow from the digestive tract to the heart, lungs, and muscles. The stomach and intestines, thus deprived of oxygen and nutrients carried by the blood, can't produce adequate amounts of digestive enzymes to dispose of metabolic wastes. As a result, the chemical breakdown of food becomes sluggish, and the resulting undigested food debris, along with the waste by-products of metabolism, turn into acidic waste. The intestines are far more vulnerable to the effects of acidic waste than the stomach because they don't have the thick mucous lining that the stomach has for protection against the acid-forming digestive chemicals it produces. (The thin mucous lining in the intestines enables digested food to pass through the intestinal walls into the blood and lymph circulatory systems, where, after purification in the liver, it's delivered to the trillions of cells that make up the body. Also the alkaline-forming enzymes and bile in the small intestine are much less irritating than the acid-forming digestive chemicals and hydrochloric acid produced in the stomach.)

Acidic waste causes injuries to the intestines in several ways. Besides inflaming intestinal tissues, it kills off the friendly bacteria that aid in digestion and extract nutrients from digesting food. This can cause diarrhea. Also, with destruction of friendly bacteria, invading microorganisms are no longer kept in check. These unfriendly germs give off such poisonous wastes as alcohol, ammonia, acetaldehyde, and formaldehyde, which, when elevated, destroy the intestines' mucous lining. Once this protective barrier is gone, the toxins make scratches, tears, and holes in the intestinal walls, and along with sharp acidic particles, sometimes wear away the lining of the colon, thinning it out until it is stretched so tight that it balloons out and forms sacs (diverticula) in which waste matter gets lodged.

Acidic waste also slows down peristalsis—the alternating contraction and expansion of the muscles. Weak peristaltic movement not only slows the movement of food and waste through the digestive tract, but also the breakdown and absorption of food, causing nutritional deficiencies and increasing the already elevated levels of acidic waste. If acidic waste is routed to the ileocaecal valve, situated near the ileum (the part of the small intestine that joins the large intestine), it becomes inflamed. This causes the valve to go into a spasm and open up, allowing solid waste and poisonous fluids from the ascending colon to back up into the small intestine, where they contaminate the digesting food mass. The waste also acidifies the normally alkaline environment in the small intestine, throwing the acid-alkaline balance in that part of the digestive tract out of kilter.

Slow peristaltic movement can also cause alternating bouts of constipation and diarrhea if the muscle action in the bowel actually comes to a stop and then starts up again with a vengeance. Sudden evacuations don't leave enough time for food to be absorbed through the small intestinal wall into the circulating blood. As a result, the body becomes deficient in vitamins A, B, C, E, magnesium, and other minerals. Chronically sluggish peristalsis has another downside. It compounds the constipating effect that acidic waste and the lack of mucus has already had on the stool, causing the hardened stool to putrefy, further acidifying the colon.

Toxicity from constipation was accepted as fact by many in the medical profession in Europe before the era of modern medicine. Lynn Payer, in her book *Medicine and Culture*, writes about the British obsession with the "toxicating effects of an unemptied bowel," and traces it back to the theory of autointoxication developed by the late Dr. Edward C. Lambert in the early twentieth century.[11] He postulated that as a result of constipation, the waste matter in the intestines putrefies and produces toxins that lead to chronic poisoning of the body.

Appendectomy

There are other causes of intestinal inflammation besides mental stress. One is the surgical removal of the appendix. This operation, from 1900 to around 1950, was almost as common as tonsillectomy. The justification for its removal was that it had become a vestigial (useless) organ. However, several studies have correlated appendectomies with an increase in cancer. A study of 1,165 patients at the Medical College in Toledo, Ohio, conducted by Dr. George Padanilam, showed that 67 percent of the patients who had developed cancer before the age of fifty had had their appendix removed;[12] and Dr. Howard Bierman of the Institute for Cancer and Blood Research, speaking at the American College of Surgeons in 1966, said that according to his studies of hundreds of cancer patients, 84 percent had had their appendixes removed whereas only 25 percent of the noncancer patients were missing their appendixes.[13]

These studies make a strong case that the appendix, like the tonsils and adenoids, is part of the immune system and as such produces antibodies that not only destroy cancer-causing viruses but also engulf and dispose of the toxins and bacteria that inflame the bowels. The appendix's location at the bottom of the ascending colon clearly indicates that its purpose is to protect the small intestine from the toxic waste in the ascending colon. According to Michael Crichton, M.D., in his book *Five Patients*, appendix operations started with the pathologist Reginald H.

Fitz's assertion that inflammation, pus, and pain in the lower right abdomen was caused by an infection in the appendix.[14] This hypothesis, Crichton writes, created a new disease. Although many physicians resisted the idea of removing the appendix, eventually the surgeons won out. The final victory for the appendix removal proponents was achieved in 1902 when England's King Edward VII had an appendectomy. Shortly after, the operation came into vogue. Physicians were not then aware, as they still aren't today, that inflammation from toxic acidic waste is the initial cause of appendicitis. When I was growing up, parents became alarmed when their children complained of a pain in the abdomen for fear that it could be appendicitis and that the appendix might burst. They rushed the afflicted child to the doctor, who did a blood analysis. As children are prone to head colds, respiratory and ear infections, it's not surprising that blood tests often showed an elevated white blood cell count. The latter, in combination with abdominal pain, was considered sufficient evidence that the appendix was infected and should therefore be removed. (In China today hospitals typically offer patients with appendicitis two choices: an appendectomy or a program of herbs and diet to detoxify the appendix.)

Other Causes of Inflammatory Intestinal Disorders

Doctors no longer remove the appendix as a matter of course, but this hasn't decreased inflammatory bowel disease because new medical interventions have come into use that are even more damaging to the intestinal tract. Irritable bowel syndrome, Crohn's disease, and colitis became commonplace when antibiotics came into widespread use fifty years ago. Bacteria that survive antibiotic treatment develop a resistance to it, possibly by producing a virulent toxin that destroys the antibiotics—and also damages the intestinal walls. The measles vaccination has also increased bowel disease. A British study of 3,545 individuals who received measles vaccinations showed that there was a threefold increase in Crohn's disease and a two-and-a-half-fold increase in ulcerative colitis as compared to a control group.[15] The formaldehyde, mercury, and diseased animal tissue in vaccines all contribute to the breakdown of intestinal tissues.

The results of a Swedish study that shows a relationship between junk food and an increase in intestinal disorders is hardly surprising.[16] According to the study, those who eat fast foods at least twice a week are 3.4 times more likely to develop Crohn's disease and 3.9 times more likely to develop ulcerative colitis. Junk food debris, like antibiotics, vaccines, and mental stress, produces acidic waste which triggers the flow of adrenal hormones. These hormones divert the flow of blood from the digestive tract to the cardiovascular system, the first step in the process that results in inflammatory bowel disease.

Curing Inflammatory Intestinal Disorders

Bowel disorders can be relieved by either treating the symptoms or eliminating the cause. The latter can be accomplished by reducing stress levels so that the two halves of the autonomic nervous system—that is, the sympathetic and parasympathetic nerves—become balanced. When this is achieved, there is a more even distribution of the blood and lymph fluids, and as a result all the organ systems receive their fair share of nutrients and oxygen, and so function at approximately the same rate of speed. This helps to assure complete digestion of foods and the speedy transit of food and waste through the intestinal tract, giving the intestinal tract a chance to heal.

Bess chose to eliminate her colitis and ileitis by eliminating the cause: her anxiety and depression. She took a supplement called SAM-e. (SAM-e is activated methionine, formed by combining ATP energy [adenosine triphosphate] with methionine.) SAM-e increases the production of the neurotransmitters L-dopa and dopamine, and phosphatidylcholine. Healthy amounts of these neurotransmitters have a calming effect and lower stress-hormone levels. Bess also took Aangamik for its ability to oxygenate the brain cells and relieve depression. After she had been on this regimen for three months, she stopped feeling anxiety-stricken over the least deviation in her daily routine. Moreover, her feelings of depression left her—she was the first member of her family to have conquered a mental disorder. This brought her autonomic nervous system into balance. The resulting increase in blood flow to the intestines normalized Bess's intestinal function.

Another underlying cause of intestinal disorder is bad diet, which is most likely a contributing factor in cases where mental stress is the primary cause. Anyone with a bowel disorder should try to reduce intestinal inflammation by avoiding foods that produce an allergic reaction and by eating only organically grown foods based on their metabolic type. Martha, a psychotherapist, improved her intestinal function by improving her diet. She began by testing herself for food allergies (see Chapter 2) and found that she was allergic to milk (lactose intolerant), the most common allergy among those with intestinal inflammation. (In a study of 77 patients with irritable bowel syndrome conducted by Italian physicians, 74 percent were found to be allergic to milk. They were put on a milk-free diet for three weeks and their condition in all cases improved.[17]) Martha's attacks of diarrhea became less frequent but didn't go away entirely, so she took three tablespoons of bran three times a day to strengthen the intestinal walls. Eating bran on a daily basis is not a good idea for anyone with normal intestinal function because it speeds up the transit time of stool too much. But for those sufferers whose food mass passes through the intestinal tract at a snail's pace, bran can bring peristaltic action up to speed. In Martha's case, however, it acted as an irritant, causing her intestines to become more inflamed. Discouraged, she went to her family doctor for treatment. He told her that raw garlic was effective for all forms of inflammatory bowel disease, but he asked her to keep it confidential—what if it got around that he had recommended a folk remedy! It always worked, he said. The patient had to eat as many raw cloves of garlic as he or she could stand, fixed in a variety of different ways to make it more palatable—on bread, in spaghetti sauce, in salads, and so on—and in two or three days, relief would be complete. Martha tried the garlic remedy and it worked.

John started having digestive problems when he was twenty. By the time he was thirty-five he had developed Crohn's disease, an extremely severe inflammatory bowel disorder. He tried to avoid foods that gave him indigestion, but his job took him all over the world and his digestive tract couldn't adjust to foods that differed from one country to the next. His intestines became so inflamed that the doctor prescribed prednisone, a steroid hormone. This didn't work and he had to have three feet of his intestines and his ileocaecal valve removed. Desperate, John began investigating alternative remedies. After narrowing down a long list of nutritional supplements suggested by various people, he asked my advice. I suggested he start by taking castor oil, the best remedy for a sluggish gut and one that has been used for many ailments since biblical times. The oil is extracted from the castor bean, which grows on a tree called the Palma Christi. According to Edgar Cayce's psychic readings, castor oil activates peristalsis in the colon by triggering a chemical action in which water splits oil into glycerol and the fatty acid ricinoleic acid.

John placed a castor oil pack on his lower abdomen for one hour every day for one week and took one tablespoon of the oil every morning before breakfast. In a week his stools, which had been either too loose or too hard, assumed a normal consistency. His abdominal cramps and pain, however, hadn't gone away because his intestines were still inflamed, a sign that his bowel was still hyperacidic. To increase the alkalinity of his intestines, I suggested that John try a far infrared pad, which he placed on top of his mattress. He also took alkaline water. (For where to buy alkaline water and far infrared pads, see Resources.) A month later he broke out in a rash and had open, running sores all over his abdomen. The acidic waste in his gut had dissolved and was disposed of by the lymph system through the skin. With this removal, the pain and inflammation in John's intestinal tract vanished.

SUGGESTIONS FOR INFLAMMATORY INTESTINAL DISORDERS

- ➤ Far infrared pad—alkalinizes the intestinal tract. (See Resources.)
- ➤ Melatonin—reduces stress hormone levels. Start out taking 0.3 milligrams and increase the dosage until the desired effect is obtained. Maximum dosage is 5 milligrams. (Do not take if you have an autoimmune disease.)
- ➤ SAM-e—200 to 600 milligrams. Lowers stress hormone levels by improving brain function.
- ➤ Aangamik—six tablets.

➤ Caprylic acid—two tablets, 365 milligrams each, every day. It destroys yeast cells in the intestinal tract.

➤ Garlic—as much as you can eat for two to three days, preferably raw. Clears up inflammation in the intestinal tract. Proceed with care if the intestinal walls are severely lacerated.

➤ Castor oil packs—on the lower abdomen for one hour once a day for a minimum of one week. (See Resources.)

➤ Castor oil—one to two tablespoons. Relieves constipation by activating the intestines.

➤ Ice pack—whenever the abdomen feels hot, use an ice pack.

➤ Slippery elm tea—drink it warm, not hot.

➤ Vitamin E—400 to 800 units as a cancer preventative. It also heals hemorrhoids. The latter are more often caused by inappropriate diet than any other intestinal inflammatory conditions.

➤ Multiple vitamin and mineral supplements—to replace the nutrients that in intestinal disease often don't get absorbed into the bloodstream.

➤ Acupuncture. It helps normalize blood circulation.

➤ Pureed carrots—good for diarrhea, especially in babies and small children.

CHAPTER 4

OBESITY

My colleagues and I were sitting around a table in the faculty lounge of the university where we teach discussing the untimely death of Jim, an administrator, from a stroke. Only forty-eight years old, he was sixty to seventy-five pounds overweight and had high blood pressure. Because of his craving for junk food he hadn't been able to follow his doctor's advice to go on a calorie-reducing diet. One colleague quoted a government survey which showed that whereas in 1980 25 percent of all adults were overweight, in 1997 the number of obese adults had gone up to 33 percent. Another cited the frightening prediction of Doctors John Frey and Ken Goodrick, published in the medical journal *Lancet*. Extrapolating from current statistical information, they wrote that by the year 2030, the entire adult population in the United States will fall into the overweight category. Being overweight, defined as twenty pounds over the norm based on height, is linked to every major degenerative disease, including cancer, heart disease, diabetes, and arthritis.

HOW THE ASHANTI KEEP SLIM

Was it possible, I asked my colleagues, for a group of people on earth to remain insulated from the chemicalized, processed fast-food diet that had spawned the obesity epidemic in the United States? One professor, who came from Ghana, West Africa, said that the Ashanti of Ghana were one such people. He said they were the envy of neighboring tribes because of their slim, willowy figures. He had been told by non-Ashanti Ghanaians that there were no fat Ashanti because they ate such huge quantities of plantains.

In fact, the plantain is just one of many foods that explains why the Ashanti are not obese. The slimming effect of the Ashanti diet is assured by the fact that many of them still obtain their food by trapping and foraging, just like their ancestors, who lived more than ten thousand years ago, before herding and planting became the way of life in most of Africa.

The Neolithic era, characterized by a planned economy and cultivation of the soil, had passed the Ashanti by, chiefly because the territory of the Ashanti is forested. In the forest there is no grassy savanna for cattle to graze on, and no sunlit fields for planting grains, so farming and herding are impossible. Instead, the Ashanti trap small animals and deer, fish in streams, dig up such root vegetables as wild yam, and pick plantains off trees. Nothing that grows in the tangled vines, swamps, and dense foliage of the forest floor has been enriched and fattened by humans. The nutritional content of these wild foodstuffs is enough for the Ashanti's energy and the repair and regeneration of their body tissues, but it is not enough to make them fat.

Raw Foods Prevent Excessive Weight Gain

We should emulate, to the extent that it's possible, the raw food–eating habits of preindustrial cultures, because for nearly all of the 300,000 years of human existence, humans ate raw meat, fish, fruit, and vegetables. It was only with the Wurm Glacial period 65,000 years ago that humans began using fire for cooking, thus destroying by heat the enzymes in foods that prevent obesity. Enzymes keep weight down, because, like workers at a construction site who use just enough bricks and mortar to put a building together, they convert the food we eat into the exact quantity of raw materials needed for maintaining and rebuilding the body. The rest is eliminated.

However, in the case of enzyme-free cooked food, there is nothing to prevent too many nutrients from being absorbed into the body. What the body doesn't need is either stored in fat cells located in loose connective (adipose) tissue or turned into toxic, acidic waste. Cooked food also causes weight gain because, taking longer to digest, it leaves food particles behind. Leftover food turns into acidic waste, some of which is stored in the body as fat.

Dr. Edward Howell, in his excellent book *Enzyme Nutrition*, writes that unlike raw food, cooked food stimulates the endocrine glands, causing them to secrete excessive levels of hormones.[1] This increases body weight because hormones regulate body functions, that is, they switch body functions on and off according to the body's needs, and an excessive level of hormones turns on the production centers in the cells too often, causing the overproduction of nutrients. Excess nutrients are stored in fat molecules under the skin. A study in which the effects on weight gain between canned and raw food are compared supports Howell's contention. Conducted by Kohman, Eddy, White, and Sanborn of Columbia University and published in the journal *Nutrition*, April 1977, the study concluded that canned food, which must be cooked at a high temperature, caused more weight gain than the same food left raw.[2]

Monosodium glutamate (MSG), which is added to many bottled and canned foods as well as poultry and fast foods, is also linked to weight increase. A review of the article "Diabetes Danger in a Taste of Chinese" states that scientists have discovered that MSG affects insulin secretion.[3] Since MSG is known to excite the endocrine glands, it is safe to conclude that the islets of Langerhans in the pancreas that produce insulin, when exposed to MSG, become whipped up and overproduce it. Excessive levels of insulin lower blood sugar excessively. The resulting low blood sugar, referred to as hypoglycemia, is associated with obesity, probably because the excess glucose that is removed from the blood is converted to fat.

MSG is not the only artificial chemical that promotes obesity. Any foods that are altered by chemical additives confuse the appestat mechanism. This is the part of the brain that signals us to eat when our stomachs are empty and our body tissues need nourishment by creating hunger pangs. It tells us to stop when our stomachs are full and nutrient requirements are met, by creating a feeling of satiety. Chemicalized foods tend to stimulate hunger, even when the body does not need nutrients. Another factor contributing to obesity is eating food deficient in such alkaline minerals as calcium, magnesium, and potassium. (This includes most processed foods.) Alkaline minerals are needed to neutralize the acidic waste that is the by-product of even the most nutritious foods. When the supply of alkaline minerals is low, acidic wastes don't get neutralized. While some of the fatty acids in the waste are stored as body fat, other fatty acids are converted to cholesterol and lactic acid. This increases the acid levels in the blood and lymph fluids, which makes the body more vulnerable to weight gain because as blood, loaded with acidic waste, circulates, it clogs organ systems. This slows down metabolism, so that correspondingly less food (fuel) is burned up.

Excessive weight gain is also caused by the consumption of refined grains. Even before our digestive machinery had a chance to adjust its digestive juices to the grains that humans began cultivating a few thousands years ago, manufacturers in the early 1900s started removing the husks—where all the vitamins and minerals are stored—from grains in order to lengthen the shelf life of bread, cereal, pasta, and pastry products.

The health benefits of whole grains are not just in the nutritional content. They take longer to digest than carbohydrates with all the nutrients removed. The advantage of slow digestion of complex carbohydrates is that blood sugar levels don't end up excessively high. Refined carbohydrates, on the other hand, are broken down so quickly that they leave excessive glucose in the blood. This is another case where high blood sugar levels are converted by insulin to fat.

Excessive glucose in the liver is converted to fat just as it is in the blood. A fatty liver is more dangerous to health than layers of fat under the skin because the fat globules in the liver interfere with the detoxification of foods that are transported to the liver from the small intestine by the portal vein.

What's Wrong with a High-Protein, Low-Carbohydrate Diet

Many individuals who want to lose weight look for the silver bullet diet that doesn't demand too much sacrifice, but still guarantees weight loss. This is usually a diet that prohibits some foods while allowing unrestricted consumption of others. For example, one diet that was popular in the 1950s was all the bananas and ice cream you could eat and nothing else. This was a one-week diet. Another allows hardly any fat but the unrestricted consumption of carbohydrates. Such diets are appealing because they promise relief from ravenous hunger by allowing the dieter to pig out on one or two foods.

Certainly the most popular diet since it first appeared in England in 1860, in William Banting's book *Letter on Corpulence*, and more recently in Dr. Robert C. Atkins's *New Diet Revolution*, is the high-protein, high-fat, low-carbohydrate diet. Its popularity is understandable because it takes weight off relatively easily, and eating lots of meats seems to lessen the hunger pangs that drive many people to binge eating—at least in the beginning of the diet.

But if the objective in losing weight is to improve health, that should be the driving force behind the choice of diet. The high-protein, low-carbohydrate diet does not fulfill that objective because it is unbalanced. Eating so little starch deprives the body of glucose, its primary source of fuel, while eating too much meat threatens the body's minerals reserves. Excessive phosphate levels in meat can remove calcium and magnesium in the teeth and bones. Another danger to the body's supply of alkaline minerals is blood nitrogen urea from the breakdown of meat. Too much meat in the diet produces excessively high urea levels that the kidneys excrete along with magnesium and calcium.

Shifting viewpoints of the medical establishment as to what constitutes a healthy meal, as well as trendiness in diets, has made us lose sight of what used to be the axiom of nutritionists and doctors: the balanced meal made up of meat, potatoes, vegetables, and salad.

We can learn a valuable lesson from traditional cultures that never lost sight of the value of balancing carbohydrates and protein, the two staples of their diet. Two exceptionally long-lived populations in which obesity is rare are the Abkasians living in the Caucasus Mountains in Georgia and the Vilcabambans in the mountainous regions of Ecuador who combine a huge variety of proteins and carbohydrates at each meal. These two cultural groups eat similar foods. A typical breakfast or dinner in both cultures consists of soured sheep's milk, sheep's cheese, chicken or mutton, whole wheat bread, yams, potatoes, rice, soup, and greens.

In most tribal societies in Africa, including both meat and starches in every meal was a time-honored tradition because it reflected the social structure of the clan. For example, among the Kaguru of central

Tanzania a meal was said to be made up of both *ugali* (starches such as maize, millet, rice, plantain, and cassava) and *nyama* (stew meat). Only when nyama was not available did *mboga*, vegetables, take its place. Ugali represented the feminine gender because it was cultivated by women, while nyama was masculine because it was obtained by man's work as herdsman and hunter. The well-balanced diets of these preindustrial cultures prevented obesity because they did not produce excessive levels of fatty acid wastes that build up layers of fat in the body.

Weight Reduction for the Morbidly Obese

Anyone fifty pounds or more overweight is considered morbidly obese. These are people whose biochemistry is often unbalanced. For many in this category hunger is not satisfied even when the stomach is filled; others become morbidly obese even when they eat moderately. For both types of individuals a well-balanced diet with a lot of raw, organically grown foods must be accompanied by nutritional and hormonal supplements.

Cheryl fit into this category. She was seventeen years old at the time I met her, weighed 350 pounds, and was five feet, six inches tall. Cheryl's mother showed me her medical records. Physical examinations by an endocrinologist which included blood tests every year since she was twelve failed to show any abnormalities in glandular function, blood lipid levels, or blood pressure. Nevertheless, Cheryl had some symptoms of ill health such as migraine headaches, depression, and swollen ankles and feet.

A ravenous appetite, however, was not one of her problems. At times she went all day without eating because she wasn't hungry. Her one liking was for sweets, and she ate two chocolate candy bars at a time once or twice a week, hardly enough to account for being two hundred pounds overweight. I believed Cheryl when she said she was not addicted to sweets, because the favorite marzipan cake her mother made for her birthday was practically intact at the end of the week. Considering the small quantities of food Cheryl ate—her mother actually worried because she was hardly ever hungry—there could be only one cause for her obesity. She was not burning up her excess body fat. Her body shape was partly responsible. Cheryl had always been chubby, but before adolescence the fat was concentrated around her hips and thighs. As she put on the pounds, the fat crept up into her abdomen and chest. Excess fat in these regions is broken down and released into the bloodstream more quickly than the fat in the lower part of the body. This can lead to heart disease and liver damage.

It was essential, therefore, that Cheryl take off the excess layers of fat around the chest and abdomen. I had Cheryl place three five-inch by twelve-inch magnetic pads over her chest and abdomen at night when she went to bed. Magnetic energy is a useful adjunct in a weight-loss program, because the negative charge of the magnets helps the growth hormone pull fat out of the fat cells. Happily, the removed fat is not deposited elsewhere. Not only do the chest and abdomen areas flatten out, weight typically drops by fifteen to twenty pounds. After about two months Cheryl's chest and upper abdomen were protruding less and she had taken off ten pounds.

Cheryl's rotund shape was not only dangerous to her health, it made it very difficult for her to burn up fat. To generate additional energy, she used coconut oil, a tropical oil that's supersaturated. At room temperature the oil is a solid, white block, so hard that it has to be melted before it can be used. But unlike meat and some dairy fats, coconut oil is not converted into cholesterol. Nor does it add to the stores of body fat. Because it's made up of medium chains of fatty acids which oxidize, it's burned up. Cheryl took two tablespoons of coconut oil a day and at the end of three months had lost twenty pounds. This weight loss seems insignificant in relation to Cheryl's total weight, but it reduced the swelling in her ankles and feet.

To further raise Cheryl's energy level, with her doctor's approval, I had her take some thyroid extract even though her thyroid function tested normal. The thyroid supplement raised her body temperature slightly above the normal waking temperature of 98.6 degrees. This caused her body to produce more energy and she burned off twenty more pounds of fat.

An increase in the production of energy is not much benefit if it isn't transported to wherever it is needed in the body, so Cheryl took 50 milligrams of CoQ-10 twice a day. But CoQ-10 did not cause further weight loss, probably because Cheryl's energy distribution system was normal. Cheryl melted away another fifteen pounds after she started playing badminton with her father for two hours, five times a week.

The weight that Cheryl lost as a result of these measures alleviated most of her health problems. While she still has migraine headaches, she no longer gets a blind spot in the center of her visual field during an attack. Her depressed moods also occur less often. Cheryl's weight stabilized at around 270 pounds—not enough weight loss for her to be taken out of the morbidly obese category, but enough to make her feel much better. That was two years ago. Her mother called me recently to tell me that Cheryl had taken off another fifty pounds by eating only one meal a day and by taking a nutritional supplement called Stacker 11 for weight loss. This supplement contains a highly concentrated dose of ephedra. (Ephedra should not be taken by anyone with high blood pressure or any other cardiovascular disease.)

Factors to Consider in a Weight Loss Diet

What can be done about food addictions? Give them all up at once and see if there are any you can do without. Cheryl did this and discovered that whereas her craving for pizza and hero sandwiches persisted, she didn't miss the sodas. In place of soda, she drinks carbonated water.

SUGGESTIONS FOR WEIGHT LOSS

➤ Nearly raw potatoes. These are effective in reducing hunger pangs. For directions, see Chapter 3.
➤ Ice pack. Placed on the lower abdomen, it takes away the appetite.
➤ Raw honey. The brand Really Raw contains the starch-digesting enzyme amylase, which disposes of excess nutrients.
➤ Raw milk and butter. These are hard to find, but worth tracking down because of their rich supply of the fat-digesting enzyme lipase and the enzyme protease, which breaks down protein.

➤ Raw beefsteak. If the steer have been raised on hormone-
and pesticide-free feed, raw beefsteak is a good diet food
because it's loaded with protein- and fat-digesting enzymes.
Bartenders recommend rare roast beef sandwiches for
hangovers because the enzymes in the beef eliminate acid
aldehyde, the poisonous by-product of alcohol, which causes
the symptoms described as a hangover.

➤ Avocados and bananas. These are filling, but when eaten raw
don't cause unnecessary weight gain, and they contain more
enzymes than fruits and vegetables with fewer calories.

➤ Vitamin E. Not only normalizes thyroid function, but also
neutralizes the poisonous by-products of polyunsaturated oils,
which interfere with thyroid function. An underactive thyroid
produces less heat energy, so less fat is burned up.

➤ ChitoPlex. The gel in this resin absorbs fat. (See Resources.)

➤ Coconut and flaxseed oil. Two tablespoons daily help increase
energy production.

➤ Raw carrots. These remove fat molecules from the body.

➤ Acidic foods. Sour-tasting foods such as grape juice, vinegar,
and yogurt reduce hunger.

➤ Bland foods. Bland foods don't excite the taste buds and
stimulate hunger.

➤ Several small meals. Eating small amounts of food often,
rather than three big meals a day, keeps the digestive process
working and burning up energy.

➤ Blackstrap-lemon drink. Detoxifying the liver is an aid to
weight loss because it gets rid of acidic waste. Add two
heaping tablespoons of blackstrap molasses and the juice of a
lemon to a glass of hot water. Drink nothing but this
concoction for three days. Sip it slowly. Repeat this
procedure every few months.

➤ Ice water. Drink a lot of ice water, especially before a meal.
This reduces weight because in order to maintain the body's
internal temperature, which has dropped due to the cold
water, the body burns up additional calories.

One hard and fast rule all dieters should follow: no junk food before breakfast. A junk-food snack first thing in the morning ferments and putrefies in the stomach. Any healthy food eaten afterward, exposed to the bacteria in the putrefying and fermenting junk-food molecules, is also broken down into toxic waste by these bacteria.

The most critical factor in any weight-loss program is the efficient digestion of foods. Complete digestion means fewer acidic wastes. This has at least three advantages. First, appetite cravings are reduced (toxic acidic food residues create abnormal hunger pangs). Second, fewer acidic wastes means less fat sticks to the ribs. Third, reduction in toxic acidic wastes makes for a more alkaline environment in the body. This in turn increases the production of food-digesting enzymes. The more enzymes that break down food molecules in the gastrointestinal tract, the less food remains undigested and the better the chances to attain the ultimate in efficient digestion and consequent weight loss: oxidation (burning) of 97 percent of the food you eat.

CHAPTER 5

HYPOTHYROIDISM

A mystical teacher once wrote that an individual needs three forms of nourishment: air, food, and experience. Deprive the human of any one of these and he or she will die. There is another form of nourishment just as essential to life: light. Primitive tribes, far more than technically advanced cultures, understood that their vigor, strength, and energy depended upon exposure to sunlight. Among the Sakhas, hunter-gatherers in northern Siberia, a shaman (priest) exhorted tribal members at sunrise every morning to "let the first rays of the sun . . . give you strength." Indigenous peoples also understood that the absence of sunlight (energy) put their lives in danger. The Native Americans living in the Northwest believed that the overcast days of winter sapped their strength by causing poisons to accumulate in their bodies. They traveled long distances to hot springs in which they soaked themselves so that the steaming water would pull the toxins out of their bodies.

The Dogon peoples of Mali, West Africa, believed in the power of sunlight to support life, which they equated with energy and health, and equally in the power of evil spirits at night to cause illness and death. They felt so strongly that their lives depended upon observing this alternating cycle of day and night, because of its power over life and death, good and evil, that they patterned their way of life on it. In the built environment, they represented day and night as a series of alternating white and black squares and incorporated this pattern into the design of all their artifacts, including their villages. For example, in the morning and at sunset their two-story houses cast shadows into the adjoining courtyards. As houses and courtyards were built in rows, the sunlight on the houses and the shadow made by the upper part of the house into the courtyards created a series of alternating white and black squares. As for their way of life, the Dogon acknowledged the power of life (sunlight) by staying outside during the day and those of death (night) by building houses that let in no light, and by using them primarily as a place to sleep—a state of unconsciousness they equated with death and disease.

Medical science has substantiated the Dogon belief that darkness has a harmful effect on the body. The absence of light at night reduces the production of energy, and this slows down metabolic function and puts us to sleep. Sleeping, then, is a form of hibernation which gives the internal organs a needed rest and the time to detoxify, but at the same time places life in danger. The lack of light damages the power-generating factories (mitochondria) in the cells. This indicates to the adrenal glands that survival is threatened, and so they secrete more stress hormones. But without the energy to offset their harmful effects, stress hormones cause the blood to clot, cancer cells to proliferate, and acceleration of gallbladder disease.

The belief of indigenous cultures that the first light of day brings a renewal of energy and health has also been scientifically verified. For the pineal gland in the forebrain, which, through its regulation of the endocrine glands, controls all chemical reactions in the body, is stimulated into speeding up its actions by the first rays of light in the morning. The light, absorbed into pigment in the pineal gland, like the windup of a toy soldier which sets it marching, accelerates the flow of the pineal gland's hormonal messengers that regulate the pace at which all the chemical reactions in the body occur. As a result the output of thyroxin from the thyroid gland is increased. This increases the production of energy, which makes possible more efficient metabolic function and the reduction of acidic waste by-products that accumulate during the night.

The thyroid hormone thyroxin regulates the rate of energy production in the mitochondria in the cells. Large amounts of thyroxin supplements can even increase the number of mitochondria in the cells when they are needed to meet the body's increased energy requirements. The crucial role thyroxin plays in the production of energy is highlighted by the fact that even when depressed thyroxin levels are due to an underactive pituitary, thyroxin supplements or synthetic substitutes often normalize respiration. The many diseases associated with low thyroid function—cancer, cardiovascular problems, arthritis, and other degenerative diseases as well as infection—make clear that an underactive thyroid, resulting in insufficient energy levels, causes life-threatening health problems.

Until I reached middle age, I was unaware that the health problems I had had were symptoms of energy levels that weren't sufficient to sustain normal metabolic function and that this was due to an underactive thyroid. I was lacking in energy even as an infant. I didn't walk until eighteen months and didn't start talking until the age of three, at which time I started getting very painful canker sores—another symptom of hypothyroidism. My slowness was attributed to the "lazy baby" syndrome and the canker sores to an allergy to oranges.

By the time I was thirty, my eyes had become oversensitive to light. Even in winter on a gray day I wore sunglasses and left them on when entering a store because of the glare from the fluorescent lights. During the winter I caught one virus infection after another. Each infection lasted for two weeks, and my canker sores had become so painful that they kept me in bed for days.

I ignored the role of the thyroid in regulating the organ systems' fuel supply until treating each symptom separately no longer worked. Like a mechanic who repairs broken-down cars, I had treated each organ as a separate entity. Now taking the reverse approach, I attributed my health problems to low thyroid function. This point of view indicated that my eyes' sensitivity to light could be due to my thyroid's inability to convert enough beta carotene (the precursor of vitamin A found in carrots and other vegetables) into vitamin A, that my virus infections were caused by the thyroid's underproduction of the immune system's T cells, and that my cankor sores were the result of acidic food debris that wasn't broken down and disposed of because of a deficiency of energy. I took the basal thermometer test, a method for testing thyroid function discovered by Dr. Broda Barrens. Hundreds of studies in England have verified this test as the most reliable measurement of an underactive thyroid.[1] The test revealed that I had extremely low thyroid function. A blood test which showed that my thyroid stimulating hormone (TSH) blood levels were too high confirmed my depressed thyroid function. TSH is secreted by the pituitary gland to stimulate the release of thyroid hormones and when thyroid output is low, the pituitary releases higher amounts of TSH. My doctor prescribed Synthroid, a synthetic thyroid medication. For the year and a half that I took these supplements, I had no infections, my backache went away, and I had a little less trouble with food allergies.

After twelve months on Synthroid I began to feel restless; I itched all over, and my hair stood on end as though an electric current was running through it. I was having an allergic reaction and so switched to natural thyroid extract. The same allergic symptoms appeared. After trying two more thyroid formulas with the same results, I stopped taking thyroid supplements. This was scary because my waking temperature was just a little over 96 when it should have been around 98, my TSH pituitary blood hormone level was 20 (the normal range is between 0.4 and 6.0), and my T3 (the active form of thyroxin) blood level was 25 nanograms, far below the normal range of between 55 and 171.

Having gone off all thyroid medications, I was again plagued with virus infections. After a two-hour plane trip, I invariably came down with a temperature and sore throat. It became obvious that I was on the way to becoming a semi-invalid unless I found the cause of my underactive thyroid. The only factor that I had never considered was diet. Aware that the foods and/or beverages consumed most often are often the offending allergens, I reduced the number of cups of tea I drank every day from fifteen to one. Since then I haven't had any virus infections and my basal temperature is now 98.5, almost normal.

Testing for Underactive Thyroid

The basal thermometer test is the most reliable measurement of an underactive thyroid. To test thyroid function, take your temperature with a mercury thermometer. Place under the tongue or under your arm for seven to ten minutes three or four times a day. Upon waking before you get out of bed your temperature should be around 98 give or take two degrees; at mid-morning after you've had breakfast and been up and around for awhile it should reach the normal 98.6 degrees. This temperature should be maintained until early evening when it begins to drop to around 98 degrees. Any temperature reading below these numbers indicates an underactive thyroid. You can get an idea if foods depress your thyroid function by taking your temperature a half-hour after eating a single food and then an hour after that. (This shouldn't be confused with the pulse test.) A below-normal temperature after eating a single food item is a pretty good indication of a food allergy. Drinking one cup of tea causes my temperature to fall by about one degree; a second cup of tea causes a drop of two degrees. When I avoid tea, my temperature is 98.5.

Blood tests only measure pituitary (TSH) and T3 hormone blood levels, while temperature readings measure how much energy is actually being generated in the cells. You can use the temperature test not only to determine if you have an underactive thyroid but also how much thyroid medication you need. (Do this only in consultation with your doctor.) When you're on thyroid medication and your temperature normalizes (98.6) *without causing an increase in the heart rate or pulse*, you know you're taking enough medication to maintain normal metabolic function. Another advantage of measuring thyroid function with a mercury thermometer is that if your doctor, convinced that your thyroid function is normal because your tests have come out negative, refuses to give you thyroid medication, you can double-check with the temperature test. Some doctors are so fearful of thyroid medication that they associate an underactive thyroid only with nonspecific symptoms such as fatigue, brittle nails, and cold feet, and overlook it as a major cause of degenerative disease. This mind-set was developed by the medical media, which wrote about the thyroid "storm" caused by taking so much thyroid medication that the heart fibrillates, causing death from heart failure. What isn't mentioned in these articles is that such deaths occurred when, in the 1960s, a handful of doctors prescribed twenty-five to thirty times more thyroid medication than the average dosage.

Elevated Blood Pressure Indicates a Low-Functioning Thyroid

If you're fifty or older, you can get a pretty good idea of how well your thyroid is functioning by taking your blood pressure. In my experience, when blood pressure is elevated, body temperature tends to be below normal, indicating that waste debris from inappropriate food has raised the blood pressure by slowing down thyroid function. Monitoring your body temperature and your blood pressure to find out what foods are incompatible with your metabolism and then avoiding them is the most effective way to maintain normal thyroid function and good overall health. It's hard to imagine that anyone age fifty or older who has normal thyroid function (as determined by a mercury thermometer reading) as well as normal blood pressure could be suffering from any sort of degenerative illness because by that age in most people, acidic waste from bad diet has already lowered thyroid function and in most cases also raised blood pressure. Various studies indicate that anywhere from 50 to 90 percent of the population has a thyroid insufficiency.[2] If these figures were broken down by age, I'm sure it would show that nearly 100 percent of those over the age of fifty have an underactive thyroid. Individuals in their twenties, thirties, and sometimes even in their forties can eat horribly and still have normal thyroid function because they still have enough enzymes to neutralize excessive levels of acidic waste, which interfere with thyroid function. But by late middle age some enzyme-producing glands have worn out from overproduction.

Reducing Acidic Wastes to Revive Thyroid Function

Allergy-causing foods left over from incomplete digestion turn into acidic waste. Carried by the blood, this waste lodges in the capillaries near the thyroid, blocking the flow of oxygen and glucose, materials the thyroid needs to generate energy. Toxic wastes from food allergies can have same effect on the liver, further reducing energy production, since the liver stores sugar (glycogen) as well as converting thyroxin (T4) to the active T3 when more energy is needed. According to Ray Peat, Ph.D., in *Progesterone in Orthomolecular Medicine*, when the temperature of the nose, hands, and feet falls when you are hungry, and rises when you eat carbohydrates, the main cause of an underactive thyroid is the liver.[3] Detoxification of the liver with vitamins E and C, and avoidance of food allergens can heal the liver, and so restore energy production.

Besides allergy-causing foods, substances in certain foods suppress thyroid function. These foods are beans (all beans except string beans), peanuts, polyunsaturated oils, undercooked broccoli and cauliflower, cabbage, muscle meat, and beta-carotene. Goiter (enlarged thyroid) ceased to be a major health problem when iodine was added to salt, but more recently, with the use of iodide as an emulsifier used in bread dough, yogurt, and pudding to make a smooth consistency, the public is getting an overload of iodine. This can interfere with the thyroid's production of thyroxin to the same extent as too little iodine can, and is probably one of the causes of the current epidemic of hypothyroidism. Foods that promote thyroid function are heart, butter, vitamin A instead of beta-carotene, skin for its gelatin content (unless you are sensitive to MSG [monosodium glutamate]), and eggs.

Thyroid function is also inhibited by the heavy metal residues in processed foods and food additives which come from the metal used in their manufacture. Two examples are the aluminum used to hydrogenate oils, and sulfuric acid and chromium in the production of food additives. Estrogen, a stress hormone, is also responsible for increasing the heavy metal levels in our bodies because it stimulates the absorption of iron. Excess iron depletes oxygen needed for respiration, so less oxygen means a lower rate of respiration and lower energy levels. Avoiding processed foods that are contaminated with heavy metals improves thyroid function and lowers excess estrogen levels. This in turn will prevent surplus iron from being stored in the body which in older people becomes a problem, as an aging body absorbs heavy metals more readily than a young one.

Low thyroxin levels in the blood, which inhibit thyroid function, are also caused by water pollutants. Sir Robert McCarrison, a British physician who spent a lifetime traveling to remote areas of the world looking for the cause of goiter, found one answer on the side of a mountain in Kashmir, India. Nine villages built one above the other shared the same water supply that flowed in a channel down the mountain. This water served every purpose: drinking and cooking, irrigation of crops, bathing, washing utensils and clothes, as a latrine, and as a basin for catching manure-saturated runoff water from cultivated fields. While the water was relatively clean at the top of the mountain, as it flowed downward it gradually filled up with organic pollutants so that the lower a village was situated the more polluted the water and the greater the incidence of goiters. It would be hard to find a cause of goiter among the people in these nine villages other than the amount of pollution in their water supply, since the incidence of goiter in each village correlated directly with the degree of pollution in the water they used.

SUGGESTIONS FOR THE MAINTENANCE OF NORMAL THYROID FUNCTION

➤ If your temperature is subnormal, check for food allergies and food incompatibilities (see Chapter 2) before you start taking thyroid medication.

➤ The most effective thyroid medication is one that contains the active form of thyroxin, T3. In fact, many experiments show that medication that contains only T4 is dangerous. If the liver is sluggish and can't convert all the T4 into the active T3, the excess T4 suppresses thyroid function. So as not to overload the liver with T4, even if you are taking a supplement that contains some T3, break up the tablet into two pieces and take one piece in the morning and one at night. (For information on the thyroid medication Cynoplus, see Resources.)

➤ Vitamin E—400 to 800 units a day helps normalize thyroid function whether you have a hypoactive thyroid or a hyperactive one.

➤ Vitamin A—25,000 units daily. It converts cholesterol to progesterone, a hormone that enhances thyroid function.

➤ Mineral complex—preferably in liquid form, essential for the conversion of tyrosine, an amino acid, to thyroxin and for the conversion of T4 to T3 in the liver.

➤ A good source of glucose and minerals to ensure normal respiration is either orange or grapefruit juice. The minerals such as magnesium, potassium, sodium, etc. in these citrus juices are present in the right balance, and the sugar in the juice provides the chemical energy needed by the respiratory organelles for the manufacture of the form of energy the body uses for metabolic function.

➤ Vitamin B complex and C—to eliminate side effects of thyroid drug medication in individuals with hardening of the arteries.

➤ Coconut oil—two tablespoons daily. As an additional source of fuel, it counteracts the toxic effects of unsaturated oils on the thyroid gland.

➤ Raw eggs—Use only eggs laid by hens fed organically grown grain. Promotes thyroid and progesterone function. Also protects the fat in the body from degenerating.

➤ Progesterone—five to fifteen drops of progesterone oil applied locally wherever the blood vessels are close to the skin, for example, in the neck, improves thyroid function. The natural progesterone, derived from yams, has a different chemical structure than the pharmaceutical medication, which, along with estrogen in the hormone replacement therapy preparation, has been implicated in female reproductive cancer. (See Resources.)

➤ Pregnenolone—Lowers excessive levels of thyroxin in people with a hyperactive thyroid. Two symptoms of an overactive thyroid are bulging eyes and Graves disease. (See Resources.)

In the United States we don't have a problem with organic water pollutants since chlorine, a poisonous gas added to the water supply, kills off the bacteria that thrive on this waste. There is no mineral, however, that neutralizes the toxic chemicals that have infiltrated all the ground-water tables. Examples of water contamination by chemical wastes are resorcinol and dihydroxol by-products of coal mining operations in Kentucky. These have been discovered in the water supplies in towns in the Appalachian mountains where there is a high incidence of goiter, especially among children. Fluoridated water is also an inhibitor of thyroid function. Because the thyroid absorbs waterborne pollutants so easily, it's difficult to maintain normal thyroid function unless water used for drinking and cooking has been distilled or comes from underground springs that are tested regularly.

There isn't a mental or physical health problem in existence that can't be caused by an underactive thyroid—and therefore not one physical ailment that can't be improved by normalizing it. One of the factors extremely important in maintaining normal thyroid function is the one mentioned so often in this chapter because it is the original source of energy in our bodies: the sun. Direct sunlight converted into chemical energy (ATP) and imbedded in the glucose molecules in the food we eat provides the raw material for cellular respiration. We obtain a supply of chemical energy when we eat, say, an apple. After it is digested some of the glucose molecules in the apple are carried by the blood-stream to the mitochondria in the cells where they are split up to release their energy, which is used to create heat energy. But for this respiratory process to take place, red light, the longest light wave of the sun, must be present. Gaining entry into the body through the eyes and wherever there are a lot of blood vessels near the surface of the skin, the red spectrum rays of sunlight are carried by the blood to the pineal gland in the brain. They are absorbed into the pigment in this gland—much as sunlight is absorbed into the chlorophyll pigment in the chloroplasts in leaves so that photosynthesis (manufacture of glucose) can take place.

The quality of sunlight varies, depending upon the degree of clarity in the air. One place where sunlight has phenomenal health-giving potential is in Vilcabamba, Equador, one of a handful of mountainous enclaves in the world where people living on the mountainsides commonly live more than one hundred years. Visitors comment that the sky is so clear and the sun so sparkling in Vilcabamba that it defies explanation, and the inhabitants describe sun-storms that remove toxins from their bodies. There are still relatively unpolluted areas in the mountains and national parks in the United States where you can expose your body to a few weeks of good quality sunlight once a year—the most important factor in the generation of energy.

CHAPTER 6

CARDIOVASCULAR DISEASE

S am, my colleague at City College, who was born and raised on the African coast of Ghana, had a father who died at the age of 103 in full possession of his mental faculties. Sam believed he had inherited his father's longevity genes since in looks and mind-set he was his image. His father, however, had lived on freshly caught fish, fiber (from yams, plantains, and cassava), and coconut milk, which he drank straight from the shell when he got up in the morning. In addition, he sprinkled his food with what is considered the best salt in the world—mineral rich, reddish colored, and sweet tasting, it is raked up from the shoreline of the Ghanaian coast. Sam, on the other hand, had immigrated to the United States as a young man and had eaten processed foods most of his life. Now at age eighty-six his chances of living to be as old as his father were virtually nil since he was suffering from hardening of the arteries, a disease unknown among Ghanaians—despite their high intake of salt.

I recommended to Sam that he change his diet, but he chose to follow the advice of his doctors and underwent an angioplasty. This minor operation, in which a balloon is threaded through the arteries to the heart and expanded, clears away the plaque blocking the arteries. The operation appeared at first to be a success. With his arteries cleared, Sam's chest pains went away and the increased flow of blood through the widened arteries now carried a sufficient supply of oxygen to the cells for the production of energy. Once again full of vigor, Sam no longer swayed and tottered when he walked, and his voice lost the gravelly sound typical of people who are seriously ill.

Sam's return to health, however, was short-lived. Within six months the inside walls of his arteries were once again encrusted with fatty plaque and his symptoms had returned. What caused his arteries to harden after they had been cleared of cholesterol, calcium, and various other kinds of debris? Scientific researchers have come up with the culprit: a virus called cytomegalovirus located in the walls of blood vessels.

Several studies support the connection between the presence of the virus and the regrowth of plaque. In one study of seventy-five patients who had had an angioplasty, fatty plaque recurred in 75 percent of those patients who were infected with the cytomegalovirus, while only 8 percent who were not infected had a recurrence of plaque. Another study shows that patients with no symptoms of heart disease who were taking tetracycline were 30 percent less likely than those who were not taking antibiotics to have a heart attack.[1] A nutrient-poor diet can lead to virus infections in the cardiovascular system because, not digested properly, it leaves behind food molecules that turn into acidic waste. Viruses and bacteria thrive on these wastes and multiply. In this regard it is instructive to remember the bitter conclusion that the famous German pathologist Rudolf Virchow (1821–1902) came to after spending a lifetime doing research based on the belief that germs were the cause of disease. "If I could live my life over again I would devote it to proving that germs seek their natural habitat—diseased tissue. For example, mosquitoes seek the stagnant water but do not cause the pool to become stagnant."[2]

Another condition present in individuals with heart disease is inflammation of the inside walls of the veins and arteries. This connection has been established in many studies. One such study, published in the April 1999 issue of the *New England Journal of Medicine*, found that men whose arteries have been inflamed for several years are three times more likely to have heart attacks and two times more likely to have strokes as individuals whose arteries are not inflamed.[3] Currently, the most popular theory holds that inflammation in heart patients is caused by bacteria-induced infections. Antibiotics, vaccines, and strong anti-inflammatory drugs are given to eliminate infections and prevent the regrowth of plaque after an angioplasty. They succeed in doing so for a while, but studies have not been made on the long-term effectiveness of these treatments. It seems unlikely that the health of the arteries can be maintained in this way indefinitely when the condition that caused the infection and inflammation is not addressed. *That is the acidic waste in the blood flowing through the arteries and veins.*

Bacteria and viruses live off the acidic tissue of dead organisms—they are nature's primary decomposers. The fermentation and putrefaction (rotting) of undigested food circulating in the blood provides germs in the body with the same kind of acidic brew as the dead bodies of wild animals and plants provide the bacteria in nature.

Acidic waste in the blood makes scratches and tears on the inside walls of the blood vessels. The injured cells die off and turn into acidic waste, adding to the accumulation of acidic waste in the blood from undigested food debris. The larger the quantities of acidic waste the more rapidly germs multiply, forcing the immune system to defend the walls of the arteries and veins by triggering the growth of tumors to encapsulate germ colonies, patching the injuries in the lining of the vessels with fatty plaques to prevent life-threatening leaks, and reacting to arterial degeneration the same way it does to bodily injury from accidents—by triggering the flow of blood to the area which inflames the walls of the arteries. These measures prevent imminent death, but set up the conditions for a heart attack. All that has to occur is for a blood clot to form, which blocks the flow of blood to the heart. This typically happens when a calcified plaque on the vessel wall breaks loose. The most common symptoms of a heart attack are nausea, a feeling of suffocation, dizziness and fainting episodes, tightness in the chest, or pain in the region of the heart and/or left shoulder accompanied by feelings of anxiety. If, however, a pain in the chest occurs at the same time as the hands and feet become cold and breath becomes short it is usually a sign of indigestion.

Why was the role of "bad guy" in coronary heart disease assigned to cholesterol—that waxy, gray-yellow substance in our bodies that is vital to the growth of tissue, development of the brain, and manufacture of hormones? The answer lies in the mind-set of the medical establishment, which holds that when a medical problem arises, a "bad guy" is responsible: a virus, bacteria, or some harmful substance the body itself manufactures such as cholesterol. Medical researchers have ignored studies conducted by Rudolf Virchow in the nineteenth century. He discovered that degeneration of the blood vessels started before cholesterol plaques appeared in the lesions. The late Dr. G. E. Barnes reaffirmed Virchow's conclusions. He examined 50,000 autopsies of people who died in Europe during World War II when saturated fats like meat and butter were scarce. These autopsies showed advanced hardening of the arteries in spite of the low cholesterol diet in individuals who had died too young to have heart attacks. Legions of statistics show similar results, among them the fourteen-year Framingham study, which found that one-half of the individuals in the study who died of heart attacks had normal cholesterol levels.[4] This indicates that there is no definitive link between moderately high cholesterol and cardiovascular disease.

Dirk Collier was forty-eight years old and president and CEO of a Fortune 500 financial services company when he had a heart attack. He had just finished playing a tennis match when he felt a sharp pain around his heart and numbness in his left arm. His tennis partner called an ambulance, which delivered him to the nearest hospital just three blocks away from the club where they were playing tennis. The hospital confirmed that Dirk had had a coronary occlusion. I saw Dirk the day after he got out of the hospital. He couldn't believe that he was sitting in bed with a damaged heart, pain in his chest, and out of breath, when, for the last ten years, he had jogged three times weekly, taken a multiple vitamin and mineral complex, a B complex, and vitamin C. There was one vitamin he had overlooked, and that was vitamin E. The fifty units of E in his multivitamin was not enough to prevent his blood from clotting if he lacked the antithrombin (clotting) factor. Although Dr. Wilfred E. Shute, the first physician to use vitamin E for heart and artery disease, gave all his patients who were having or just had a heart attack 1,600 units of vitamin E a day, he started anyone who was recuperating from a heart attack with 800 units. That was the amount that Dirk took. After six weeks he had not regained his energy, so we upped the dosage by 200 units to 1,000. A month later Dirk had regained his strength and vigor, no longer felt pain in his chest, and had reverted to the peppy and exuberant personality he had been before his heart attack. Now, twenty years later, in retirement in Scottsdale, Arizona, he continues to take vitamin E—along with the other supplements he had taken before his heart attack. Vitamin E healed Dirk's cardiovascular system so effectively there is no medical evidence that he ever had a heart attack. Vitamin E also strengthened the walls of the varicose veins in his legs by reducing the swelling.

Nutrients for Cardiovascular Health

How did vitamin E heal Dirk's cardiovascular system? Its anticlotting factor prevented the formation of blood clots and its oxygenation of the blood neutralized the acidic waste that provided food for bacteria and injured the lining of the vessels and heart. Without the presence of these toxic acid particles, the self-healing powers of the circulatory system went into effect, generating new cells and breaking down and eliminating injured ones. Dr. Piero Anversa of the New York Medical College in Valhalla, New York, found evidence that the damaged heart muscle grows new muscle cells, although not enough to heal the damage done by a heart attack.[5]

Individuals who suffer from hypoxia (oxygen deficiency) are more vulnerable to heart disease than those who don't. It's not easy to recognize hypoxia. I had it and one of my symptoms was an inability to stand still for longer than five minutes without feeling faint—I broke out in a sweat and had to hold on to something to keep from keeling over. After I began taking vitamin E, I could stand still indefinitely without feeling light-headed. Vitamin E not only overcame an oxygen deficiency in my brain, but also increased the oxygen capability of my lungs. I can now swim twice the distance underwater that I could before I began taking vitamin E.

The B vitamins are also important in the prevention of cardiovascular disease. Their effect on cardiovascular health has only recently been brought to light through publication of the research that Dr. Kilmer McCully conducted at Harvard University more than thirty years ago.[6] McCully discovered that deficiencies in vitamins B_6, B_{12}, and folic acid give rise to abnormally high levels of a protein called homocysteine, which is a major factor in the development of heart disease. The left-over homocysteine not used for the repair and regeneration of cells turns into acidic waste because there is not enough folic acid, B_6, or B_{12} in the body to help the liver dispose of it. The acidic waste damages the lining of the blood vessels.

The importance of adequate vitamin B levels in the body is underscored by studies that reveal that people with low levels of folic acid have high levels of homocysteine, and a study of 14,000 physicians confirms the link between high homocysteine readings and heart disease. Those physicians with homocysteine levels higher than 95 percent of the population had three times the risk of heart attacks as those with normal homocysteine levels. Another study found that people who took B vitamin supplements had half the heart disease rate of those who didn't.[7] These studies indicate that even healthy individuals should take B vitamin supplements.

But vitamins B_6, B_{12}, and folic acid are not the only B vitamins whose shortage triggers heart disease. A deficiency in B_1, a vitamin that aids the heart in the production of energy, also increases the chances of having a heart attack. A diet heavy in refined carbohydrates, particularly sugar, depletes the stores of vitamin B_1 in the body.

Other nutrients essential to heart health include magnesium (an anticoagulant), vitamin C, and copper. Magnets and far infrared (FIR) energy—the heat generated by red light—have also been shown to help, as has hawthorn berry extract. Hawthorn berry's wide-ranging healing powers are due mostly to the fact that its beneficial effects begin *as soon as it is swallowed and enters the digestive tract*. The berry's abundant food-digesting enzymes step up the speed at which food in the stomach is broken down so there is little undigested food left to acidify. Hawthorn berries also contain an alkaline factor that binds with acidic particles and neutralizes them. When no acidic waste is formed in the digestive tract, the arteries, veins, heart, and kidneys have a chance to heal and the fatty plaque "bandages," no longer needed, are dissolved and carried away by the blood.

Another important step in promoting the health of the cardiovascular system is to eat enough omega-3 fatty acid found in oceangoing fish such as cod and salmon, and also in green leafy vegetables and eggs.

The health of the heart and the arteries depends on a balance between fats from fish and such vegetables as spinach, collard greens, and kale, and those from meat and butter fat. A recent study shows that diets rich in fish and green leafy vegetables lower the incidence of heart disease.[8] According to this study, in Japan and the Mediterranean countries where people eat large quantities of fish and green leafy vegetables, individuals with high blood pressure are three times less likely than Americans and Northern Europeans with high blood pressure, who eat very little of these omega-3 rich foods, to die of a heart attack.

SUGGESTIONS FOR CARDIOVASCULAR HEALTH

➤ Vitamin C—500 units.

➤ Vitamin E. Begin taking 800 units a day. Increase the dose by 200 units every six weeks until your symptoms disappear. Don't take more than 1,600 units. For heart disease prevention, women should take 400 units daily, men 800 units, and children no more than 100 units.

➤ Vitamin B complex—containing at least fifty milligrams of B_1, B_2, B_3, and B_6. Your daily intake of folic acid should be 1,000 micrograms. For prevention, take 800 micrograms of folic acid daily, along with 500 micrograms of B_{12} (take the sublingual tablet), and 100 milligrams of B_6.

➤ Hawthorn berry extract. Begin with twenty drops and work up to fifty drops three times a day. Even if you don't have heart disease, when you reach the age fifty, take twenty drops twice a day to prevent decomposition of the heart. Hawthorn berry extract lowers blood pressure by dilating the peripheral blood vessels that are responsible for a rise in blood pressure.

➤ Taurine—two to four grams a day. This amino acid is used extensively in Japan to treat congestive heart failure and heart arrhythmias (irregularities).

➤ Mineral complex that includes at least 400 units of calcium, potassium, and magnesium and 200 micrograms of selenium.

➤ Thyroid supplement—speeds up the efficiency with which waste products are eliminated from the body by speeding up metabolism. (For how to obtain one such medication, Cynoplus, see Resources.)

➤ CoQ-10—involved in the production and transportation of energy in the heart. There is more CoQ-10 in the heart than in any other organ. The heart patient should take at least ninety milligrams of this nutrient daily. For maintenance of the cardiovascular system, take thirty milligrams.

➤ Multiple enzyme tablets with each meal.

➤ Carpain—an enzyme found in papaya that is good for the heart.

➤ Hot water with lemon juice—drink the first thing in the morning. It removes plaques from arterial walls, detoxifies the liver, and stimulates the production of food-digesting enzymes.

➤ Cooked asparagus and raw or cooked celery. The arsenic in these vegetables, which is in phosphate form and therefore not dangerous, aids in the regeneration of heart tissue.

➤ Celastyn (cetyl myristate). Six tablets daily of this fatty acid lowers high blood pressure caused by hardening of the arteries. (See Resources.)

➤ Pycnogenol—fifty milligrams twice a day. Extracted from pine bark, it's the most easily assimilated bioflavonoid. Reduces inflammation and strengthens the inner lining of blood vessels, so it's also effective for varicose veins. Helps dissolve blood clots in phlebitis.

➤ L-carnitine—1,500 to 3,000 units. Decreases cholesterol and triglycerides, and aids in the transport of fatty acid used by the heart to manufacture energy.

Allergies and High Blood Pressure

High blood pressure occurs when the walls of the blood vessels become constricted and cause a rise in the pressure exerted by the blood against the blood vessel walls. If the blood vessels are healthy (that is, if they are not inflamed or hardened), they can take this added pressure without being injured or endangering the heart. If there is some hardening in the arteries, however, even when the high blood pressure is caused only by food allergies, constricted blood vessels can cause a heart attack or stroke because increased pressure on arteries and veins encrusted with calcified plaques can force a calcified plaque loose. This triggers the formation of a blood clot.

In devising a diet that will lower your blood pressure, first test for food allergies, then take a test to determine whether you have a grain-eating or meat-eating metabolism. When you eat according to your metabolic type and avoid food allergens, you avoid the acidic waste that injures the heart and blood vessels and starts the process of calcification that causes blood clots to form.

CHAPTER 7

KIDNEY DISEASE

Everyone who has ever watched boxing knows there is one part of the body it is against the rules to punch—the lower abdomen in the back where the kidneys are located. The kidneys are vulnerable for two reasons. First, they're vulnerable because of their location: unlike the heart, lodged between the breast bone and the backbone; the lungs, tucked behind the rib cage and in front of the backbone; and the stomach, liver, pancreas, and intestines shielded in times of danger by the reflexive action of the arms and legs, the kidneys have no such buffers to protect them. Second, they're vulnerable because of the role they play in the body.

In the center of each of the two fist-sized kidneys, located on either side of the spinal chord in the lower back, are millions of microscopic structures called nephrons. They do the work of the kidneys—filtering the blood. They are microscopic, very fragile, number in the millions, and are encircled by a network of blood vessels. Each nephron is made up of a cuplike structure called the glomerulus which is attached to a long, narrow tube, referred to as a tubule. The glomerulus resembles a bent-over, partially opened bud, while the tubule connected to it forms a loop like the outline of a test tube. The blood vessels in this structure remove all the compounds in the blood plasma except the protein and red blood cells. The separated compounds—water, urea, glucose, minerals, and enzymes—then flow into the capillaries in the tubules where most of them are reabsorbed into the main bloodstream. What's left behind—excess water, salt, urea, and uric acid—constitutes urine. It leaves each kidney through a tube (ureter) connected to the bladder, where it's stored until the nerves in the bladder signal the brain that it needs emptying.

If water, salt, urea, and a small amount of uric acid were all that the kidneys had to filter from the blood, kidney failure would be unknown. However, to prevent death from toxemia (blood poisoning), which is to say, excessive blood acid levels (a lowering of the alkaline pH in the blood from the normal 7.4 to 6.9 is fatal), the kidneys must filter acidic waste from the circulatory system, which they weren't programmed to handle. What the liver can't process because of congestion and/or over-work is dumped back into the main bloodstream and carried by the blood to the kidneys for removal.

There are many different kinds of toxins and acidic waste in the blood that are left to the kidneys to dispose of. Some of the toxins come from the serum used in immunization shots. (One of the worst vaccines is the polio shot, which contains twenty-eight compounds foreign to the body, among which are diseased monkey tissue and formaldehyde, an embalming fluid. This vaccine and the rest of the immunization pro-gram given to children, starting just a few days after birth, is estimated to have caused millions of cases of kidney degeneration in the young.) The kidneys also have to filter mercury, lead, iron, and cadmium out of the blood when there aren't enough alkaline minerals and phagocytes in the liver to neutralize these heavy metals. Another source of acidic waste sometimes left for the kidneys are the end-products of incom-plete digestion. An example is serum protein. A healthy liver neutral-izes serum protein by converting it into salts. When it fails to do so, the kidneys have to filter this strong acid "as is." The kidneys are also burdened at times with the removal of acetic, lactic, and sulfuric acid, the by-products of body (metabolic) function which the liver hasn't had the time or energy to convert into weaker acids. Excess blood sugar is still another acidic waste which the kidneys have to handle when insulin levels are too low to do so.

As these acids are filtered out of the blood by the capillaries in the nephrons, they act like harsh cleaning solvents, scraping and scratching the inside walls of these micro blood vessels. And just as large injured blood vessels are patched up with calcium-encrusted fatty plaques, so the damaged walls of these micro vessels in the nephrons get filled in with microscopic particles of calcium and fat. While it usually takes decades before arteries and veins become completely clogged, the nephrons' tiny capillaries are stopped up in much less time.

As nephrons are knocked out, the remaining ones need more plasma (liquid) in the blood to strain the filtrate (the solid part of the blood). The hormones that regulate water levels comply by directing the flow of more water into the blood plasma, enabling the nephrons to filter the blood with ease. The downside is that with the increase in blood volume, blood pressure rises. Doctors react by prescribing a diuretic. Thus the action taken by the body to protect the nephrons is reversed as the diuretic drug reduces the liquidity of the blood, and the nephrons once again have to overwork to filter the solid materials out of the blood. The nephrons are injured in still another way. Once the acids cause the arteries to harden so that they can no longer absorb the pressure of the circulating blood, the kidneys have to bear its impact.

The kidneys are more vulnerable than other organs not only for all the reasons mentioned above, but also because they are less versatile. For one thing, unlike the liver, the kidneys can't convert acids and other toxins into less noxious substances. Nor do the kidneys have the regenerative power that the liver and lungs have. The liver, like the crab, which grows a new claw to replace a missing one, can regrow a part that has been surgically removed or destroyed by disease. Emphysema and tuberculosis patients have been healed when their deteriorated alveoli (air sacs) were rebuilt by a steady diet of dark green vegetables, and natural chemicals have stimulated the production of new air sacs in the lungs of rats. (Scientists at the Georgetown University School of Medicine treated rats who had emphysema-like lesions in their lungs with retinoic acid, a derivative of vitamin A. It caused the growth of new alveoli sacs.[1]) But nephrons have never been revived or regenerated to my knowledge to the point where kidney failure has been reversed.

One of the kidneys' tasks is to regulate the concentration of salts in the body. When the kidneys' management of salt metabolism is normal, each atom of sodium picks up twenty-one molecules of water which is excreted from the body as urine. The fact that urine enters the bladder from the kidneys drop by drop gives an indication of how slowly the kidneys filter water and waste products out of the blood. When water is poured into the digestive tract like torrents of water from a faucet turned on full, it stretches the walls of the capillaries in the nephrons to the breaking point. The best way to synchronize drinking water with the rate of speed with which the kidneys process it is to sip it. Another way to supply the body with water at the same rate at which the kidneys remove it from the blood is to eat raw those vegetables and fruits that have the highest percentage of water, such as tomatoes, cucumbers, lettuce, and oranges. The much slower process of eating as opposed to drinking ensures that the amount of water ingested won't be more than the kidneys can filter out of the blood at any given time.

Nephritis and Kidney Stones

During his childhood, Gordon had one ear infection after another in the winter, a possible indication that the ear malformation he was born with extended into his inner ear. Antibiotics hadn't yet come into use, so his mother used aspirin to bring his temperature down. A few days after he had gotten over a particularly severe ear and throat infection, Gordon came down with a fever, chills, nausea, and a headache. A blood test showing that he had albumin (a water-soluble amino acid), and red and white blood cells in his urine, substances which the nephrons shouldn't have filtered out of the blood, indicated that he had nephritis—inflammation of the kidneys. One good piece of news, shown by the absence of hyaline casts in his urine, was that his nephrons hadn't deteriorated. The doctor recommended aspirin to reduce the inflammation, plenty of water, and bed rest. Gordon recovered in two weeks and the doctor assured his mother that his kidneys hadn't suffered any permanent damage, that he still had "fine filtration." He didn't comment on how the nephritis had changed Gordon's appearance. His complexion was now gray and pouches had formed under his eyes.

The cause of Gordon's nephritis could have been all the aspirin he took for the dozen or so ear infections he had each winter for five successive years during his childhood. Although aspirin and other analgesic compounds are anti-inflammatory agents, in the long run they have the

opposite effect. Their hyperacidity destroys the alkaline-forming minerals in the blood. This acidifies the blood and as a result, as the kidneys filter it, they are damaged by the high blood acid levels. That the
acidic particles targeted Gordon's kidneys rather than any of his other
vital organs was due to an inherent infirmity. Gordon's malformed earlobes provide the clue. Because ears and kidneys grow in the embryo at
the same time—which might explain why both organs are shaped like
a kidney bean—a malformed earlobe can be a sign of kidney problems.[2]

Once Gordon got over his ear infections, he had no health problems
for many years. He became a chemical engineer, married, and had five
children. He got a job with Dupont right after he graduated from Texas
A&M. At the age of forty-two he developed symptoms that reminded
him of the way he felt when he had nephritis as a child. He had a dull
ache in his lower back, urinated more frequently, had blood in his urine,
and felt so nauseated that he vomited. The doctor ordered an MRI,
which revealed kidney stones. He arranged for Gordon to be admitted
to the hospital. As Gordon was packing his suitcase for the trip to the
hospital, he suddenly felt pains in his lower abdomen which were so
sharp that he doubled up in agony. The pains disappeared as suddenly
as they had come. It turned out that they were caused by the passing of
his kidney stones through one of the ureter tubes connecting the kidney to the bladder. Once in the bladder, the stones passed through the
urethra along with the urine without causing any discomfort.

The doctor advised Gordon that to prevent a recurrence he should
drink a lot of liquids, eat less meat, and avoid all green vegetables. As
Gordon was addicted to soft drinks, he convinced himself that drinking more soda would be just as good for his kidneys as drinking a lot of
water. He was not successful in keeping his meat protein intake to the
recommended seven ounces daily, but had no trouble giving up green
vegetables. Given his halfhearted commitment in the matter of diet and
the misguided advice of his doctors to give up all greens, it's not surprising that five years later Gordon felt the familiar dull ache. Only this
time he felt it not only in his lower back, but also in his legs and groin;
nor did the pain stop as it did with the first kidney stones. The stones
were too big this time to migrate through the urinary tubes and pass
out in the urine. Gordon had to have them removed. After that, his kid-

neys formed stones every five years. By the time he reached his early seventies, Gordon had had his kidney stones removed six times: four times by traditional surgery, once by laser, and once by sound waves. He had also had two recurrences of the nephritis

It's not unusual in older age for the organ system that was infected in childhood to degenerate. For example, those who were crippled as children from polio but with exercise and massage managed to walk again are often confined to wheelchairs in old age. Likewise, children who had repeated mastoid operations when their ear infections spread to the mastoid bone often need a hearing aid as they get older, or have strokes in the auditory center of the brain. This happens because as the body ages, acidic wastes accumulate in the areas that were injured in childhood.

In Gordon's case, the acidification of his kidneys began with the huge quantity of aspirin he took as a child to relieve his ear infections. The acidic condition of his kidneys was reinforced when during his teenage years he became a habitual cola drinker. He continued devouring soft drinks as an adult. Gordon was proud of the fact that he rarely drank alcoholic beverages. What he didn't know was that the sugar in the soda, combined with the other ingredients, fermented in his stomach. He was getting a high without drinking alcoholic beverages, but was paying the price. Filtering alcohol out of the blood places a burden on the nephrons. Moreover, fermented liquid prevents the breakdown of food in the digestive tract. This deprives the body of nutrients, and the undigested food turns into acidic debris that can lower the blood's pH factor. The acid-forming phosphorus in the colas also increases the acidity of the blood—and the kidneys, in the process of filtering it, break down.

The combination of his habitual consumption of cola, along with the aspirin compounds he had as a child, could have caused Gordon's kidney stones, but his overconsumption of meat was probably also a factor. The effect of a heavy meat diet on the formation of kidney stones is made clear in an experiment described in an article in the *Journal of Urology*.[3] Because of increasing contact with the West since World War II, the Japanese have been eating more meat and fewer vegetables. To prove that this change in diet is responsible for the tripling of the rate of kidney stones among the Japanese, researchers at Kinki University in

Osaka divided 370 men into two groups and put each on a different diet. One group was on a low-meat, high-vegetable diet and the other simply increased their intake of fluids. The former group of men were 40 to 60 percent less likely to have a recurrence of kidney stones than the latter.

The problem with large quantities of meat in the diet is that urea, the by-product of protein breakdown, causes too much urine to be excreted. This has the effect of throwing out the baby with the bathwater, because alkaline-forming mineral molecules are excreted when urine output is excessive. Without enough alkaline-forming minerals to neutralize the excess acidic waste in the blood, the urine becomes highly acidic. This causes particles in the urine to stick together and gradually get bigger until they form stones.

Kidney stones are usually composed of calcium and oxalic acid. (Urates from uric acid and sulphates from sulphuric acid have also been found in stones.) What most people with kidney stones don't know is that oxalic acid, like calcium, is vital to metabolic function. Ninety-eight percent of the oxalic acid in the body is produced internally and is used for moving food through the digestive tract by peristalsis (the contraction and expansion of muscles). Oxalic acid also aids in the absorption of calcium into the cells.

Leftover oxalic acid, along with excess calcium, is removed from the blood by the kidneys, and passes into the urine. Calcium oxalate permeates the urine generally, but only in those people whose urine is overloaded with acidic waste does it form stones.

It would seem therefore that the way to prevent kidney stones would be to alkalinize the urine. But urologists, unaware apparently that the acid-alkaline pH factor in the urine determines whether or not stones are formed, recommend reducing the levels of calcium and oxalic acid in the diet. Kidney stone patients are instructed not to eat any green vegetables, especially broccoli, which is high in calcium, and spinach, beet greens, and chard because of their high oxalic acid content. By doing so, doctors are depriving their patients of valuable nutrients, one of which, calcium, actually helps prevent kidney stones by alkalinizing the urine.

It's probably a good idea for anyone who has a tendency to form stones to avoid cooked spinach, beet greens, and rhubarb, the only foods that are extremely high in oxalates (although oxalates from these foods constitute only 2 percent of the oxalates in the body, hardly enough to be considered responsible for creating stones). They can, however, use these greens in salads.

SUGGESTIONS FOR KIDNEY STONES AND NEPHRITIS

➤ Vitamin E—800 to 1,600 units daily. Reduces inflammation through its oxygenating effect.

➤ Vitamin A—50,000 units daily for three months; 25,000 units thereafter.

➤ Cranberry juice—eight ounces three times daily.

➤ Vitamin C—1,000 milligrams daily.

➤ Raw asparagus juice—eight ounces two times daily.

➤ Magnesium oxide—400 to 800 milligrams daily.

➤ Vitamin B_6—100 to 250 milligrams daily.

➤ Choline—250 milligrams four times a day.

➤ Lower consumption of meat—no more than seven ounces daily.

➤ Vegetables—raw, whole, and juiced—should be the major part of the diet until the kidney stones are dissolved and/or the inflammation is gone.

➤ Hot water with the juice of one lemon—one glass every day in the morning upon waking for its detoxifying effect.

CHAPTER 8

MENTAL AND NEUROLOGICAL DISORDERS

Neuroscientists map abnormal brain function. The challenge they have taken up is to devise experiments that show how the mood-disordered brain reacts to emotional stimuli and how these reactions differ from those of normal brains.

Dr. Rodolfo Llinas, a professor at New York University Medical School, discovered an aberrant chemical reaction common to many brain diseases (depression, Parkinson's disease, obsessive-compulsive disorder, and tinnitus [ringing in the ears]), but he didn't go one step further and explore the connection between brain disorders and abnormal blood chemistries.[1] To do so would amount to an admission that curing brain disorders depends upon improving blood chemistry rather than manipulating brain function. The problem lies in the neuroscientists' focus on the brain's extracellular activities—the motions of cells, the directions in which neurotransmitters convey thoughts and feelings, or the abnormal shapes of cellular brain tissue—rather than on the internal function of the brain cell. It is what is going on inside the cells that determines how a cluster of brain cells behave. There is as yet no way of visualizing the internal functions of cells. Since, however, the capillaries deliver nutrients, hormones, and other raw materials to the cells and pick up the acidic waste by-products of their metabolic functions, a blood profile gives some idea as to the quality of intracellular function.

The connection between abnormal brain function and abnormal blood chemistry is obvious. The typical blood chemistry of someone with a mental disorder shows elevated levels of such heavy metals as copper, iron, and lead, of ammonia, estrogen, histamine (an indication of allergies), and in schizophrenia alien chemicals called porphyrins and kryptopyrroles. Even some nutrients, if present in such large amounts that not all of them are used, break down into acidic toxic waste. Excessive blood levels of copper, lead, iron, and estrogen are toxic, and their overload in the blood indicates that they have also accumulated in excessive amounts in the cerebrospinal (intercellular) fluid in the brain and in brain cells whose membranes have developed leaks.

Wastes such as ammonia, heavy metals, lactic acid, and other debris in the blood accumulate in the brain (rather than in some other organ system) when it has sustained an injury, or when a key enzyme or coenzyme in the brain is missing due to a genetic defect. There are plenty of studies linking schizophrenia and other mental disorders to fetal brain injury due to maternal viral infections, misplacement of the fetus in the uterus, difficult pregnancies, and so on, and even more so to a family history of mental illness. Genetically defective or injured tissue becomes overloaded with toxic waste because such tissue either lacks the chemicals (enzymes, vitamins, or minerals) or the energy needed to neutralize the residue by-products of such cellular functions as assimilation of food, respiration, and the manufacture of protein. This accretion of acidic waste in and around injured areas of the brain, with nothing to keep it in check, grows. Excessive levels of acidic wastes, heavy metals, and ammonia in the blood are most likely responsible for the swelling (inflammation) of the corpus callosum and of the ventricles that Fred Bookstein of the University of Michigan's Medical Center found in the brains of schizophrenics.[2] And the elevated estrogen so commonly found in individuals with brain disease may be the real reason for the aberrant chemical reactions that Llinas found.

Symptoms of fear, anxiety, and/or depression worsen mental disorder because they trigger the flow of the adrenal hormone cortisol. When the release of cortisol (which is ordinarily liberated in big doses only as a response to life-threatening situations) is prolonged because of persistent feelings of anxiety and fear, it destroys brain cells in the hippocampus (a part of the primitive limbic system where long-term memories are stored). This explains why most schizophrenics have a smaller than normal hippocampus. Emotional and physical abuse during childhood also causes injury to this region of the brain, and these injuries can give rise to intellectual and emotional disabilities.

Brain disease can also lead to degenerative disease in other parts of the body. While acidic waste in the neurons clogs the organelles (machinery) inside the cells until they grind to a halt and the cell dies and turns into acidic waste (again adding to the acidic pool in the injured brain tissue), another portion of the waste is carried off by the capillaries and gets into the general circulation. The high levels of toxic chemicals in the blood solidify when they bond with alkaline minerals and are deposited in other organ systems, giving rise to degenerative disease elsewhere in the body.

Energy Deficiency in the Brain

A lack of energy is the biggest problem in brain disorder because enzymes and coenzymes (vitamins and minerals) can only neutralize the accumulated waste in the brain tissue if they have enough fuel. A fuel deficiency can be caused by a thyroid that doesn't produce enough of the hormone thyroxin to maintain normal energy levels. Low energy levels in turn inhibit the production of glucose. Thus a deficiency of thyroxin has a snowball effect. The mitochondria are not stimulated (because of a lack of thyroxin) to produce enough energy to fulfill the brain's energy requirements and the resulting lack of energy interferes with the liver's ability to produce an adequate quantity of glucose, the raw material out of which energy in the body is made. Since the brain generates more energy than any other organ in the body—although the brain is only 2 percent of the body weight, it uses up 60 percent of the body's glucose reserves (and 25 percent of its oxygen supply)—a shortage of glucose is more injurious to the brain than to any other organ.

Another cause of deficient energy levels in the brain is a lack of the hormone progesterone. Because anxiety and depression trigger the continuing circulation of cortisol in the blood, there is not enough of this hormone left over for its conversion into progesterone. A deficiency of progesterone raises estrogen levels, and estrogen lowers energy production by destroying glucose and oxygen. Progesterone is so important to the brain's production of energy that it lessens and sometimes even eliminates symptoms of a whole range of brain diseases (bipolar depression, schizophrenia, Parkinson's disease, epilepsy, neuritis, and migraine headaches)—in some cases only forty minutes after it is taken.

Low thyroid hormone and glucose levels and excessive estrogen are not the only problem with the inability of diseased brains to generate enough energy. If the oxidoreductase enzymes in the mitochondria of the cells that carry out the process of respiration are sluggish, even higher than normal levels of thyroxin and glucose can't increase the production of energy. Dr. William H. Philpott, an expert on the therapeutic use of magnetic energy, states that the stumbling block in the cure of mental disease with nutritional protocols is the paralysis of these enzymes. According to Philpott, the oxidoreductase enzymes can be activated by removing acidic wastes in the affected brain area with a negatively charged magnet placed on the head. (See Resources for where to obtain magnets.)

Besides thyroid supplements, progesterone, and magnetic energy, nutrients that stimulate respiration (energy production) include saturated meat fats (and the avoidance of polyunsaturated oil, which poisons the thyroid), vitamin B_1 (thiamin), and vitamin C. Vitamin C helps produce the amino acid tyrosine, which is converted into the thyroid hormone thyroxin. Although most individuals with mental disease have excess levels of copper in their blood, anyone with a deficiency of copper needs to supplement their diet with copper since it is the receptor for the red light waves of the sun inside the energy manufacturing plants (the mitochondria) in the cells.

Few people realize that sunlight is a vital part of the cellular respiratory process by which the chemical energy in glucose is converted into heat energy. The importance of sunlight in energy production in the brain is underscored by the fact that in Third World countries, although coronary heart disease, cancer, and diabetes have become common (since the introduction of refined sugar, flour, soda, and canned goods), schizophrenia and depression are still rare. While the inhabitants of these countries have given up their traditional foods, because of the tropical climate they still spend a great deal of time in the sun. It would seem then that as far as the health of the brain is concerned, sunlight for the manufacture of energy is more important than a healthy diet.

Cellular respiration in the brain can also benefit from a raw material not ordinarily associated with respiration, and that is glutamic acid, an amino acid. Taken in the form of L-glutamine, it can get through the highly selective membrane (blood-brain barrier) of the brain capillaries where it produces a special, concentrated energy useful for those with or without brain disorders who suffer from inertia. Glutamic acid also gets rid of excess ammonia in the blood, a problem in most mental disorders. (Dr. Roger Williams recommends one to four grams per day for schizophrenics.) There is however, a downside to glutamic acid. Individuals who are allergic to this amino acid when it is separated from other amino acids (as in the flavoring MSG or meat broth) must avoid it since in these people it acts as an excitotoxin, distorting the functions of neurons by accelerating their movements and causing them to heat up.

Nutritional Therapy for Mental Disorders

Individuals with mental disorders also tend to have a deficiency in the B vitamins, vitamins E and C, and such minerals as zinc, magnesium, calcium, and manganese. Magnesium and vitamin B_6 have a calming effect on the agitated brain, but magnesium has an importance of its own. This was pointed out by the French scientist M. L. Robinet in the *Bulletin of the Academy of Medicine* published in France back in 1934.[3] He found that more people commit suicide in regions where the magnesium content of the soil is low. But it's not only the lack of minerals in the foods grown in mineral-deficient soil that is responsible for the low magnesium levels in the bodies of those with mental disorders. Excessive amounts of stress hormones circulating in the blood of emotionally disturbed people deplete blood magnesium levels. But when magnesium and/or other nutrients are supplied in large enough quantities—provided energy levels in the brain are sufficient—symptoms of mental disorder can disappear. Magnesium in combination with B_6 is effective in alleviating learning disabilities and emotional disorders in children. Megadoses of niacin (vitamin B_3) cures pellagra, a vitamin B_3 deficiency disease which causes such symptoms as paranoia and hallucinations, as well as elevated blood levels of porphyrins. In 1964, Dr. J. McDonald Holmes wrote in the *British Medical Journal* about a number of studies that revealed that individuals who have a deficiency of vitamin B_{12} suffer memory loss, hallucination, paranoia, and epilepsy— until they receive injections of B_{12}.[4] The B vitamins are vital to brain function because the myelin sheathing covering the neurons in the brain and the rest of the nerve cells in the body contains greater concentrations of B vitamins than any other organ tissue in the body.

Dr. Abram Hoffer, a pioneer in the holistic treatment of mental disorders, was successful in curing schizophrenia with vitamins B_3, B_6, and B_{12}. That stems from the ability of these B vitamins to eliminate porphyrins, the alien chemical that causes hallucinations, paranoia, and delusions. Hoffer typically started out adults with schizophrenia and/or chronic depression on three grams of B_3 in the form of niacin and an equal amount of vitamin C and went up depending on need to as high as twenty-two grams. Beyond that amount, he found that there was no improvement. In individuals who had longstanding cases of schizophrenia he included one to two grams of B_1 and B_6 as well as magnesium, calcium, manganese, and zinc.

Vitamin C, along with niacin, picks up the "garbage" in the blood, while vitamin B_6 enables the schizophrenic to dream, an ability which is lost as the disease worsens and the thought processes dry up. B_6 may accomplish this by neutralizing the lactic acid that typically accumulates in the blood of people with mental disorder. Anxiety causes the buildup of lactic acid in the body because, like aerobic exercise, it uses up oxygen and as a result energy has to be generated without it. The by-product of this type of respiration (glycolysis) is lactic acid. By destroying excess lactic acid, vitamin B_6 has a calming effect as well as activating the dream structures in the subconscious. Several other nutrients also reduce anxiety. The high alkaline content of calcium and magnesium makes lactic acid physiologically inactive, while vitamin E lowers anxiety levels by slowing the transmission of anxiety impulses as they move between the amygdala and the cortex. Vitamin E also blocks the action of porphyrins, the alien chemical that causes disordered thoughts and bizarre behavior in the schizophrenic. Zinc and calcium are two other nutrients that reduce blood toxicity by lowering excessive levels of copper and lead, which are toxic to brain cells.

It's just as important to eat a metabolically appropriate and allergen-free diet (see Chapter 2) as it is to take nutritional supplements if you have a mental disorder. Mild brain disease, for example, occasional depression or a mild obsessive-compulsive disorder, may be cured by avoiding an allergy-causing food. People with all kinds of mental disorders are particularly allergic to the proteins gluten and alpha gliadin in wheat, and often to the protein in other grains as well. I believe that grains eaten during pregnancy by mothers whose fetuses are allergic to wheat is the greatest single cause of brain injuries that lead to mental disorder. This agrees with the research of Dr. Chris M. Reading, an orthomolecular physician in Australia. Reading found a link between celiac disease, an inherited digestive disorder caused by an intolerance to wheat gluten, and Down's syndrome. He contends that if a pregnant woman whose fetus is allergic to wheat eats wheat products during pregnancy, it can cause a doubling of chromosome 21 in the fetus. The result is Down's syndrome, a form of mental retardation which develops because the extra chromosome triggers the production of chemicals the body doesn't need. These clog the blood vessels, preventing the delivery of adequate levels of oxygen and nutrients to the brain cells, resulting in a drop in intelligence and emotional stability. Reading's study of eighteen children with Down's syndrome substantiates his premise. It showed that a diet free of wheat products vastly improved the mental functions of these youngsters.

The glutens in grain may also cause schizophrenia and depression in people allergic to it by depleting the supply of the minerals zinc, calcium, magnesium, iron, and manganese and vitamins B_1, B_3, B_{12}, and folic acid. Mental disorders, like other degenerative diseases, came into existence when the cultivation of wild grain plants began, so it's not surprising that mentally disturbed people feel more balanced on a diet that emphasizes meat, vegetables, and saturated fats and avoid food products made of grain.

Signs of the onset of schizophrenia are a change in behavior, attitude, and personal appearance that can't be explained. But this isn't always the case. The first sign of schizophrenia in Helen, a middle-aged woman who was as stable and free of complexes as anyone I know, was a hallucination, a symptom that ordinarily occurs when the disease is well advanced. Helen and her husband lived on the floodplain of a small rural town north of Seattle where, along with most of the other farmers in the area, they grew tulips. One day Helen was sitting on her front porch gazing at a large field of red tulips across the street from her house when the tulip blossoms suddenly broke off from their stems and began doing the polka. Helen recognized this vision as a symptom of schizophrenia, and the doctor confirmed her diagnosis when a blood test revealed excess kryptopyrroles in her blood and urine. (Kryptopyrroles are referred to as the "mauve spot" because of the reddish color they give urine.) Helen's hallucinations disappeared as abruptly as they had come on, when, after hearing that schizophrenics are often allergic to wheat, and knowing that an allergy to gluten ran in her family, she gave up all wheat products. It's amazing how quickly the body returns to normal even when afflicted with a seemingly incurable disease once the offending food allergens are removed.

Depression: A Matter of Nature or Nurture?

There is a theory supported by numerous studies that while everyone has ups and downs in moods irrespective of circumstances, our overall sense of well-being is preset by our genes. In a study by the National Health and Nutrition Examination, the state of happiness of 6,000 men and women was tracked over ten years. The results showed that the people who were happiest in the beginning of the study were also the happiest at the end of ten years. The study further concluded that those who have a high set point for happiness rebound from tragedy within six months to a year, whereas unhappy people who experience a loss fall into a depression that persists over time. By the same token, unhappy people after they, say, win the lottery or get a promotion, lose their happy feelings by the end of a year.[5] The conclusion drawn from this and similar studies is that the threshold of happiness is as genetically determined as the color of the eyes or the shape of the nose.

The studies on which this conclusion is based, however, focused on individual differences in mood. If we compare groups of people, specifically technologically advanced cultures with preliterate ones, a different scenario emerges. While unhappy individuals are common in modern society, in preindustrial cultures happiness was the rule. Explorers in Africa, in the Australian outback, and in the Arctic who kept diaries wrote about the continual joking and laughter among the native porters they hired to carry their luggage, and movies of the Eskimos and Australian aborigines before they adopted the ways of the Europeans reveal people who laughed together continually as they went about their daily tasks. Such consistently high levels of happiness are a phenomenon peculiar to preindustrial cultures. That they don't exist in "civilized" society suggests that the lack of a sense of well-being is a mental disorder like clinical depression, rather than an inborn personality trait. What sets the level of happiness, according to Dr. Richard Depue, a psychologist at Cornell University, is the dopamine level in the brain. He found that people who have a higher dopamine level have more positive feelings than those with lower levels. Thus a low set point of happiness, like chronic and bipolar depression, has a physical component that may reflect a genetic weakness, but the high level of happiness of preliterate peoples indicates it is not a fixed trait. With the right nutritional environment it can be "reset" upward.

Fatima and her husband Fawaz and their two teenage daughters had emigrated from Lebanon to New York and opened up a dry-cleaning establishment in my neighborhood on the upper east side of Manhattan. I had been taking my clothes to them to be dry-cleaned and having Fatima alter my clothes for several years when Fatima, with whom I had become friendly, told me that she was depressed. It's seldom that a single nutrient within a few weeks can erase all feelings of depression, but that is what happened in Fatima's case. I recommended that she take four tablets (500 milligrams) of Aangamik (vitamin B_{15}) daily. Within three weeks she noticed her depression lifting and in two months all traces of it had vanished. No one quite knows how B_{15} works, but scientists speculate that it oxygenates the brain, thereby increasing the brain's ability to generate energy. Fatima got another benefit from B_{15}. It eliminated the arthritis in her hands that had begun to interfere with her work as a seamstress. Several years after she had started on the Aangamik, one of her daughters, while visiting relatives in Florida, committed suicide. Fatima and Fawaz had had no idea that she was depressed. I often wondered if B_{15} would have cured their daughter's depression like it did Fatima's.

SUGGESTIONS FOR CHRONIC AND BIPOLAR DEPRESSION AND SCHIZOPHRENIA

➤ Vitamin B_3—three to twenty-two grams daily, preferably in the form of niacin.

➤ Vitamin C—three grams or more if niacin dosage is high.

➤ Vitamin B_6—250 to 1,000 milligrams.

➤ Vitamin B_1—100 to 3,000 milligrams.

➤ Folic acid and vitamin B_{12}—1,000 to 3,000 micrograms.

➤ Vitamin E—1,600 to 2,000 units can lift depression. May take three months to take effect, but individuals with mild depression may find it goes away in two or three days.

➤ L-glutamine—one to four grams for schizophrenia.

➤ Mineral complex—including calcium, magnesium, manganese, and zinc.

➤ Thyroid supplements containing T3 as well as T4—to increase energy production. (See Resources.)

➤ Progesterone—three to fifteen drops a day. Take natural progesterone (see Resources), which is extracted from yams, instead of the pharmaceutical preparation, Provera, which is chemically different and which increases the likelihood of getting breast cancer.

➤ Ginkgo biloba—120 milligrams daily. Relieves depression by increasing the flow of blood to the brain.

Migraine

A migraine occurs in two stages. In the first stage the sufferer sees light-ninglike zigzags, wavy lines, and/or dark spots. This is caused by hyper-active neurons in the visual center of the brain whose blood supply has been cut off by the constriction of the blood vessels. In the second stage the blood vessels covering the skull become enlarged and the head begins to throb painfully. Speech, hearing, and muscle problems develop during this stage.

Researchers are at a loss to explain what initiates the first stage of a migraine—the constriction of the blood vessels that causes the neurons to misfire, and in some cases to stop transmitting visual messages alto-gether. However, there are a couple of theories as to the cause of the symptoms that define the second stage: the noticeable bulging of the blood vessels on the skull and the throbbing headache. In the 1990s researchers found that a rare type of headache called familial hemi-plegic was caused by a genetic mutation that leaves the nerves in these outer blood vessels covering the brain in a permanent state of hyper-activity. Presumably this condition makes the blood vessels more vul-nerable to dilation. The cause of the enlarged blood vessels in the other 98 percent of the migraine cases, according to Michael Cutrer, a neu-rologist at Boston's Massachusetts General Hospital, is potassium.[6] Messages get transmitted between neurons when sodium enters a neu-ron and potassium leaves it. This exchange of minerals continues as long as messages are being transmitted. But when the neurons stop transmitting messages—which occurs when the capillary vessels that feed them constrict—the potassium, now out of the loop with nowhere to go, is carried by the blood to the vessels covering the brain, where it triggers their dilation and extreme sensitivity.

Another, more likely explanation of the second stage of a migraine as well as the first is injured brain cells and acidic waste. The fact that the blood vessels on the side of the head where the migraine occurs become enlarged and painful confirms Coutrer's hypothesis that some-thing in the blood is responsible. Acidic waste, which causes inflam-mation by depleting oxygen, seems a far more likely suspect than potassium. An ancient Arab remedy for severe headaches supports the acidic waste theory. The Arabs placed a clove of garlic under the skin in the region of the temple. As soon as a pocket of pus developed under the garlic, the blood vessels shrunk, and the headache vanished. It would seem that the garlic drew out pus from the blood in the dilated vessels. The presence of pus, which contains phagocytes (white blood cells) that destroy bacteria and cell debris, indicates that acidic waste from cell debris, and bacteria that feed on acidic waste are what expand the blood vessels on the skull.

But what causes the initial stage of migraine, the constriction of the blood vessels inside the brain? Injured neurons in the visual center of the brain interfere with the ability of the capillary vessel cells to dispose of acidic waste. As the acidic waste accumulates, two things happen. The acidic waste constricts the capillaries and blood flow increases to dilute the acidity of the waste. This is a double whammy because the constricted capillaries can't expand in response to surges in the flow of blood. This cuts off the neurons' supply of oxygen and nutrients, which excites them and they begin moving back and forth at high speed. The result is that the migraine sufferer sees neon spots and zigzags—or becomes temporarily blind if the vibrating neurons come to a stop. The second stage of migraine begins when the acidic wastes circulating in the microscopic blood vessels in the visual center of the brain flow into the veins that cover the skull, causing these much larger blood vessels to go into spasm and widen instead of narrowing like the brain capillaries. They also become inflamed, giving rise to the throbbing characteristic of the second stage of a migraine.

An effective treatment for migraine headaches was developed by an otologist, Dr. Miles Atkinson. Atkinson described the results of the vitamin B therapy he gave to his patients. B complex, particularly B_3, helped maintain normal dilation in the brain's blood vessels in his patients who suffered from migraine headaches. He made this discovery quite by accident. His patients with gastrointestinal problems who took bacterium lactobacillus acidophilus not only got relief from their intestinal problems, the patients who had migraine headaches noticed that some of their migraine symptoms disappeared. Atkinson came to the conclusion that by replenishing the bacterial colonies in the intestines that aid in the manufacture of vitamin B, the body was supplied with enough B vitamins to normalize the dilation of the blood vessels covering the skull. (He also gave vitamin B injections and prescribed oral B.) Vitamin B_3 (niacin) also cures mental disorder by eliminating acidic waste by-products in the brain, and this factor may also have helped relieve the migraines of Atkinson's patients.

Individuals with injuries in the visual center of the brain only get migraines if they eat foods that their digestive systems can't handle or if they react to airborne allergens. These incompatible factors cause acids to form that accumulate near the brain injury. Migraine sufferers are known to react to coffee, tea, alcohol, wheat and other grain products, red wine, chocolate, citrus fruit, and cheese, chain smoking, and pollen. Avoiding these factors also normalizes the thyroid so energy levels increase enough to eliminate the metabolic wastes and toxins that trigger migraines. Migraine sufferers, like people with other mental disorders, usually do best on a diet high in meat protein and relatively low in carbohydrates.

SUGGESTIONS FOR MIGRAINE HEADACHES

➤ Diet. Test for metabolic type and food allergens (see Chapter 2). If you have a grain- and meat-eating metabolism and therefore have a choice, choose a meat protein diet, low in carbohydrates.

➤ Thyroid supplements containing the active T3 (under medical supervision).

➤ Progesterone—three to fifteen drops. Start with three drops and work up to the number of drops that relieves symptoms. (See Resources.)

➤ Vitamin E—400 to 800 units a day to bolster energy production and eliminate free radicals.

➤ Omega-3 fats and oil—in green leafy vegetables, eggs, and saltwater fish, particularly mackerel, salmon, anchovies, and sardines, and omega-3 supplements.

> ➤ Air cleaner—ionizer with an ozone maker to clear the air of allergens, bacteria, molds, and toxic particles. (See Resources.)
> ➤ Acupuncture—prevents migraine headaches in almost 60 percent of the sufferers who use it.
> ➤ B complex. Take three B-complex capsules, each containing 100 milligrams of B_1, B_2, and B_3 daily. If you don't get significant relief, take additional B_3—up to 3,000 milligrams.

Alzheimer's Disease

Before Rebecca developed Alzheimer's she suffered from atherosclerosis. She said that the hardening of her arteries started when she was a child. At the age of four she had severe pains in her feet; in her teens the pain had crept up into her legs. Then in her early forties she developed chest pains. Five years after I last saw her, at the age of seventy, she was showing symptoms of Alzheimer's. I believe that the same condition that had injured the inside walls of her veins and arteries, triggering the formation of fatty plaques, also killed the neurons in her brain.

Modern science views Alzheimer's and cardiovascular disease as two different pathologies because the plaques in the arteries that trigger the development of blood clots are made up of fat, triglycerides, and calcium, and the beta-amyloid plaques that cause Alzheimer's are composed of protein. Moreover, fatty plaque adheres to blood vessel walls while beta-amyloid plaques float in the watery lymph-like fluid surrounding the brain cells.

However, before the protein strands in the neurons are broken up into segments to form amyloid plaques, they performed the same function for the brain cells as arteries and veins do for the organs: transporting materials to and from the destination. Thus both the cellular protein strands in the membranes of the cells and the veins and arteries of the circulatory system are exposed to acidic wastes; the protein strands from the acidic by-products of the metabolic processes that go on inside the cell and the acidic debris in the cerebrospinal fluid surrounding the cell; and the veins and arteries from the acidic waste by-products the blood picks up from metabolic function.

The formation of beta-amyloid plaques in the brain begins when enzymes cut the protein filaments in the cells into shorter strands. An enzyme, beta-protease, snips the section of the protein strand that protrudes from the cell and another enzyme cuts a segment off the other end which extends into the cell. Cut strands accumulate outside brain cells in clusters which are covered with a sticky, waxy substance. Because these amyloid plaques are considered the cause of Alzheimer's, medical researchers are looking for ways to eliminate them. A compound developed by Prana, a biotech company, causes beta-amyloid plaques to fall apart by sucking the copper and zinc structure out of the plaques. Prana is also developing a vaccine in which amyloid is injected into the body to elicit an immune response. Such a vaccine would trigger the immune system into identifying and eliminating amyloid plaques. The discovery of the beta-protease enzyme has opened up the possibility of preventing the formation of amyloid plaques altogether by inhibiting their production. Several drug companies are working on medications that would accomplish this.[8]

Efforts to eliminate amyloid plaque in the brains of Alzheimer's patients or those who show signs of it, if successful, would interfere with normal brain function. Protease enzymes that cut the protein strands into segments are programmed to get rid of excess protein strands—presumably those that are worn out or have deteriorated. Amyloid plaques may therefore act as waste deposits for protein strands that have outworn their usefulness. The fact that these plaques are held together by a protective structure of metals and a waxy, cholesterol-like substance reinforces this possibility and makes the prevention of amyloid plaques tantamount to interfering with the brain's waste disposal system. Even the genetic basis of Alzheimer's doesn't strengthen the case of the researchers who see the elimination of amyloid plaques as the solution to Alzheimer's. The gene for producing extra amyloid plaques—found on chromosome 21 by Dr. Rudoph Emilio Tanzi—is only a strong risk factor in offspring when both parents carry this gene (called apoE-4) and when the disease sets in before the age of seventy. (Tanzi states that individuals with Down's syndrome get Alzheimer's in middle age because the doubling of chromosome 21, which causes Down's syndrome, also causes the gene making amyloid to double.) The most convincing evidence in favor of not eliminating these plaques is that *only those beta-amyloid plaques that have become inflamed destroy brain cells* (by tangling up the protein strands inside the cell). How did they become inflamed? The highly selective blood-brain barrier, which keeps toxic waste matter out of the brain, deteriorates and acidic waste slips through the leaks between the cells in these capillaries into the brain fluid. The acidic waste in the intercellular fluid depletes the oxygen and this inflames the amyloid plaques. When brain cells come in contact with these inflamed plaques, they die off. With the death of a critical number of brain cells, Alzheimer's becomes symptomatic.

Acidic wastes inflame amyloid plaques in Alzheimer's either because a genetic mutation (a doubling of chromosome 21 or of the gene apoE-4) programs the manufacture of too much amyloid—although this appears to play a minor role—or an injury in the brain disables the respiratory machinery so that there isn't enough energy to dispose of acidic waste debris. A study from the National Institute on Aging at Duke University found that serious head injuries increase the chances of developing Alzheimer's in old age. Of the 1,800 marine and navy veterans who were the subjects of the study, 548 had suffered a head injury and 1,228 had not. While family history, tobacco, and alcohol abuse played a small role in the disease, the veterans with serious head injury—those who were unconscious for more than twenty-four hours—had four times the risk of developing Alzheimer's or other dementia as opposed to the men who had suffered no head injuries. While these head injuries must have affected different areas of the brain, they resulted decades later in some form of dementia, particularly Alzheimer's—rather than some other brain disease such as Parkinson's or obsessive-compulsive disorder. According to scientific researchers, this is because the cells in the brain that perform the most complicated tasks like those in the hippocampus, the part of the brain affected by Alzheimer's where memories are stored, are the most vulnerable to trauma.

Nutritional Supplements for Alzheimer's Disease

Many health care professionals still don't seem to be aware of vitamin E's ability to delay the worsening of Alzheimer's symptoms. One study cited by Jane Brody in the May 28, 1996, issue of the *New York Times* reveals that in middle-aged and older animals, supplements of vitamin E prevented the conversion of the protein strands in the cellular membrane into beta-amyloid plaques. Another study showed that humans with Alzheimer's as well as animals can profit from vitamin E. Directed by Mary Sano, an associate professor of clinical neuropsychology at Columbia University, it showed that patients who took high doses of vitamin E delayed having to go into a nursing home by seven months.[9] By making more oxygen available (by preventing its breakdown), vitamin E heals inflamed tissue or prevents the inflammatory process from happening in the first place. But vitamin E could also prevent the inflammation of protein strands by clearing away toxic acidic waste before it gets the inflammatory process going. Like vitamin C, vitamin E removes toxic waste, but unlike vitamin C it's fat soluble so it can go through the double-layered fatty membrane surrounding the cell where the main portion of these protein strands are located.

Vitamin E is most effective in delaying the onset of Alzheimer's because by oxygenating brain tissue it neutralizes the acidic condition that causes inflammation. Another effective anti-inflammatory supplement is huperzine A, a type of club moss that has been used for thousands of years by the Chinese to treat inflammation. Huperzine can cross the blood-brain barrier and in animal experiments has been shown to soothe, protect, and even regenerate neurons.

Maintaining cellular energy is the best way to protect the brain cells from toxic acidic waste. Besides thyroid supplements and vitamin E to normalize thyroid function, and progesterone to ensure a balance of steroid hormone function, coenzyme Q-10 and acetyl-L-carnitine help maintain energy levels in the cells: CoQ-10 by transporting electrons that are involved in respiration and acetyl-L-carnitine by transporting fats into cells where they are burned for cellular energy.

SUGGESTIONS FOR ALZHEIMER'S DISEASE

➤ Thyroid—(containing T3 as well as T4) extract. (See Resources.)

➤ Progesterone—three to fifteen drops at a time, no more than every half-hour.

➤ Coenzyme Q-10—30 to 100 milligrams daily.

➤ Acetyl-L-carnitine—500 to 1,500 milligrams a day.

➤ NADH—five to ten milligrams daily.

➤ High intensity light—one-half hour to one hour every morning to restore the mitochondria's ability to manufacture energy.

➤ B-complex capsule—three times daily to reduce homocysteine levels. Excess homocysteine becomes acidic waste and destroys brain cells. According to Robert Clark, M.D., of Oxford University, people with low blood levels of folic acid, B_{12}, and B_6 have the highest levels of homocysteine and are three to four times more likely to develop Alzheimer's disease.

➤ Vitamin C—1,000 milligrams daily to pick up and dispose of acidic wastes.

➤ Omega-3 fats and oils—omega-3 found in saltwater fish and leafy green vegetables has an anti-inflammatory effect that helps offset the inflammatory effect of omega-6 polyunsaturated oils.

➤ Removal of silver/mercury dental amalgams has been known to stop the progression of Alzheimer's, but the removal must be done according to the system devised by Hal Huggins, D.D.S.[10]

Epilepsy

While little is known about epilepsy, electroencephalograms give a clue as to its underlying cause by showing that the brain waves in epileptics, even when the brain is not undergoing a seizure, contain an excess of electrical activity. (Medications such as Dilantin and Depecot prevent grand mal seizures by reducing electricity in the brain.) Electricity is generated by the overactivity of neurons that have become inflamed. Inflammation—from exposure to toxic waste, estrogen glutamate, heavy metals, and so forth—causes the electrons orbiting around the nucleus of the neurons to speed up so that they generate too much electricity. Excessive electrical activity in turn heats up the neurons, causing them to spin so fast that they can no longer communicate with other cells. The degree to which the neurons "go crazy," which determines whether symptoms will be relatively minor (petite mals) or will escalate into grand mal seizures, depends on how inflamed the neurons are.

I suspect that the pathology of epilepsy is no different than that of most other neurological disorders since the neurons in particular areas of the brain in Parkinson's disease, obsessive-compulsive disorders, tinnitus, and depression, like those in epilepsy, are overactive. That the symptoms presented are epilepsy rather than one of these other mental disorders is due to the location of the brain injury.

The Ketogenic Diet for Epilepsy

When epilepsy is accompanied by frequent headaches, food allergies are suspect. Acidic wastes from food allergens that accumulate around the injured area in the brain could cause seizures by causing the neurons to spin out of control. A ketogenic diet is one in which four times more fat than protein and carbohydrates combined is eaten. Saturated fats such as butter, cream, cheese, bacon, fatty pork, and beef fat are best. In an impressive number of cases this diet has prevented seizures where drug medications haven't worked. Saturated fat is said to prevent seizures because fat rather than sugar is burned as energy, producing ketones which, absorbed into the blood, calm the nerves, thereby lessening the severity of seizures or stopping them altogether. Saturated fats may also act by patching up the holes and tears in brain cellular membranes, through which toxic wastes can infiltrate the cells.

Medical research is based on the premise that cures for brain disease depend on discovering how the brain functions. But the thrill of discovering unknown brain functions—for example, the way neurons

---

SUGGESTIONS FOR EPILEPSY

➤ A ketogenic diet in which four times as much saturated fat as protein and carbohydrates is consumed, that is, four grams of fat to one gram of protein and carbohydrate foods. (See Resources.)

➤ Coconut oil—supersaturated fat that is completely burned up and is therefore the best single source of fat for an epileptic individual on the ketogenic diet.

➤ Progesterone—three to fifteen drops a day. According to chemist Ray Peat, Ph.D., progesterone works in three stages: it soothes, then protects, and finally causes the brain cells to regenerate.[11] (See Resources.)

➤ Vitamin B_6—seizures in babies and small children have been relieved with 50 to 100 milligrams of B_6 daily. For adults, 200 to 300 milligrams have been effective.

➤ Vitamin D—1,000 units daily help one out of three people who take it.

➤ Magnesium—700 milligrams broken up into three doses daily. In combination with B_6, magnesium seems to have a calming effect on injured brain cells.

➤ Taurine—one to five grams a day.

➤ L-tyrosine—500 milligrams three times daily.

➤ Avoid polyunsaturated oils, which become rancid, lowering thyroid function and poisoning the respiratory machinery (mitochondria) in the cell.

transmit or store memory or the amount of fuel the brain uses up during problem solving—clouds the real issue: healing the brain injury that causes mental disorder. This depends on three factors: individual differences in food metabolism and eating habits; the condition of the thyroid and respiratory brain machinery; and nutritional deficiencies in the brain. When any or all of these factors causes the brain to malfunction, since the brain controls the thought processes, regulates mood, and coordinates movement, a variety of behavioral and muscular disorders follows.

CHAPTER 9

LUNG DISORDERS

Asthma

I met Christina shortly after my family and I moved into an inner-city neighborhood in Harlem. Waiting for the same bus at the same time every morning to take us to work, we talked to wile away the time. Christina, forty-five, divorced and a mother of three, had immigrated to the United States from the Dominican Republic twenty years before. Soon after her arrival, she became asthmatic. Her case was so severe that she had an asthmatic attack at the least physical exertion. Picking up a toy, making a bed, or just standing to do the dishes could bring on an attack. She had been taken by ambulance to the hospital fifty times between 1987 and 1998 when her breathing passages were so constricted that she almost suffocated. Her doctors considered her disabled enough to authorize Medicaid payment for a full-time housekeeper.

Christina's life, however, took an unexpected turn for the better due to a chance encounter. Sitting in the waiting room of a clinic waiting to see her doctor, another patient told her about a folk remedy for asthma used in the rural areas of Puerto Rico: grapefruit juice mixed with peeled and finely chopped aloe vera, a cactuslike plant found in supermarkets and bodegas (corner grocery stores) in Hispanic neighborhoods. Christina was open to this suggestion because she no longer wanted to take the daily dose of corticosteroid hormones prescribed by her doctors (corticosteroid hormones are produced in the cortex of the adrenal glands). The painful joints, the swelling of her entire body, and the dizziness—side effects of these anti-inflammatory hormones—were worse than the drowning sensation when her bronchial tubes narrowed so much that she couldn't get her breath. The same day she was given this recipe for asthma Christina made a five-gallon container of the mixture and started drinking several glasses a day. She has not had an asthmatic attack since she began drinking the mixture two years ago. She has started a business selling clothes from her apartment, jogs every day with her boyfriend, and has set a wedding date with her jogging partner. "Best of all," she says, "I still have my housekeeper!"

Like most people who have asthma, Christina used antispasmodic inhalers when she had trouble breathing. Just a few sprays from these inhalers almost instantly open up the air passages in the lungs. Those asthma patients who rely most heavily on inhalers, however, run twice the risk of dying. Two studies conducted in New Zealand and Canada documented the dangers of bronchodilators.[1] These statistics became real to me when a friend of mine, Jacob, died from the overuse of an inhaler. Jacob pulled the inhaler out of his pocket whenever he wheezed. One day he had a full-scale asthmatic attack. He used the inhaler, but it didn't open up his breathing passages. He had used it so often that it had lost its effectiveness. With no one around to rush him to a hospital he died.

The high mortality rate of inhaler users indicates that forcing the expansion of constricted bronchial tubes and air sacs can ultimately cause the loss of their ability to expand when the constriction of air passages is severe. The inhaler or bronchodilator is also dangerous because it gives sufferers a false sense of wellness. Relieved when the inhaler has given them their breath back, they don't realize that their bronchial tubes and alveoli (air sacs) are still inflamed.

Doctors have become increasingly concerned about lung inflammation that is chronic in individuals who have frequent asthma attacks. Not only does inflammation make the lungs more prone to future attacks of asthma, it also causes lung tissue to deteriorate. This has changed the medical profession's perception of asthma from a disease that strikes periodically and is largely a problem during childhood to one that is chronic and lasts a lifetime. The current practice is to recommend medication—corticosteroid hormones—for moderate and severe asthmatics on a continuing basis.

The persistent use of corticosteroid hormones has its downside. While they reduce inflammation, they also cause weight gain, dark moods, anger, and, when taken long term, can stunt growth. Side effects in adults are elevated blood pressure and blood sugar, cataracts, and osteoporosis. So while prednisone and cortisone have saved many from immediate death, they reduce the quality of life and lay the foundation for degenerative disease. The problem for asthmatics in the long run, then, is perhaps less the acute breathing problems that can be alleviated with injections of medications than the chronically inflamed bronchial tubes and air sacs that make it necessary to use corticosteroid (stress) hormones.

For asthmatics who are hypoglycemic, the conditions that precipitate an attack are present when blood sugar levels become too high, eliciting a strong insulin response that causes the blood sugar to take a sharp plunge. (Insulin, a hormone, regulates sugar levels in the blood.) The steep rise in blood sugar and the overresponse of the insulin-producing glands (the islets of Langerhans in the pancreas) occur for a number of reasons: when sugar is burned too slowly it accumulates in excessive amounts in the blood; with the ingestion of large quantities of refined carbohydrates that are broken down too quickly, sugar levels rise; when the insulin-producing glands misread a normal blood sugar level as too high and secrete excessive amounts of insulin to take some of the blood sugar out of circulation, or conversely the adrenal glands misread sugar levels as too low and "order" an overload of sugar to be released from the liver (where it is stored in the form of the starch glycogen). Excessively high insulin levels in the blood grab the attention of the immune system, which interprets these hyped-up hormonal insulin secretions as a fight-or-flight reaction against pathogens that are endangering the survival of the individual. The lungs' immune cells help to mobilize the lungs against its "enemies"—normal particles such as pollen, mites, or cat dander—by triggering the release of histamine. Histamine causes blood to flow to the lung tissue just as it does when there is an injury or infection. This inflames the bronchial tubes and alveoli (air sacs). If they become spastic, an asthmatic attack is likely to occur. That high insulin levels are a major factor in asthmatic attacks is confirmed by the fact that Type I diabetics who have low insulin levels don't get asthma or any other type of allergic reaction.

To protect the lungs against immune reactions that occur partly as a result of the malfunctioning of the insulin-producing glands and the adrenals (the adrenal cortex in asthmatics is not secreting enough cortisone; if it were, allergic reactions would not occur) supplements of pancreatic enzymes and adrenal extract should be taken. Vitamin C (which is stored in the adrenals) also helps normalize the function of these glands. Harry N. Holmen, Ph.D. describes the relief of eighteen asthmatic patients who were given vitamin C supplements.[2] Avoiding the consumption of white flour and white sugar is the most important factor in keeping insulin levels on an even keel. Honey is a good substitute for white sugar if it is unfiltered and unheated because it contains levulose, a type of sugar that, unlike dextrose, maltose, and sucrose, is absorbed into the blood so slowly that it doesn't cause blood sugar levels to rise excessively. Dark honey is preferable because it contains the most levulose.

Causes of Asthma

While allergic reactions are undoubtedly related to defects in the adrenal and insulin-producing glands, it is not by chance that the lungs become the site of immune reactions rather than some other organ. Any number of factors can sensitize the lungs to normal airborne substances, including injury.

Lung injury can occur during the prenatal stage of fetal development. The croup, bronchitis, and asthma my brother and I had when we were young and passed on to our children was most likely the result of injury to our fetal lungs. My mother, who smoked through both of her pregnancies, inhaled the smoke from four packs of Pall Mall cigarettes each day. (Pall Mall, a popular brand in the 1930s and 1940s, was referred to as a chest breaker because the cigarettes' high level of nicotine wrecked the lungs of most of the people who smoked them.)

Air pollution is also a factor in asthma. A study by Dr. E. M. Drost found that air pollutants destroy the elastic fibers in the alveoli.[3] But even when air pollutants don't appear to damage the lungs, the immune cells in the lungs, unless supplied with sufficient enzymes to neutralize airborne pollutants as they pass through the air sacs, will react to toxic particles the same way they react to an injury: by triggering the release of histamines.

An article in the May 2000 issue of *The Atlantic Monthly* by Ellen Ruppel Shell rates the borough of the Bronx in New York City as the asthma capital of the United States with three times more hospitalization of asthma patients there than in any other area in the United States. Shell attributes this asthma epidemic in the Bronx in part to the fact that it is the hub of trains and trucks delivering cargo from all parts of the country, and to Interstate 95—the major truck route from Florida to Maine—which cuts through the middle of the Bronx.[4] This statistic and the fact that asthma rates are highest in the inner cities clearly establishes the connection between severe asthma and motor vehicle exhaust.

When possible, families with asthmatic children should avoid living in areas where there are major freeways and frequent traffic jams. When an acquaintance of mine, a teenage girl, moved from the Bronx to the upper west side of Manhattan—some would say she moved from the frying pan into the fire—her asthmatic attacks amazingly became less threatening. Since, however, air pollution is endemic in all parts of the country, the only way you can breathe relatively pure air is to buy an air cleaner with an ozone maker, which destroys harmful bacteria and molds. (See Resources for where to obtain an air cleaner.)

Toxicity inside the body as well as in the environment can sensitize the lungs to allergens. Acidic toxic gases enter the bloodstream from the colon and are carried by the blood to the liver and kidneys for detoxification. But when these two organs are already overburdened with the processing of toxins, they pass these toxins on to the lungs. The task of absorbing the toxins and exhaling them, along with its normal function of diffusing oxygen into the blood and removing carbon dioxide, can injure the lungs. Acidic waste gravitates to injured tissue. This inflames the tissue. All it takes then is exposure to allergens to cause the inflamed lung tissue to become spastic. This narrows the bronchial tubes and causes wheezing, an asthmatic condition.

That acidic waste (in the form of gas) is a factor in all asthmatic lung problems is confirmed by the discovery of Dr. Benjamin Glaston, associate professor of pediatric pulmonary medicine at the University of Virginia. According to Dr. Glaston, an asthmatic's breath is 1,000 times more acidic than normal breath. Normal breath is slightly alkaline with a pH of 7.4, but when asthmatics are sick and wheezing, their breath pH drops to 5—into the acidic range of the pH scale. That asthma sufferers have acidic breath is not surprising, given that acidosis, a blood pH that is below the normal alkaline pH, has long been associated with asthma. It's possible that just the presence of toxic acidic gas in the lungs can bring on an asthmatic attack.

Nutritional Treatments for Asthma

The asthmatic's problems with acidic blood and breath and acidic toxic gas in the lungs call for the reduction of acidic waste not only in the lungs but in the entire body. The high alkaline content of celery and dandelion leaf juice neutralizes some of the acidity in the body. Celery, carrot, and endive juice clear mucus and acidic debris from the lungs and help eliminate carbon dioxide from the system. Since asthma is often triggered by a backup of toxic waste that flows into the lungs from the liver, kidneys, and colon—waste that is the product of incomplete digestion of food in the stomach and small intestine—these organs need to be detoxified. Potato and carrot juice is a good general cleanser of all these organs, while the chlorine in cabbage cleans the debris from the mucous membranes in the stomach, and carrot juice detoxifies the liver. Detoxification of the colon is the most effective means of preventing asthmatic attacks because it is in the colon that acidic waste matter gives off toxic gas that diffuses from the liver or kidneys via the bloodstream into the lungs. My students at City College who are from the Caribbean islands described an old folk remedy—a dose of castor oil once a month—which proves that by removing toxins from the colon, asthmatic attacks can often be prevented. When asked why this remedy works, they replied, "Clogged colon, clogged lungs." The fact that garlic often heals respiratory and intestinal disorders at the same time supports the contention that detoxifying the colon clears up the lungs. Professor E. Roos of St. John's hospital in Freiburg, Germany, used garlic to cure a patient of diarrhea.[5] Not only was her intestinal function normalized, the swelling and redness of her tubercular lungs went down.

Asthma as well as other lung diseases is associated with a green vegetable deficiency. The healing of a severe asthmatic with a "green" drink is an example. Myron Cheminrow, a vegetarian, long distance runner, and fan of the health guru Gary Null, teaches children who are homebound because of illness. He had a student, age twelve, who had asthma so severe that he was on seven different drug medications. Kevin spent more time in the hospital than at home and was too drugged to do much of anything, let alone his schoolwork. A bright boy with an above-average IQ, Kevin was three grade levels behind in reading and could hardly hold a pencil in his hand. Kevin's mother told Myron that she knew that her son's life, the way it was, was not worth living. Both mother and son were ready and willing to follow any nutritional advice that Myron had to offer.

He recommended what Kevin referred to as "a whole plateful of vitamin pills" as well as four teaspoons of green powder made up of green freeze-dried vegetables every day in juice or water. He also attached a water filter to the water line under the kitchen sink and to the faucet in the bathtub because Kevin gets hives from the chlorine in the water. At Myron's suggestion, Kevin's mother bought an air cleaner. This regimen brought Kevin back to life. He is now on only one drug medication, he can run and play outside for the first time since he was a toddler in preschool, and his handwriting has become legible. Myron asked Kevin's mother, what, out of everything he recommended, helped Kevin most. Without hesitation she said the green drink.

Why is it that green vegetables, but not red, purple, orange, or white, have worked miracles for people with asthma and other lung conditions? Several studies show that pregnant women who eat lots of green leafy vegetables and fish during pregnancy are less likely to have asthmatic children. Fish and green vegetables are two out of three solid foods—the other is eggs—that contain omega-3 fatty acid (a fatty acid is a precursor of fat). Chlorophyll, the green coloring that is found in large amounts in dark green leafy vegetables such as spinach, chard, and collard greens, is the repository for omega-3 fatty acid through its association with vitamin F. Unsaturated omega-3 fatty acid, along with some monounsaturated and saturated fatty acids, is one of the building blocks of the cell membrane (the wall that surrounds the cell). The role of omega-3 fatty acid in assuring the integrity of cell membranes explains why omega-3 in green vegetables and fish is so healing to the asthmatic's lungs. Strengthening the membranes of the lung cells helps prevent inflammatory histamines from entering cells and triggering an attack of asthma.

Asthma has also been associated with an immature immune system. Protecting children against germs by using antibacterial agents, immunization shots, and antibiotics may prevent a host of childhood diseases, but it doesn't give children's immune systems the exposure to harmful bacteria, viruses, and other parasites they need to learn the difference between disease-causing germs and harmless ones. Paoli Matricardi, an immunologist in the Italian Air Force, conducted a study comparing two groups of male cadets, 240 subjects altogether. Allergies were rare among those who had been exposed to three common food-borne pathogens, while the group that had no exposure to these pathogens had elevated allergic responses.[6] Supporting these findings is the well-known fact that children living in rural areas of Third World countries who are exposed to parasites and bacteria rarely develop asthma.

The modern world is a breeding ground for asthma wherever factories are built or modern foods are introduced. Medical interventions also contribute to the increase in asthma. Antibiotics, by killing off harmful bacteria, prevent the immune system from learning what germs it must guard against, and give the immune system the impression that it is no longer needed to defend the body against disease-causing microbes. Another downside to the use of drug medications for asthma is that when used routinely they destroy coenzymes that assist enzymes in carrying out lung function. Chemical food additives have a similar effect.

But drug medications and other man-made chemicals are most dangerous because, not being natural substances, the body has not developed the mechanisms for eliminating them. They remain in the body, forming acidic residues that lower the pH factor of the blood, and clog and inflame the blood and lymph vessels near the lungs. This prevents the delivery of digested food particles and oxygen to lung cells. Starving lung cells develop injuries that make them sensitive to airborne particles.

Genetics also appears to play a role in asthma. This is indicated by the lives of the members of a religious sect called the Hutterites who live in South Dakota. Carole Ober, a professor of human genetics at the University of Chicago, has found a genetic basis for the 15 percent of the Hutterites who have asthma. But because they live in rural areas where they are exposed to parasites from farm animals, where fast-food restaurants are not accessible and where all infants have been breast-fed for at least nine months, asthma never becomes a serious problem. It is so mild that many of the Hutterites didn't even know they had asthma before she told them.

SUGGESTIONS FOR ASTHMA

➤ Avoid all refined carbohydrates.

➤ Test for your metabolic type and for food allergies.

➤ Green powder—take four to six teaspoons a day in juice or water. Freeze-dried green vegetables build healthy cellular membranes.

➤ Omega-3 fatty acid capsules—1,000 to 2,000 milligrams daily.

➤ Raw adrenal extract—two tablets of freeze-dried capsules per day.

➤ Pancreatic tablets—two to three tablets with each meal— only for individuals who are thirty-five years old or over.

➤ Vitamin A—25,000 to 50,000 units per day for healthy mucous membranes and as an immune system booster.

➤ Vitamin E—400 to 1,200 units oxygenizes the asthmatic's oxygen-deficient lungs.

➤ Vitamin C—1,000 milligrams two to six times per day to detoxify allergens in the blood.

➤ Vitamin B$_6$—100 to 200 milligrams three times per day. B$_6$ acts as an antihistamine.

➤ Garlic—two to three capsules with each meal to clear out the lungs and colon.

➤ Aloe vera—peel and chop finely. Add either to fruit juice or to beaten egg whites.

➤ Melatonin—check with your doctor before using. A study at the Hebrew University Hadassah Medical School and

Cardiopulmonary Laboratory in Israel found that melatonin administered to dogs intravenously dilated the lungs as effectively as drug medications. People with autoimmune diseases should not take melatonin.

➤ Ginkgo biloba extract—the first plant to grow after the atomic bombing of Hiroshima, it diminishes asthma-stimulating allergens and airborne bacteria in the blood.[7]

➤ Ice pack—rub on chest, usually for a minimum of two to three hours during an asthmatic attack. This treatment gradually opens up the constricted bronchial tubes.

➤ Sea salt—add sea salt to warm water and place two or three drops of the solution in each nostril. This destroys the pollen and other airborne allergy-causing particles that cause wheezing and/or colds that can lead to asthmatic attacks.

➤ A combination of one teaspoon of cod liver oil, one teaspoon of honey, and a few squirts of lemon mixed together once a day (an old West Indian custom).

➤ Eliminate dust mites. Place an air cleaner on the bed and cover with a sheet for one hour a day, or use mattresses made of organic cotton, flame-retardant wool, or natural latex. (See Resources.) These natural products prevent the proliferation of mites by absorbing body sweat.

Some of the factors that make certain individuals vulnerable to asthmatic attacks, such as genes, immature immune cells, and lung injuries that occurred during the fetal stage of the lung's development, can't be changed. But these factors alone don't trigger asthmatic attacks, and the other factors involved in asthmatic attacks can be controlled by diet and/or nutritional supplements. These are blood sugar levels, adrenal and insulin function, the integrity of the lungs' cellular membranes, the quality of air, and the acidic waste in the organ systems that often ends up in the lungs. Indeed, judging by the hyperacidity of the blood and breath of the asthmatic, acidic waste particles and toxic acidic gas are at the root of the chronic inflammation that turns asthma from a minor complaint, as it is among the Hutterites, to a lifelong degenerative disease that shortens life. A diet, customized to fit the metabolic needs of the individual, that also includes a lot of green vegetables and raw, unprocessed foods is the most effective weapon against the inflammation that triggers asthma.

Emphysema

The trachea (windpipe) in the throat branches into two bronchial tubes, each of which leads to a lung on either side of the chest. In design, the bronchial tubes look like a slightly diagonal, upside-down tree trunk from which progressively smaller branches, called bronchioles, radiate. Hanging off these bronchioles, like bunches of grapes, are millions of microscopic alveoli (air sacs) that do the work of the lungs.

Inhaled air flows into the trachea in the throat, through the bronchial tubes, into the bronchioles, and finally into the air sacs. From there it diffuses through the membranes of the air sacs into the blood vessels lining the air sacs' surface. The oxygen is then carried by the blood to the cells, where it's used to produce energy. The waste product from energy production, carbon dioxide, takes the reverse route. It's picked up by the blood in the intercellular fluid surrounding the cells and carried by the blood to the lungs. Its dropoff points are the same blood vessels encircling the air sacs into which oxygen from the air sacs flows. Once inside the alveolar sacs, carbon dioxide is expelled from the lungs.

In emphysema, the deterioration of the air sacs interferes with this exchange between oxygen and carbon dioxide. The air sacs break down largely because of air pollutants. Cigarette smoke is often cited as the worst offender. Inhaled smoke paralyzes the lungs' built-in cleaning system: the hairlike cilia lining the trachea and bronchial tubes that catch particles of dirt, tobacco, etc., in the air before they reach the air sacs. These pollutants eat up oxygen, which inflames the air sacs. Chronically inflamed air sacs eventually rupture and combine to form large air pockets. The walls of these air pockets aren't permeable enough to enable the oxygen to diffuse into the blood vessels. As a result, circulating blood, deprived of oxygen, is unable to deliver enough oxygen to satisfy the cells' needs. Moreover, the loss of elasticity in the air sacs makes it impossible to breathe out all the carbon dioxide in the lungs. It remains trapped inside the alveoli, taking up space intended for oxygen. The emphysema victim's scarcely moving chest swells up with the carbon dioxide that he or she can't exhale and with oxygen that hasn't been absorbed into the circulating blood. What happens to the cells that don't receive enough oxygen to satisfy their energy needs? They rob Peter to pay Paul, grabbing one oxygen atom from each carbon dioxide molecule (CO_2), and in doing so, turning carbon dioxide into carbon monoxide (CO), a highly poisonous residue, which further damages the alveoli in the lungs.

Another source of toxins that contribute to the destruction of the alveoli are metabolic wastes that the liver and kidneys are too overworked to process. When the liver can't detoxify poisonous gas from the colon, the latter is carried by the blood out of the liver and, circulating in the bloodstream, ends up in the lungs, where it is exhaled along with carbon dioxide. The lungs become a dumping ground for the kidneys as well. The gaseous wastes the kidneys can't handle are carried by the blood to the alveolar sacs in the lungs. Processing these metabolic wastes is hard on the lungs because they were designed to eliminate carbon dioxide, not toxic waste. While they harbor macrophages and other white blood cells that devour germs and dust, unlike the liver, kidneys, and lymph nodes, the lungs have no structures to neutralize or filter out acidic waste.

One of the most impressive studies showing the relationship between cigarette smoking and lung disease is the five-year study conducted by the Harvard School of Public Health and Brigham and Women's Hospital in Boston. Ten thousand teenagers, tracked from 1990 through 1995, showed that adolescents who smoke as few as five cigarettes a day have undersized lungs. A previous study of the same group of children, who were examined every year from 1974 to 1989, revealed that while 25 percent of the nonsmoking teens wheezed, of the smokers, wheezing was a problem in 56 percent of the girls and 47 percent of the boys. Dr. Frank E. Speizer, a member of the research team, said that the high rate of asthma even in the nonsmoking teenagers in the study was related to the highly polluted areas in which they lived. The role that pollutants other than tobacco smoke play in lung disease should be the subject of more research studies.

The problem with focusing most of the research on the effects of cigarette smoking on the lungs is that, given prominent space in the media, the evils of cigarette smoking have acquired a monopoly on the public's and Congress's attention. It's the tobacco companies that have to issue a warning on their cigarette packs and whose product is highly taxed to discourage customers. This lets other air polluting industries off the hook. They can spew pollutants into the air without having to take the consequences because the tobacco industry has taken the heat off them.

However, research studies carried out over the decades in which industrialization expanded by leaps and bounds and the automobile was introduced, indicate that industrial air pollutants are even more responsible than cigarette smoking for the startling increase in emphysema, lung cancer, and asthma. Dr. Eugene Houdry, an inventor and lifetime researcher of the petroleum industry, stated that the nearly 2,000 percent increase in lung cancer between 1914 and 1975 corresponds with the increase in gasoline consumption.[8] Strengthening the connection between lung cancer and the burning of petroleum are statistics showing that lung cancer decreased 35 percent between 1941 and 1945 during World War II when gasoline was rationed. This establishes vehicular exhaust as a major factor in lung cancer and brings up the possibility that if cars hadn't been invented, lung cancer might be rare.

Emphysema, like lung cancer, is attributed almost solely to smoking. Yet emphysema was rare until around 1960, although during the previous thirty years, smoking was even more prevalent than it is now. However, between the end of World War II in 1946 and 1960, there was a tremendous growth in air polluting industries. This transformed emphysema, which before that time was a rare disease, into one of epidemic proportions.

Anna and her husband Olaf, who lived in Malmö, Sweden, moved to New York City when Olaf, who worked for a multinational paper company, was transferred to the New York office. Anna had never smoked a single cigarette, but her lungs were so sensitive to the pollutants in the New York air that she had pneumonia six times during the twenty years she lived there. Pneumonia, a bacterial or viral infection that inflames the alveolar sacs and causes them to fill with fluid, is a causative factor in emphysema. After her last bout of pneumonia, Anna developed emphysema. On the advice of her doctor she and Olaf left New York and settled permanently in their summer place in Nantucket, Massachusetts. Anna hasn't had pneumonia since.

Nutrition for the Lungs

Juiced vegetables, especially celery juice, detoxifies the lungs. The circulating blood carries the juice to the liver, which uses the alkaline minerals in the juice to neutralize metabolic wastes, heavy metals, uric acid, and lactic acid. The detoxified blood leaves the liver and eventually circulates in the lungs, where it neutralizes carbon dioxide and other wastes trapped in the alveoli. Once cleared of this garbage, the inflamed air sacs and bronchioles heal.

The chlorophyll molecules in vegetable juice play a big part in healing the alveolar sacs indirectly, by rebuilding the hemoglobin in the red blood cells. The answer to how this happens lies in the similarity between the chlorophyll molecule in vegetables and the hemoglobin molecule in human blood. Chlorophyll and hemoglobin (hemoglobin contains a protein compound, *globin* as well as *hematin*) both contain a mineral—in chlorophyll it's magnesium; in hemoglobin, iron—surrounded by carbon, nitrogen, and oxygen atoms. When any of the elements encircling the iron in hemoglobin are missing, the iron molecule loses some of its magnetic properties. The chlorophyll in the vegetable juice replaces the missing atomic elements in the iron molecules in the blood and they regain their magnetic charge. Thus reconstituted, hemoglobin can once again exert its magnetism to pull out the oxygen molecules in the air sacs of the lungs, with the result that more oxygen is absorbed into the blood. The body's oxygen needs are taken care of and space is made available in the air sacs for newly inhaled oxygen. The lungs are also strengthened by the great concentration and range of vitamins—A, B, C, D, and K— in the carrot juice, while the carrot juice molecule, nearly identical to a molecule of blood, rebuilds the blood's red blood cells, enabling the blood plasma to carry more nutrients to the lungs.

Other Ways to Strengthen the Lungs

An organ is most likely to break down through exposure to toxins in the substances it processes. The digestive tract is injured by the chemicals in the processed food it breaks down, the kidneys by the toxins in the blood it filters, and the alveolar sacs by the pollutants in the air that diffuses through them. Thus the quality of the air that flows into the lungs is the most important factor in maintaining their health. The best way to improve the air in the home and workplace is by using an air cleaner that produces negatively charged ions—or preferably, one that emits negative (alkaline) and positive (acidic) ions in the same ratio as in the unpolluted air in nature. Not only do the negative ions eliminate the positively charged pollutants from the air we breathe, but absorbed by the lungs, the negative ions reduce acidity, which normalizes the lungs' acid-alkaline pH factor. This balance is vital to the health of the lungs because it facilitates the absorption of oxygen from the air sacs into the blood. Negatively charged ions also cause the cilia, hairlike projections lining the trachea and bronchial tubes, to move more vigorously. The faster their motion, the more dirt particles and pollen they catch before they're deposited in the alveoli. Drs. Krueger and Smith of the University of California in their research studies showed that cigarette smoke slows down the movements of the cilia, while negative ions counteract the effects of the smoke by increasing the ciliary beat.[9]

The volume of air we breathe into the lungs is also a factor in their health. Most of us don't breathe in enough air and, as a result, don't exhale the stale air lodged in the alveoli. This residual oxygen and carbon dioxide has no function and therefore constitutes waste that is harmful to the lungs. It also takes up space, reducing the lungs' oxygen capacity. The only way to get rid of this stale air lodged in the lower lobes of the lungs is to become a deep breather. You can't do this by reminding yourself to breathe deeply because it's not possible to be conscious of how you breathe all the time.

You can, however, develop the habit of breathing deeply by strengthening the muscles involved in breathing: the muscles that move the ribcage, since they initiate the breathing process, and the muscles that make up the diaphragm. As we breathe in and out, the diaphragm underneath the chest moves up and down, causing the chest to alternately expand and contract. How large the chest becomes and how much it shrinks determines how much air we can inhale and exhale. By strengthening the diaphragm muscle, the chest cavity automatically expands more during inhalation and becomes correspondingly smaller when breathing out. This increases the air pressure, and when the pressure is great enough, the stale air is pulled out of the lungs.

The best exercise for strengthening the diaphragm and rib muscles, described at the end of this chapter, is an exercise that promotes something dogs do frequently: panting. One individual who profited from this exercise was Jack Smith, a professional photographer. Jack developed emphysema at the age of seventy-three. He believes his exposure to asbestos was responsible. When Jack was twenty-seven, he took pictures of the interior of a naval ship while it was being sprayed with asbestos. He had forgotten about this until the diagnosis of emphysema jogged his memory. Jack's chiropractor recommended panting as a way to strengthen the alveoli, and Jack has performed this exercise for an hour each day ever since. He also bought an ionizing air cleaner for his apartment. A breathing test, taken a year after he began exercising his lungs and using an air cleaner, showed that his breathing was almost normal (95 percent).

Unlike vigorous exercise—jogging, basketball, volleyball, tennis, or even calisthenics—panting involves only the muscles in the chest and abdomen. As a result, the oxygen level in the cells doesn't fall as in aerobic exercise, and there is no buildup of acidic waste (lactic acid and ascetic acid) which lowers thyroid function. Overexercise appears to have the same effect as emphysema in terms of preventing the lungs from breathing in enough oxygen. At least this is indicated by the results of the breathing tests taken by two groups of individuals, one with emphysema and the other highly trained athletes. These tests were conducted by Carl Stough, a former opera singer who trains people with lung problems to breathe correctly. He writes in his book, *Dr.*

Breath, that the results of the breathing tests of his emphysema clients were about the same as those of the Olympic sprinters in the control group![10]

SUGGESTIONS FOR EMPHYSEMA OR PNEUMONIA

➤ Dark green vegetables—including spinach, collard greens, chard, and kale—should be eaten at least once a day, preferably raw.

➤ Raw vegetable juice—one pint of celery juice and three pints of a combination of carrot, spinach, and a small amount of watercress or parsley daily.

➤ Ionizing air cleaner (see Resources).

➤ Castor oil packs on the liver—one hour a day for five to ten days (see Resources).

➤ Vitamin A—50,000 units a day. Before taking more than this amount, sometimes necessary in emphysema, consult your doctor.

➤ Vitamin E—800 to 1,600 units a day. It lessens the need for oxygen.

➤ Vitamin C—1,000 to 3,000 milligrams a day.

➤ Chlorophyll—two or more tablets three times daily (made by Food Science Labs).

➤ Aangamik (DMG)—250 milligrams three times a day (made by Food Science Labs).

➤ Panting—stand in front of an open window or outside, raise your arms above your head, open your mouth slightly, and pant until you feel tired.

➤ Tea tree oil—one-quarter teaspoon three times daily for seven days for pneumonia.

CHAPTER 10

ARTHRITIC CONDITIONS

Rheumatoid Arthritis

Stephanie, age sixty, a children's dress designer and a mother and grandmother, had two staphylococcus infections early in life followed by two autoimmune diseases, one of which was rheumatoid arthritis. She had her first staph infection at the age of nine—osteomyelitis in the bone marrow of the right femur (the leg bone that extends from the knee to the thigh). The infection left her with minor bone damage and a slight limp. She developed the second staph infection when she was in her early thirties. While planting flowers in her garden, her index finger suddenly swelled up and turned bright red. Within a half-hour the swelling and redness spread to the rest of her hand and up her arm. The doctor was called to the house and gave her antibiotic injections that killed off the infection and saved her life. Staphylococcus bacteria had gotten into a joint in her finger through a small cut in the cuticle, and meeting no resistance from her immune system, had multiplied so fast that were it not for the antibiotics it would have overrun her entire body within hours and killed her. Stephanie had no aftereffects other than a deformed finger.

In her late thirties Stephanie became pregnant with her third child. During the second trimester of her pregnancy she developed an autoimmune disease. Her spleen, programmed to dispose of worn-out red blood cells, devoured the healthy ones instead. Stephanie's red blood cell count fell drastically, her complexion turned a waxy yellow, and her gums were gray. The doctor gave her cortisone injections, and when that didn't work, had her spleen removed. The instant the spleen was taken out, her face turned a healthy pink.

Stephanie had no more serious illnesses until the age of fifty, when she developed a second autoimmune disease, rheumatoid arthritis (RA). It began with the swelling of the joints of her fingers in both hands; the pain and swelling gradually extended to her wrists and then to her back. An MRI (magnetic resonance imaging) showed that the cartilage between the vertebrae had worn away. The agonizing pain when the vertebrae rubbed against each other and pinched the nerves persuaded Stephanie to undergo an operation to have the vertebrae fused. This relieved the pain somewhat, but she still had to wear a brace in bed to prevent back pain. Another inconvenience was having to ride the train when she traveled long distances because sitting on a plane in the same position for hours was too painful. A trip to visit her son, which she took three times a year, traveling from Boston where she lived to Portland, Oregon, took four days on the train.

Rheumatoid arthritis, like all autoimmune disease, occurs when the immune system mistakes the body's own tissues for antigens and destroys them as if they were infestations of deadly germs. According to medical science, this happens because the immune system has become overactive. Stephanie's staph infections, however, would seem to indicate that her immune system was under- rather than overactive. The damage to her leg bone would not have occurred if the immune system had reacted vigorously against the staph germs in the bone marrow, and her immune system didn't react at all to the rapidly multiplying bacteria that infected her finger while she was gardening. Autoimmune disease is much more prevalent among individuals with underactive immune systems. For example, rheumatoid arthritis is thirty times more common in individuals who have an immune deficiency disease called Bruton's syndrome.[1]

The inability of Stephanie's immune system to combat infection was due in part to a genetic predisposition. Her mother died at the age of thirty-three, two days after she caught pneumonia. The fact that Stephanie developed osteomyelitis as a child indicates that toxic waste had already accumulated in large enough quantities in or near her genetically defective immune cells to make them sluggish. As she grew older and her immune cells were exposed to more acidic waste, they became disoriented and mistook her own body tissue for alien germs.

The immune cells that attack the body in autoimmune disease are most likely the lymphocytes (a white blood cell) because they were concentrated at the sites of all Stephanie's illnesses. The spleen where her red corpuscles were destroyed and the bone marrow where Stephanie's first staph infection took root are both production centers of lymphocytes. The synovial fluid surrounding the bone joints, where rheumatoid arthritis begins, is loaded with lymphocytes—in fact this fluid is practically identical to lymph fluid. Stephanie's case is not unique. Spleen malfunction is a common occurrence in individuals with rheumatoid arthritis, although it usually occurs during its active phase. This supports the conclusion that lymphocytes are the rogue cells that cause rheumatoid arthritis.

Normal lymphocytes protect the body from infectious disease by producing antibodies that bind to the germs and disable them. This prepares the way for scavenger cells called macrophages that engulf and devour them. Lymphocytes poisoned by acidic waste, however, produce antibodies that are cross-matched. They link up with the body's protoplasm instead of with disease-causing germs.[2] This is what happens in rheumatoid arthritis. Malfunctioning lymphocytes, however, are not the only cause of bone and soft tissue degeneration in this autoimmune disease. The inability of lymphocytes to recognize dangerous germs and destroy them means that in the synovial fluid these germs are free to multiply unchecked. With no immune cells to stop their growth, bacteria in the synovial fluid break through cell membranes and establish colonies of germs that die out and become acidic waste. At the same time rogue lymphocyte and macrophage immune cells eat up the collagen that binds the cells together. These destructive actions cause edema by increasing synovial fluid levels, inflaming the membranes covering the bone joints and muscles, and making pits and grooves in the bones.

Nutritional Treatment for Rheumatoid Arthritis

To cure her rheumatoid arthritis, Stephanie had to detoxify the fluid in her bone joints and lymph ducts and then rebuild these fluids. The most effective detoxifier of synovial and lymph fluid is freshly squeezed organic vegetable juice because it is made up of water, minerals, and protein, nearly the same composition as the lymph and synovial fluids. Stephanie drank a juice made from grapefruit, celery, spinach, and carrots that provides a balance of alkaline and acid electrolytes, making it an effective detoxifier. The salicylic acid in the grapefruit helps dissolve calcium that encrusts the membranes and bones and also removes toxins from the lymph fluid; celery juice keeps the sludge in solution, and carrots and spinach facilitate its elimination from the colon.

Stephanie juiced twice a day, in the morning before breakfast and again in the evening before dinner. She also stopped eating wheat because she was allergic to the gluten (wheat protein), a common allergy among individuals with RA. This got rid of the acid-producing histamine in her synovial fluid. Avoiding food allergens and taking one gram of the amino acid histidine a day raised Stephanie's depressed histidine levels in the blood and synovial fluid. RA sufferers have low histidine levels because they are prone to food allergies. In an allergic reaction histidine is converted into histamines, which explains why rheumatoid arthritis sufferers have low histidine levels. Histamine not only inflames the joints, it also produces an acid in the stomach that causes digestive problems and raises acidic waste levels in the body in general.

The best supplement for RA sufferers, perhaps because they have below-normal blood levels of fatty acids, is a fatty acid called cetyl myristate (see "Celastyn" in Resources). Stephanie took the prescribed dosage of six tablets a day for the required length of time, which was six weeks. At the end of this time period, Stephanie said she felt as though the arthritis had actually been lifted out of her body. Cetyl myristate also lowered her elevated blood pressure. The effectiveness of this fatty acid is confirmed in a study conducted by Harry Diehl, an employee of the National Institutes of Health, who isolated the fatty acid from Swiss albino mice. Of the forty-eight participants in the study, all of whom had advanced RA, only two failed to show any improvement. Diehl attributed this to their prolonged use of cortisone, which had severely damaged their livers.

While the effectiveness of cetyl myristate is partly due to its lubrication of the bone joints and muscles, its greatest value lies in its ability to repair cell membranes that have sprung leaks due to insufficient amounts of fatty acid, the principal building block of the membranes that cover the cells. Congenitally damaged lymphocytes might very well have fragile membranes that allow acidic waste and bacterial poisons to pass through them to the inside of the cells where they damage the immune response mechanism.

Bursitis and Gout

Emily, fifty-one, a Romanian by birth, immigrated to the United States with her husband and five-year-old daughter fifteen years ago and settled in New York City. Shortly after their arrival her husband developed a brain tumor and could no longer carry out his duties as the superintendent of a fifteen-story apartment building. Emily was also unwell. But despite the aches and pains of arthritis that had gotten gradually worse, Emily, "to put bread on the table," she said, took over her husband's job. Every morning she hauled loaded garbage cans in the basement up a flight of stairs and picked up trash from the incinerator rooms on each floor of the building. She took the cans and loose trash to the curb outside for the sanitation truck to pick up. She also swept the stairs and hallways twice a week, and in the winter shoveled snow off the sidewalk in front of the building. Emily carried out these tasks despite wrists that were so stiff she couldn't turn a doorknob to open a door, throbbing pain in her toes, and heel spurs that made her feel, while walking, as if she couldn't carry the weight of her body. She also had bursitis in her shoulders and pains in most of her muscles.

Emily had inherited a tendency to arthritis from her father, Joseph, who had had gout. While that was his only arthritic problem, it caused him more pain than all of Emily's arthritic joints and muscles put together caused her. Gout is caused by elevated levels of uric acid in the blood that are converted into sodium urate crystals and deposited in the toes, wrists, and/or earlobes. Joseph's gout started in the joints of his big toes and spread to the rest of his feet, inflaming and swelling the muscles. This eventually caused the muscles in his feet to degenerate. This made him flatfooted, and he had to wear slippers even when he went out.

Emily used the best remedy possible for gout. She ate cherries, a treatment that Dr. Ludwig E. Blau tried on twelve individuals with gout, every one of whom experienced great relief. The remedy worked whether the cherries the subjects ate were canned or fresh, juiced or eaten whole. Dr. Blau found that they were also effective in healing bursitis (calcification of the pockets of synovial fluid into which the bone joints in the shoulder fit).[3]

Cherries remove the sodium urate crystals in and around the bone joints by dissolving them. Because uric acid blood levels aren't raised as a consequence, it would seem that the sodium urate, made soluble by the cherries, is further broken down in the lymph system and eliminated. How cherries dissolve the sodium urate crystals in the bone joints is another question, but it is likely that the acid in the cherries breaks them up, just as vinegar breaks down the calcium deposits in arthritic bone joints. Perhaps the red pigments in cherries play a role in healing the bones and muscles injured by the sharp points of the sodium urate crystals. Many ancient cultures believed that the color red had great healing powers. (The Southwest Indians, when ill, would live for a time among the red rock cliffs in the area now known as Sedona, Arizona, in order to absorb their healing power.) Instead of eating raw cherries, Emily drank cherry liquor which she made from an old Romanian recipe. She mixed sour cherries, unfiltered honey, blueberries, and vodka in a flat pan and left it in the sun for two weeks to ferment, and then strained it. Drinking three cups of this highly nutritious drink of low alcoholic content daily for two to three weeks cured her gout as well as the bursitis in her shoulder.

J. P. Seegmitten in his book *Gout* writes that humans suffer from gout because they lack an enzyme called uricase that in animals converts uric acid into a more soluble substance.[4] In fact, humans don't need this enzyme. As long as normal levels of uric acid are maintained it's easily excreted from the urine. It is only when blood uric acid levels go so high they endanger the stability of the blood's acid-alkaline balance (pH factor 7.4) that the excess uric acid is removed from the blood and deposited as far away from the major blood supplies as possible—usually in the toes.

Lowering Uric Acid Levels in the Blood

How can elevated uric acid blood levels be lowered? Because purine (a white crystalline compound) and nucleic acid break down into uric acid, doctors recommend that individuals with gout avoid eating foods with a high purine and/or nucleic acid content such as liver, sweetbread, game, herring, anchovies, lobster, crab, sardines, pork, and avocados. With the possible exception of pork, however, foods rich in purine and nucleic acid are not standard fare. Foods that aren't eaten on a regular basis are not apt to cause gout, so there is no reason why gout prone individuals can't eat these foods every so often. It is particularly unwise to avoid sardines and avocados because the abundance of nucleic acids in these two foods help regenerate body cells. Men and women living on the coast of Portugal who work in the sardine industry and eat sardines every day of their lives are famous for their youthful appearance and robust health in old age.

Individuals with gout invariably develop osteoarthritis, a disease in which acidic wastes are solidified by mineral salts and deposited in bone joints just as they are in gout. There is, however, one important difference. Gout is caused by an excess of uric acid only; osteoarthritis, by a variety of acidic wastes, including the poisonous by-products of such fatty acids as cholesterol, acetic acid, and lactic acid. The difference between these two kinds of arthritis then is in the nature of the acidic waste that is deposited in and around bones and in muscles. Whether individuals develop gout or osteoarthritis depends on what they eat and in which enzymes they are deficient.

The different types of arthritis Emily suffered from showed that she had a wide range of enzyme deficiencies. To remedy this, Emily took a supplement that contained enzymes that break down fat, protein, and starch, as well as ox bile powder (see Resources) to emulsify fat globules. This enzymatic complex lessened the pains in her muscles by improving her digestion. Good digestion eliminates the acidic waste by-products of undigested food debris that end up in mineral deposits on bones, tendons, and muscles.

To reduce the size of the spurs in her heels, Emily underwent an ultrasound and paraffin wax treatment in a hospital. Her feet were dipped in hot wax ten times and then subjected to eight minutes of high-frequency sound waves. This alternative treatment, which is very popular with doctors in Germany, dissolved Emily's heel spurs. A few years later she took her husband to the hospital to have the same treatment, but the hospital had stopped the procedure, claiming that it didn't work. Emily said that no one had asked her whether the treatment helped her. She wonders if the medical staff at the hospital found it too much trouble to administer—or too controversial.

Emily had one problem left to solve: the pain in her arthritic wrists. She used magnetic energy to accomplish this. Attaching a magnetic pad to each wrist with a Velcro band, she wore them to bed at night. In a few days her wrists felt better. She continues to wear the magnets when she sleeps because when she takes a night off, her wrists hurt the next day.

Osteoarthritis

My mother, who had both osteomyelitis and osteoarthitis, wondered why she had excess calcium deposited on her bones where it wasn't supposed to be, but didn't have enough calcium inside her bones. The calcium deposits on the surface of bone joints and vertebrae were once part of the bone structure. My mother had suffered a loss of calcium either because there was a more pressing need for calcium elsewhere in her body or because acidic waste in the watery fluid surrounding the bones had dissolved some of the bone (bone is made up mostly of calcium and phosphorus). The resulting loss of bone mass in my mother's wrist bones when she was only thirty-five was so great that, according to an x-ray, the bones were actually hollow.

Alkaline-forming calcium is leached from the bones and absorbed by the blood for several reasons. Calcium alkalinizes the nerves and blood when they are too acidic. In cases of hyperacidity, calcium is more important to the nervous and circulatory system than it is to the bones, so bone mass is sacrificed. Excessive acid in the arterial blood, a pH of 6.95, not that much lower than the normal 7.4, can cause coma and death. To prevent this, calcium combines with the excess acid and solidifies. Going full circle, the calcium, in the form of calcium carbonate, is deposited on the bone joints and vertebrae. Sufficient calcium blood levels are also needed by the nerves to perform such vital functions as controlling the heartbeat, regulating the secretion of hormones, and the digestion and assimilation of food.

The body not only reduces bone mass to obtain calcium but also to replenish its supply of energy. Enzymes split up calcium molecules to release the units of energy, adenosine triphosphate (ATP), inside the calcium. The bone, deprived of the leftover calcium particles that were absorbed into the blood, undergoes a further reduction in bone density.

Osteoporosis

Individuals with osteoporosis can take several measures to rebuild their bone mass so as to avoid the two major health problems that it causes: fractures of the lower forearm and, in later life, of the hip; and loss of height from curvature of the spine and legs. Calcium is the most obvious need, along with magnesium and vitamin D to help the bones absorb calcium. Dr. Herta Spencer of the Veterans Administration Hospital in Hines, Illinois, conducted eighty studies with twenty-one patients to find out what amount of calcium is effective.[5] She concluded that individuals with osteoporosis should take 1,200 units of calcium daily, but no more since larger amounts didn't bring any greater improvement. The most effective way to slow down loss of bone mass is to reduce acidic waste in the body. To do this, avoid the formation of acidic waste by eliminating processed, nutrient-deficient foods as well as foods that are not attuned to your particular metabolism. For those who can't overcome the temptation to eat such foods, there is either alkaline water or the far infrared (FIR) heat energy sleeping pad (see Resources), both of which dissolve and remove acidic wastes from bone joints and muscles more effectively than from any of the other organ systems.

Fibromyalgia

Shortly after Dorothy turned fifty-five, she retired as private secretary to the executive vice president of a major pharmaceutical company. This was when she first began feeling a stabbing pain in her muscles. The pain gradually spread to all of her muscles and never let up. Around this time Dorothy's sleep patterns changed. She went from sleeping seven hours at night to sleeping most of the day as well as at night. Besides muscle pain and fatigue, Dorothy experienced memory loss, and such extreme dizziness that she became disoriented and bumped into furniture. On one occasion she fell flat on her face. Dorothy went out only once in the twelve months before she finally got a hold on her illness: a close friend drove her to Atlantic City on her birthday to gamble on the slot machines. She regretted the outing because the exertion intensified her pain for several days afterward.

Dorothy had fibromyalgia. Her mother Jean had had rheumatoid arthritis. The only medication that had relieved Jean's pain caused her death: an extremely powerful aspirin compound prescribed by her doctor. The abrasive substances in the aspirin gave her stomach ulcers that became malignant and metastasized. (The aspirin has since been taken off the market.) Dorothy first went to a chiropractor, but his manipulations and the nutritional supplements he recommended didn't help her, so she switched to a rheumatologist who prescribed steroids. They made her life a little less unbearable.

Very little is known about fibromyalgia. However, a hypothesis is possible from the few facts that are understood. The debilitating pain of this disease begins in muscles located near the bone joints. This suggests that acidic wastes in the synovial fluid surrounding the bone joints cause inflammation and injury in fibromyalgia just as it does in rheumatoid arthritis. There is no evidence, however, of damage or inflammation in the muscles. This, plus the fact that individuals with fibromyalgia experience chemical changes in the nervous system, indicates that damaged nerves cause the pain, dizziness, fatigue, and poor memory of fibromyalgia. The systemic nature of fibromyalgia is additional evidence that the nervous system is the injured organ in this disease, since the pain impulses travel along nerve pathways that extend to every part of the body.

It was hard to help Dorothy because of her unwillingness to make an effort to help herself. Her chiropractor had tried without success to get her to detoxify her liver, but Dorothy didn't want to change her diet. Being too ill to do much of anything, she needed a treatment that took no effort and so she agreed to try one such remedy, a far infrared sleeping pad. Placed on top of a mattress and switched on, the heat produced by the electrical current goes through a layer of carbon inside the pad, creating the red spectrum of light that radiates deep inside the body and raises the internal temperature. This melts the crystals of acidic toxic waste which is then eliminated through the kidneys, colon, or skin. After sleeping on a FIR pad for three months, Dorothy woke up to find that the chronic pain in her muscles had practically disappeared and the lymph nodes on the inside of her legs, under her arms, and on her neck were no longer sore to the touch. The explanation was obvious from the huge open sores all over her body. These were caused by the acidic waste that had been dissolved by the far infrared heat energy and transported by the lymph system to the glands under the skin, which had excreted it through the pores.

Dorothy now felt well enough to play a more active part in her recovery and began taking cetyl myristate. Judging by her complete recovery six weeks later, the fatty acid had made her nerves impervious to acidic wastes by strengthening the fatty myelin sheathing that covers them.

SUGGESTIONS FOR ARTHRITIS AND OTHER BONE DISEASES

➤ Cetyl myristate—six capsules daily for a maximum of six weeks (see Resources). This is by far the most effective supplement for rheumatoid arthritis and fibromyalgia, but it is also useful in relieving the symptoms of other forms of arthritis. This fatty acid works even better if it is taken with the other nutrients listed below.

➤ Gerovital—200 milligrams daily (see Resources). This medication is made up of procaine, which chemically is almost identical to the anesthetic dentists use. Gerovital can prevent arthritis. (My friend Ann, forty-five, who has been taking Gerovital since she was in her early twenties and whose family all developed arthritis and gray hair by the age of forty, is still free of both these signs of aging. She attributes this to Gerovital.)

➤ Glucosamine sulfate—1,000 milligrams daily. This nutrient, along with chondroitin, forms cushioning and lubricants in joints.

➤ Chondroitin—1,000 milligrams daily.

➤ Vitamin E—800 to 1,600 units of vitamin E daily prevents the destruction of fatty acids needed to build strong cell membranes to keep out acidic toxins that injure cellular function.

➤ A formula consisting of fish, primrose, and flaxseed oil— relieves the swelling and pain of osteoarthritis. Don't take it without vitamin E, which prevents the toxic breakdown of these essential fatty acids.

➤ B complex—two to four capsules daily of a formula containing 100 milligrams each of vitamins B_1, B_2, B_3, and B_6 and at least 1,000 micrograms of folic acid.

➤ B_{12} injections—Dr. I. S. Klemes successfully treated shoulder bursitis with B_{12}. Since B is important in nerve function, B_{12} injections might also be effective in treating fibromyalgia.[6]

➤ Thyroid extract—low thyroid function is one of the causes of arthritis. (See Chapter 5.)

➤ Calcium microcrystalline hydroxyapatite—800 to 1,200 milligrams This is the most effective form of calcium because it's dissolved into such tiny molecules that it can penetrate bone mass.

➤ Magnesium aspartate—800 milligrams daily.

➤ Raw egg yolk—one raw egg yolk daily. Eat only fertilized eggs from chickens that have been fed organically grown grains to avoid any chance of contracting salmonella. Raw eggs contain an abundance of pantothenic acid, which most individuals with arthritis are deficient in. When guinea pigs' diets were supplemented with egg yolk, they didn't contract allergically induced arthritis.[7] A good reason for pantothenic acid's effectiveness in preventing arthritis is its role in helping the body dispose of acidic wastes.

In arthritis, as in all other degenerative diseases, inheritance plays a role. In fibromyalgia the nerve cells have a built-in weakness and in rheumatoid arthritis the lymphocytes are defective. As the nervous system forms a network of nerve clusters that are laid out in the far reaches of every organ system and the lymphocytes are present in both the lymph fluid and the blood, fibromyalgia and rheumatoid arthritis become systemic diseases, unlike osteoarthritis and osteoporosis, which usually remain localized. Sufferers of these latter two conditions have a congenital problem handling metabolic wastes, particularly the by-products of incomplete digestion. In gout and bursitis too much uric acid waste is produced in the process of breaking down purine because of a deficiency in the protein-digesting enzymes involved in breaking it down.

Organ tissues in which there is an inherent weakness have to be exposed to acidic wastes before muscle, bone, and nerve degeneration occurs. That's why arthritic conditions generally occur in the later years of life. As the years pass, and the acidic waste piles become bigger and bigger, the exposed muscles and bone joints deteriorate. The cells, deprived of vital nutrients by acidic waste–clogged blood and lymph vessels, can't build strong membranes to protect the machinery inside the bone and muscle cells. Membranes become porous, allowing acidic waste to filter into the cells. This is what causes rheumatoid arthritis and fibromyalgia. In osteoarthritis, acidic waste is encapsulated in calcium and deposited on and near bone joints, in soft tissue, and in the heels. In osteoporosis excessive levels of acid in the watery fluid that surrounds each bone cell dissolves the calcium and phosphorous in these cells. Both osteoporosis and osteoarthritis result in reduced bone mass. While the process of deterioration and the location in which it occurs differs in each condition, acidic waste is always involved.

CHAPTER 11

EYE DISEASE

Cataracts

Frank, a career army officer, had been on combat duty in Korea. After the war he returned to the United States and was sent to an army base in the state of Washington. Maybe it was because he was too relaxed after his war years in Korea, where he had to be constantly alert for danger, that back in the United States he became the victim of a freak accident. Waiting in the office at army headquarters to obtain some papers, he was in a large open space that was being subdivided into smaller units. Frank heard the sound of a drill, but it never occurred to him that the carpenter was drilling a hole on the other side of the partition he was leaning against. What happened next took place in a fraction of a second. The drill broke through the composite board with such force that it went straight through Frank's eye all the way to the optic nerve and destroyed his sight.

The loss of his right eye didn't hold Frank back. Leaving the army a year after his accident, he went to college, received a B.A. in the classics (Latin and Greek), and was made a professor at a nearby community college. There was just one downside to the loss of vision in one eye. He could no longer play tennis and Ping-Pong because he had lost the three-dimensional vision necessary for judging the distance between himself and the ball. Depth perception is dependent upon the blending of two separate images. This is what gives us a sense of the distance between the objects in our visual pathway, just as the convergence of the two separate light rays from a car's headlights at night makes it possible to estimate the length of the road ahead. Because Frank sees only one image, objects flatten out and look as though they are lined up in a row. However, Frank found two sports he loved for which depth perception isn't necessary—skiing and mountain hiking.

Frank's wife Lorraine worried that his good eye, doing the work of two eyes for over forty years, had come under too much strain, and urged Frank without success to take antioxidant vitamins. (The National Eye Institute and the Chinese Academy of Medicine in Beijing showed that in subjects between the ages of forty-five and seventy-four who took antioxidant vitamins the incidence of cataracts was reduced by 43 percent.[1]) Shortly after Frank celebrated his sixty-fifth birthday he began complaining that the red walls in the living room were so bright they hurt his eyes—although it was he who had insisted on painting the walls red. Now he wanted to repaint the walls blue, a color he had never liked. When eyes become sensitive to a bright color, it is usually because particles have infiltrated the lens or cornea. The transparent cornea covering the front of the pupil and iris, along with the clear lens behind them, bend the light rays containing the images we see so that they focus on the retina in the back of the eye. When these light rays are filtered through a lens and/or cornea that is cloudy, they are broken up. This distorts the images they carry. Furthermore, the particles in cataracts give the images a yellowish tint, and this changes our perception of colors. For when the layers of tissue that make up the lens and cornea lose their transparency and yellow, the colors with longer wavelengths such as red, orange, and yellow become too luminous, while those with shorter wavelengths such as blue and violet are by contrast restful. Although Frank didn't have the more common symptoms of a cataract such as haloes around images, fogginess, or loss of vision, the fact that he felt differently about colors meant that he was seeing them differently because his lens or cornea had become indistinct. The doctor examined his eye and found that in fact his lens was opaque in spots, a sign that a cataract was beginning to form.

The lens is a series of transparent layers of epithelial cells composed of approximately 60 percent water and 40 percent soluble materials, mostly protein. A lens "grows" a cataract for the same reason that arteries harden and bones become arthritic. They have been injured by acidic waste, and calcium bonds with the waste to prevent further injury to the cell. The epithelial cells in the lens are also vulnerable to the destructive effects of crystallized sugar. The problem starts when excess blood sugar (from the overconsumption of refined carbohydrates) initiates a blast of insulin. The insulin converts the surplus sugar in the light-sensitive cells in the lens into less soluble sugars such as sorbitol and fructose. These sharp crystalline sugars stick to the pits and holes made by acidic waste on the membrane surfaces of the protein molecules in the epithelial cells. This creates a sticky surface that causes the protein molecules to stick together and harden, a condition called cross-linkage. The result is more insoluble than soluble protein in the lens. As the amount of insoluble protein increases, so does the lens's opacity, until finally the entire lens is cloudy.

When cataracts are present, respiration (energy production) is depressed because the lens, thickened by the cataract, can't absorb vitamin B_2 (riboflavin), which carries oxygen to it. The lens must rely on B_2, and to a lesser extent vitamin C, for its oxygen needs because it has no capillaries to supply it with oxygen. Dr. Sydenstricker of the University of Georgia and University of Georgia Hospital gave fifteen milligrams of riboflavin daily to forty-seven subjects. After nine months the cataracts in all forty-seven patients disappeared.[2] Inadequate respiration has two effects. Less energy means fewer wastes are burned up. The leftover waste either adheres to the cataract and makes it thicker or gravitates to the cornea, causing it to cloud over. Second, as carbon dioxide is the by-product of respiration, when respiration slows, there isn't enough carbon dioxide to help keep the lens clear by disposing of free radicals from the breakdown of lactic acid. The importance of carbon dioxide in the prevention of cataracts is underscored by the fact that in Nepal, a country that is 15,000 feet above sea level, despite stronger sunlight at that altitude, cataracts are 2.7 times less common than in areas situated at lower altitudes.[3] The reason for this is that in mountainous areas where there is less oxygen, respiration is more efficient, giving off generous levels of carbon dioxide. When the cells in the lens make sufficient energy, normal levels of carbon dioxide are maintained. This assures the transparency of the lens because the means are at hand for the disposal of free radicals created by acid waste. Elimination of free radicals prevents damage to the cells' DNA that hinders the ability of the epithelial cells to repair and regenerate themselves.

Frank wondered how he could have developed cataracts when he was such a careful eater. He shopped organic, ate vegetarian foods, the diet for his metabolic type, and drank a lot of carbonated bottled water. He found the answer to his question when he took his basal temperature. Over three days it averaged ninety-seven degrees, an indication that his thyroid activity was depressed and therefore that his lens didn't have enough energy to burn up the waste products generated by its metabolic activities.

Since foods that the digestive tract can't break down properly can lower thyroid function, and since Frank was also experiencing severe stomach pains from gas, it became apparent that a digestive problem had initiated his hypothyroid condition. Frank tested the foods he ate, one by one. When he eliminated whole wheat bread his gas pains went away. This puzzled him because he could eat other wheat products like couscous, wheat crackers, and whole wheat pita bread without any ill effects. Bread, however, contains yeast, which none of the other wheat products did. By avoiding bread Frank also brought his temperature up to 98.6 degrees. For his cataract-thickened lens to produce enough energy to eliminate his cataract, Frank needed to take extra amounts of vitamin B_2 (riboflavin). He did so and in six months his cataract had disappeared. Thanks to sufficient energy levels in the lens, the cataract had been broken up, dissolved, and removed, leaving Frank with a lens as clear as crystal.

SUGGESTIONS FOR CATARACTS

➤ Thyroid supplements—first check basal temperature for thyroid function (see Chapter 5).

➤ Vitamin E (400 to 800 units) and coconut oil assist the thyroid supplements in normalizing thyroid function.

➤ Riboflavin—fifty milligrams daily. Riboflavin, along with thyroid supplements and vitamin E, helps assure efficient energy production in the lens.

➤ Vitamin B complex—100 milligrams each of B_1, B_2, B_3, and B_6 three times a day.

➤ Vitamin D—1,000 units daily. Vitamin D assists in the absorption and utilization of calcium, so that it doesn't become waste and harden the lens and cornea.

➤ Vitamin A—25,000 to 50,000 units a day.

➤ Vitamin C—one gram per day.

➤ Avoid the use of microwave ovens. Cataracts have been linked to microwave radiation.[4] Just as cooking an egg causes the white part of the egg to lose its transparency, so heat radiating from a microwave can elevate the temperature of the eye to the point where over time the lens becomes opaque.

Glaucoma

The interior of the eyeball is filled with a transparent gelatinous fluid called vitreous humor. The pressure this fluid exerts gives the eyeball its balloonlike contours. There is another transparent fluid, more watery than vitreous fluid, called aqueous humor. This fluid is located in a tiny chamber between the pupil and iris and the lens suspended behind the pupil. As this fluid flows through the chamber, it drops off nutrients and oxygen to the cornea and then drains out of the chamber in the eye through a narrow canal. The drainage canal however, can become blocked by acidic wastes, just as a toilet can become clogged. But in the case of a clogged toilet, the water can flow freely out of the top; in the blocked canal in the chamber between the pupil and lens there is no alternate outlet and the fluid builds up. This reduces vision and can lead to blindness because the pressure of this fluid on the vitreous fluid in the interior of the eyeball puts pressure on the retina in the back of the eye. When this pressure destroys the nerve cells (the rods and cones), a portion of the vision is lost.

The fastest action to unclog the chamber that causes the buildup of fluid in the drainage canal in the eyes can be accomplished by massive doses of vitamin C. Dr. Michele Virno in an experimental research study used one-half gram of ascorbic acid for every 2.2 pounds of body weight and published a paper in *Eye, Ear, Nose, and Throat Monthly* that described how massive amounts of vitamin C dramatically reduced the intraocular pressure in glaucoma.[5] Vitamin C reduces the pressure inside the eyeball by converting toxic waste to a soluble form so that it can be carried away by the capillary blood vessels in the eye. Once the volume of acidic waste in the eye fluids is reduced, the swelling of the drainage canal goes down and the excess fluid drains out of the canal.

Taking huge amounts of vitamin C for long periods isn't a good idea because it increases the toxicity of iron in the body. Iron toxicity is especially hazardous in older people because iron levels increase with age. An elevated iron level can trigger hardening of the arteries and has also been implicated in Alzheimer's disease. (Charles Darwin wrote that low iron levels in the blood prevented infection because germs feed on iron.) Another fallout from long-term use of megadoses of vitamin C is that the diarrhea and gas pains it causes can injure the intestinal tract.

In glaucoma, acidic waste from the capillaries passes into the fluid-filled chamber between the cornea and lens because the collagen in the vessel walls that hold the cells in place crumbles, leaving open spaces for acidic debris to slip through. Vessel walls can be strengthened by taking three grams of vitamin C and twenty drops of bilberry extract three times a day for its bioflavonoid content. Vitamin C and bioflavonoids are two of the most important building blocks of collagen, the cement that holds the cells together.

Lutein, a yellow pigment similar to the beta carotene found in carrots, prevents further deterioration to the cone and rod cells in the retina caused by pressure. Lutein replenishes a purple pigment called rhodopsin in the rod cells. Rhodopsin, consisting of the orange pigment retinene and a protein called opsin, helps us "see in the dark," which means being able to see objects in very dim light since sight is not possible in the total absence of light. When the light strikes rhodopsin, it splits into its component parts—retinene and opsin—which when blended together enable us to see in darkness. Some of the retinene, a form of vitamin A, is lost every time this split occurs. To heal the rod cells, this orange pigment must be replaced. Even in healthy eyes good night vision depends upon its replacement on a daily basis. Vitamin A maintains healthy eyes, but for glaucoma patients lutein, a carotenoid pigment, is more effective. Besides the rod cells, lutein also bolsters the function of the cone cells on the periphery of the retina that help us see in bright light. Egg yolk is rich in lutein as well.

SUGGESTIONS FOR GLAUCOMA

➤ Vitamin C—one-half gram for every 2.2 pounds of body weight until healed.
➤ Liquid bilberry extract—twenty drops three times daily.
➤ Lutein—twenty milligrams daily.
➤ Vitamin A—25,000 to 50,000 units daily.
➤ Copper and manganese—three milligrams daily.
➤ Vitamin B_1—100 milligrams twice a day.
➤ Niacin—100 milligrams twice a day.
➤ Vitamin B complex—two capsules daily.
➤ Vitamin E—400 to 1,600 units daily.

Macular Degeneration

The macula is a yellow-pigmented area in the middle of the retina at the back of the eye. Along with the rest of the retina, it picks up the image-filled light rays that are passed along to it from the lens. It relays these light rays to the optic nerve. While the outer area of the retina picks up peripheral images, the macula, as befits its location in the center of the retina, absorbs the images we see when we look straight ahead.

It's thanks to our central vision that we know how far and near objects are. Because as primates, depth perception is critical to our survival, nature strengthened our central vision by placing our eyes close together. However, we developed strong central vision at the expense of our peripheral vision. The significance of this in terms of vulnerability to disease is that the macula, as the visual center of the eye and therefore the most active part of the retina, is the component most likely to deteriorate. It's therefore not surprising that while in glaucoma, the retina is damaged by a factor outside it, that is, from pressure due to the buildup of fluid in the front of the eyeball, in macular degeneration, the macula triggers its own deterioration.

Macular degeneration reduces vision in two ways. First, with the progressive loss of the rod and nerve cells in the macula, the circular-shaped area of blindness gradually enlarges. Second, vision becomes blurred because as normal cells and tissue in the macula are lost or disintegrate, inappropriate tissue (blood vessels) and alien molecules move in to take their place. These abnormal chemicals and misplaced cells injure the macula and cause scar tissue to form. Scar tissue blurs vision because as light rays focus on it they are bent out of shape. The blurring of the vision increases when the insulating layer between the macula and the blood vessels that nourish it breaks down. Leftover fluids from the breakdown of the insulating tissue leak into the macula and cause scarring. In the meantime, a yellowish substance called drusen fills the space where the insulating layer had once been. This blocks off the macula from the blood vessels that supply it with oxygen and nutrients. When this blockage is complete, the more serious form of macular degeneration, the "wet" version as opposed to the milder "dry" type, develops. In an effort to supply the deprived macula with oxygen, a blood vessel inducer called VEGF stimulates the growth of blood vessels in the macula. Probably because they don't belong there they rupture and bleed. Scars cover over the ruptured spots, and this increases the blurring of the vision, sometimes leading to blindness.

In an effort to stem the loss of vision in macular degeneration, medical researchers have focused on trying to prevent the growth of blood vessels in the macula. In experimental research, attempts are being made to prevent blood vessel growth in the eye by incorporating antibodies in the protein (VEGF). As usual, researchers are out of sync with reality. The oxygen needs of the photosensitive rods in the macula are tremendous because of the energy required to absorb light rays. The blood vessel–stimulating protein (VEGF) is alerted to this oxygen need and stimulates the growth of blood vessels in the macula to satisfy it. (Oxygen needed for the production of energy takes precedence over all other eye functions, even eyesight.) The focus thus should be on finding a way of getting oxygen to the macula so that the VEGF protein won't trigger the development of blood vessels in the macula.

If the aberrant chemicals in the macula and the waste debris (drusen) that separates it from its oxygen supply were eliminated, the VEGF protein would have no need to trigger the growth of blood vessels in the macula. Thus preventing further macular degeneration depends upon reducing toxic waste levels so as to clear away the waste material that sets up a barricade between the macula and the oxygen-carrying blood vessels behind it. Zinc is the most important nutrient for this job, because enzymes whose function is neutralizing aberrant chemicals in the macula can't do so without zinc as a coenzyme. Dr. David A. Newsome of the Louisiana State Eye Center in New Orleans conducted a research experiment in which he gave half of the 151 subjects, who all had macular degeneration, 100 milligrams of zinc twice a day, while the other half got a placebo. Examined between one and two years after the experiment began, it was found that those who took the zinc had better vision than those who received a placebo.[6]

Another way of assuring that the macula gets a normal supply of oxygen is by taking antioxidant supplements like vitamins E, C, and selenium, which make more oxygen available by preventing its breakdown. Oxygenating magnetic and/or far infrared pads placed over the eyes at night during sleep have the advantage of targeting the area where oxygen is needed. The fact that a sufficient supply of oxygen helps ensure the production of normal energy levels in the rod cells in the macula is particularly important in light of the fact that 10 percent of those with macular degeneration go on to develop the most devastating form of the disease in which blood vessels grow in the macula. Oxygen is not only one of the crucial raw materials in the production of energy, it's also important because it neutralizes toxic acidic waste; vitamins E and

C also dispose of waste, including alien molecules that have invaded the macula (by absorbing them).

That a deficiency of yellow pigment (retinene) in the photosensitive rod cells in the macula is one cause of macular degeneration is indicated by a statistical research study.[7] It shows that people who eat one carrot— or any other beta-carotene rich vegetable, such as spinach—once a day have reduced incidence of macular degeneration by 40 percent as compared to those who eat such foods less than once a week. (Blueberries have also been shown to slow the loss of vision in macular degeneration, probably for the same reason that carrots do: by supplying a pigment that helps the rod cells absorb light rays.) When there is not enough pigment to absorb all the light rays that fall within the range of central vision, it's difficult for the eyes to adjust to extremes of light. Either they become oversensitive to bright light and/or have poor visibility in dim light. Sluggish intracellular function due to a lack of pigment not only causes vision problems but also gives off excessive acidic wastes.

Toxins such as tar and nicotine in cigarette smoke have ultimately the same effect on the rod cells as too little pigment. The individual who smokes one or more packs of cigarettes a day is 2.4 times more likely to develop macular degeneration than someone who has never smoked. Nicotine destroys oxygen, which causes the cells to become inflamed and deteriorate. Unfortunately, longtime smokers who give up smoking seldom reduce their chances of getting macular degeneration. The damage to the macula has already been done.

SUGGESTIONS FOR MACULAR DEGENERATION

➤ Zinc—fifty milligrams daily.
➤ Blueberries—contain bioflavonoids that build cell membranes and supply the retina with pigment.
➤ Vitamin E—400 to 800 units daily.
➤ Vitamin A—25,000 to 50,000 units daily.
➤ Vitamin D—1,000 to 2,000 units daily.
➤ Magnetic pad placed over the eyes (see Resources).
➤ Vitamin C—1,000 milligrams daily.

CHAPTER 12

DIABETES

The Native Americans who lived in the Sonora desert in Arizona before the arrival of Europeans were agriculturists, but because rainfall was seasonal they could only grow crops for part of the year. Although there was very little to eat when the rain dried up, these people didn't starve because they lived off the food that was stored as fat inside their bodies and their appetites diminished accordingly. This feat was possible because their appetite had become synchronized with the alternating wet and dry seasonal cycle in the desert. Constantly hungry during the wet season, they gorged on harvests of tepary beans, melons, squash, and corn. Most of this food was converted by the digestive system into fat in preparation for the coming season when there would be no rainfall and therefore very little to eat.

Their adaptation to this cyclical feast or famine situation served them well until Europeans moved into the area and opened a corner grocery store, making food available all year long. By now, after four to five generations of overindulging in food that has become progressively more deficient in nutrients, these southwestern desert people have become morbidly obese, a condition that starts in early childhood. By the time they reach their early thirties, over 90 percent of them have diabetes.[1] Not all fat people, however, are prone to diabetes, because the nutrient content of the diet is also a factor.

The liver and pancreas work hand in hand to regulate and distribute glucose, so that the trillions of cells in the body will have enough of it to satisfy their energy needs. The liver converts glucose to glycogen (starch) and stores it until blood sugar levels fall too low. At that point, the glucagon hormone from the pancreas directs the liver to convert some of its stored glycogen back to glucose and release it into the bloodstream.

As long as complex carbohydrates, such as whole grains, or half raw, starchy root vegetables such as white potatoes and yams that are broken down slowly are eaten, the liver isn't overworked because it receives a slow, steady stream of glucose. Also, when blood sugar levels remain normal, the insulin-producing glands in the pancreas don't have to work overtime producing additional insulin. This explains why fat people on a healthy diet don't get diabetes. Their glucose blood levels are normal, so most of the glucose is absorbed by the cells. A diet of concentrated white sugar and flour, however, is converted into glucose too quickly, overloading the liver. When the liver can't handle all the glucose that streams into it by way of the portal vein, the excess sugar passes into general circulation. The pancreas then releases insulin, which directs the removal of the excess blood sugar and its synthesis into fat or glycogen (starch). Oversecretion of insulin wears out the pancreas's insulin-producing machinery, while working overtime converting and storing excess glucose weakens liver function. The result is a diabetic condition, since without insulin, blood sugar levels remain elevated.

Diabetes and Other Degenerative Diseases

A diabetic liver can initiate lowered energy levels. When the liver becomes inundated with glucose and no longer able to break down fat, it fills up with sugar and fat. As a result, it has no space to store the thyroxin (T4) produced by the thyroid. Without T4 in storage, the liver can't convert it into the active T3, and it's T3 that stimulates the mitochondria in the cells into increasing their rate of energy production when additional fuel is needed. The rate of energy production is also slowed when the liver can no longer restructure fatty acids for use in the manufacture of energy. The shortage of insulin is still another factor that contributes to sluggish energy production. Without sufficient insulin molecules, which enable glucose to penetrate the cells, the cells can't produce energy.

The first consequence of depressed energy levels is that harmful substances in the body multiply because the detoxifying organs don't have the energy to neutralize and eliminate them. The liver can't neutralize toxic chemicals, assist the immune system in killing off harmful bacteria, or process the by-products of metabolism in the blood and lymph fluids that pass through it, for example, lactic acid, the end product of energy production in the muscles, which under normal circumstances the liver converts into glucose. The fat the liver can't oxidize stays in the liver. This causes the liver to degenerate because fat molecules replace vital structures.

Depressed energy levels also slow up the pancreas's production of the alkaline-based sodium bicarbonate and of lipase. Without enough sodium to reduce acidity in the small intestine, digestion is impaired, which means more undigested food particles that turn into acidic waste circulate in the blood and damage the inside walls of the blood vessels. Depressed lipase levels have similar results. Fat that isn't broken down becomes acidic waste, and as it flows through the arteries it adheres to the grooves and pits in the arterial walls, causing the blood vessels to get progressively narrower, so the diabetic's arteries harden.

Once the liver can no longer alter the toxic structure of poisonous compounds that pass through it via the blood, it either stores them— which depresses liver function further—or they go back into general circulation. Some of them seep from leaky blood vessels into the intercellular fluid where they scratch and tear cell membranes. This makes it possible for viruses, harmful bacteria, heavy metals, and so on, to slip into cells and infect and/or damage them. However, most of the acidic waste not processed by the liver remains in the bloodstream and the kidneys have to filter it out. As the blood, filled with acidic crystals of sugar, ammonia, urea, and lead, streams through the kidneys' filters, these crystals injure them, and over time the filters are knocked out. This condition also explains the origin of neurogenic bladder disease, which is associated with diabetes. The nerves in the bladder that signal the brain when it is time to urinate atrophy because of the toxins filtered out by the kidneys that, as part of the urine, are stored in the bladder. These toxins irritate the bladder and the resulting inflammation destroys the bladder's nerve cells. Voluntary urination becomes impossible.

In diabetes, the body turns into a reservoir of acidic wastes. Blood and other fluids in the general circulation that are overburdened with acidic wastes disrupt the physiology most vital to life: the exchange of materials between the cells and the circulating blood. First, acidic waste-filled blood doesn't have the room to transport sufficient nutrients and oxygen to the cells or to pick up the waste products from cellular metabolism. Second, the cells, injured by the acidic waste in the fluid surrounding them, harden and lose their permeability. This makes it difficult for them to absorb the few nutrients and molecules of oxygen that the blood is able to deliver. When the interchange between the blood and the cells stops altogether, the affected tissues die. The eyesight is often the first to go. This occurs when the tiny blood vessels in the retina in the back of the eye harden, a condition that causes blurred vision and, if the diabetic lives long enough, blindness. The National Society for the Prevention of Blindness has found that 50 percent of those who have had diabetes for twenty years develop neuropathy of the eyes, while 90 percent who have had diabetes for thirty years develop it. Studies by this agency also show that diabetes is the leading cause of blindness. Other parts of the body that are damaged in diabetics are the extremities, particularly the feet and legs. This begins when cuts, scratches, and rashes take longer to heal than they should. Eventually abrasions stop healing altogether. The cells, choked with metabolic wastes and starved for nutrients, die out, causing the flesh to rot and become gangrenous. Amputation prevents death—until the gangrene spreads to vital organs in the body. Kidney failure occurs when all the kidneys' filters are knocked out. Dialysis prevents immediate death, but the drugs used to prevent the immune system from rejecting the artificial kidney machine increase the chances of getting other degenerative diseases.

Type I Diabetes

There was great excitement in the press over reports of the success of the insulin transplant operation in 1999.[2] Taken from the pancreases of deceased donors, insulin-producing cells were transplanted into the liver of patients with severe Type I diabetes. The eight patients who had this procedure done two to fourteen months before it was publicized in the press no longer had any symptoms of the disease. That's wonderful news for the present. But how long will these implanted cells continue to produce insulin? Or for that matter how long will drug medications be effective in preventing the immune system from rejecting the insulin-producing cells? And what effects will a depressed immune system have on the general health of these transplant patients? The limited availability of pancreases is another downside. It takes two pancreases from cadavers to collect enough insulin-producing cells for two separate injections of these cells into the liver. Moreover, the operation can't restore eyesight, bring back kidney function, or heal injured nerves in the legs, commonplace complications in Type I diabetics. It's possible to restore insulin function through diet and nutritional supplements, and this is the avenue that Type I diabetics should explore before undergoing transplant surgery or consigning themselves to a life of insulin injections.

Don, like his mother, older sister, and younger brother, developed the severe form of diabetes, Type I, as a small child. From the time Don was diagnosed, he had to have three injections of insulin a day. By the age of ten he was giving injections to himself. He had learned by practicing on an orange. Don came from a poor, working-class family in Brooklyn and had a New York accent that could be cut with a knife, but he was determined to make something of himself. He worked his way through medical school and married a girl from one of Boston's "blue-blood" families. At the age of twenty-eight and still in apparent good health, he and his wife, Caroline, moved to Portland, Maine, where he established a successful family practice. Don's brother Roger, whose diabetes was more severe than Don's, had already gone blind, and ten years after Don moved to Portland, his sister Phyllis died. She had caught a virus infection that lowered her blood sugar and raised the acid levels in her blood. This caused her to go into a diabetic coma from which she never regained consciousness.

Until Phyllis died, Don hadn't given a thought as to how diabetes might undermine his health as he got older. Now he felt so apprehensive that when he read about a simple self-administered test that indicates whether or not a diabetic will develop such complications as hardening of the arteries and gangrene, he took it. According to the test, if you can bend your fingers back so that they are not in line with the palm of your hand, your prognosis is good. Don took the test but his fingers wouldn't budge. While his colleagues at the clinic laughed at him for putting stock in such an unscientific test, Don didn't believe it was an old wives' tale. Because the fingers weren't accustomed to being bent back, it made sense that their immobility was an indication that the muscles and tendons that joined the fingers to the palms had hardened. This indicated that other tissues in the body would be likely to harden.

Caroline persuaded Don to see a homeopath, who prescribed liquid extracts of herbs and minerals that had been diluted millions of times until only the energy from the substances was left. Don took hundreds of drops three times a day, and after two months was able to reduce the strength of his insulin injections from sixty-five to fifty-five units. Since the homeopathic drops had only caused a slight drop in his blood glucose levels and the process of adding specific numbers of drops to separate glasses of water every day was time consuming, Don discontinued the treatment.

Ten years passed and Don's medical practice continued to flourish and he and Caroline adopted a baby girl. The only negative in their lives was a gradual decline in Don's health. By the time Don was forty-five he looked sixty, his vision even with glasses was blurred, and he felt pressure behind his eyeballs. He also felt tired most of the time, had lost weight, and his muscles had stiffened. He used to joke that he didn't need a costume when he went trick-or-treating on Halloween with his daughter. He could pass for a skeleton. When he was fifty-two, Don felt a tingling sensation in his legs and feet and walking became painful. These symptoms were diagnosed as neuropathy (nerve damage). Like many men, Don believed that exercise was a panacea for all health problems, so to relieve the pain in his leg muscles he bought a video of low-impact aerobic exercises. As long as he did these exercises for a half-hour, three times a week, he felt no pain in his legs and feet. Once he skipped exercising for a week, and the nerves in his feet became so numb that when he stepped on some broken glass on the beach and cut his feet badly, he didn't feel the slightest twinge of discomfort. He didn't know that he had cut his feet until he stooped down to pick up a seashell and saw a pool of blood.

But the euphoria over the success of his exercise program was short-lived. Don's blood sugar had begun to fluctuate wildly. One day while driving to work he started sweating profusely and trembling. He reached Caroline on his cell phone, but his speech was so slurred that she couldn't understand a word. Recognizing that he was in insulin shock, Don stuck a hard candy in his mouth, stopped at the side of the road, and waited for his blood glucose level to rise. He had always carried some candy with him for this purpose, but this was the first time he had ever had to use it.

In addition, Don's vision began to deteriorate rapidly, so much so that he became legally blind, and the pressure in his eyes was so intense he felt as though his eyeballs were about to pop out.

These factors convinced Don to change his diet and take nutritional supplements. He took the niacin test, which indicated that he had a meat-eating metabolism (see Chapter 2). If he was to eat foods that were in harmony with his metabolic type, Don had to change his diet. He had believed the propaganda about the harmful effects of red meat, and hearing that diabetes among Asians who eat brown rice, fish, seaweed, and tofu is rare, Don had been on this Asian diet for years. Now realizing that what is sauce for the goose is not sauce for the gander, he became a meat and potato eater, and also ate more vegetables.

To boost the alkaline reserves in his body, Don drank a combination of raw, juiced asparagus and celery juice every morning and took thyroid supplements and vitamin E so his energy levels would increase and speed up the removal of acidic wastes in his body. He took alpha lipoic acid because it helps glucose slip through the surface membrane of the cell when insulin fails to do so. (Fatty acids are both water and fat soluble, so they can transport sugar into the cell either through the fatty part or water soluble part of the membrane.) He also bought an ionizing air cleaner because its negatively charged particles alkalinize the body.

Don's blood sugar stopped fluctuating wildly, but because he was still stiff he added vitamin B_6, B_{12}, folic acid, and vitamin C to reduce excess homocysteine. This made his ligaments and muscles more flexible. His vision, however, was still blurred and his feet still numb. The nerves had degenerated in Don's eyes and legs because the myelin sheathing covering them had hardened. Increased energy levels from the thyroid and vitamin E supplements he took probably reduced the acidic wastes that had collected around his nerve cells and destroyed the myelin sheathing, but fatty acids were needed to rebuild it. Don took 400 milligrams of primrose oil for this purpose. His eyesight improved, he felt less pressure behind his eyeballs, and his feet no longer felt numb.

Don's insulin requirements also dropped; he now takes just twenty-five units of insulin a day. He recently started drinking the juice of brussels sprouts, string beans, carrots, and lettuce for their insulin-generating properties in the hope he will be able to go off insulin entirely.

Type II Diabetes

Type II diabetes, formerly referred to as adult-onset diabetes because it usually affected individuals past fifty, is the most common form of the disease—90 percent of those with diabetes have Type II.[3] In recent years, however, it has become a disease of young adults as well. Dr. Frank Vinicor, director of the diabetes division at the Centers of Disease Control and Prevention, states that according to a study completed by that agency between 1990 and 1998, there was a 76 percent increase in diabetes among people in their thirties. Young adults are harder hit by Type II diabetes than preceding generations, because the processed foods they eat were less common when older generations were growing up.

Agnes, fifty, who worked as a secretary for an insurance company, had pain, numbness, and tingling in her wrists, the symptoms of carpal tunnel syndrome, a health problem associated with diabetes. (John Ellis, M.D., wrote that 27.2 percent of the carpal tunnel patients of a Dr. George Phalen either had diabetes or had a family history of it.[4]) Two years later she developed insulin resistance, a condition in which insulin, although produced in sufficient quantities, isn't able to lower blood sugar or inhibit the release of fatty acids into the blood. Shortly after that, Agnes's blood sugar became elevated and she was diagnosed with Type

II diabetes. She had trouble believing that carpal tunnel and diabetes were related, since the conditions that trigger them are entirely different. The inflamed tissues in carpal tunnel, a narrow passageway in the wrist, are associated with repetitive wrist motions involved in using a computer, while the excessive consumption of sugar and other refined carbohydrates causes diabetes. Agnes spent her entire work day transcribing tapes on a computer. She also consumed plenty of sugar. The company she worked for kept its underpaid employees happy by having the best bakery in New York deliver a cake, consisting mostly of icing, to the office every afternoon. Agnes had been eating two hefty slices of this cake every day for the last twenty years, the period of time she had been working for the firm.

The condition that diabetes and carpal tunnel syndrome have in common is a deficiency of vitamin B_6. Dr. Kilmer McCully's research into homocysteine as the cause of atherosclerosis laid the groundwork for Dr. John Marion Ellis's discovery of the role it plays in diabetes and carpal tunnel. (For more on atherosclerosis, see Chapter 6.) McCully proved that excess homocysteine (an amino acid used in the repair and creation of new cells), caused by a deficiency of vitamin B_6 and vitamin B_6–dependent enzymes, triggers hardening of the arteries. The supplements McCully gave his research subjects, namely, vitamins B_6, and B_{12} and folic acid, made their arteries more flexible and acted as heart attack preventatives. Ellis, a medical doctor and researcher, noting that his patients with diabetes and carpal tunnel syndrome, like McCully's heart patients, suffered from a vitamin B_6 deficiency, concluded that they also had elevated homocysteine levels. He prescribed 100 to 200 milligrams of B_6 daily for these patients. The treatment alleviated both the carpal tunnel syndrome and the diabetes, indicating that excess homocysteine not only injures the arteries, but is also a contributing factor in these two diseases. On the basis of this research I recommended that Agnes take 150 milligrams of B_6 every day. Before long her blood sugar normalized and the pain and tingling in her wrists went away.

It's most likely that in carpal tunnel syndrome, excess homocysteine accumulates in the ligaments in the carpal tunnel area of the wrist and causes them to become inflamed. Homocysteine's role in diabetes isn't quite so obvious. But given the high blood levels of glucose in diabetics who have normal insulin levels, a logical explanation is that glucose (transported by insulin) can no longer penetrate the cell because the membranes of the cells have been hardened by homocysteine wastes.

SUGGESTIONS FOR DIABETES

➤ Vegetable juice. The alkalizing effect of vegetables has been known to reverse diabetes if it hasn't become chronic.

➤ Vitamin E. Taking 400 to 800 units helps normalize thyroid function and improve the sex drive in male diabetics.

➤ Thyroid extract (see Chapter 5).

➤ Alpha lipoic acid. Take 200 to 600 milligrams daily. For diabetic neuropathy, 600 milligrams improves nerve function.

➤ Evening primrose oil. Taking 360 to 480 milligrams strengthens nerve function, as do flaxseed and fish oil.

➤ B_{12}—1,000 micrograms; B_1—100 milligrams; B_6—100 to 200 milligrams; and folic acid—800 micrograms. These B vitamins help reduce excess levels of homocysteine, which in turn reduces hardening of the veins and arteries in the liver and pancreas.

➤ Chromium picolinate. A daily dose of 400 to 600 micrograms helps insulin transport glucose into the cells.

➤ Stevia. A plant whose leaves are a natural sweetener, stevia can be used either in the powder form sold at health food stores, or the leaves of the plant can be squeezed and added to a hot drink or cereal.

➤ Gelatin. Start with one-half to one ounce in liquid or sprinkled on food (see Resources). The mucilage in gelatin stabilizes blood glucose.

CHAPTER 13

INSOMNIA

We take for granted that before the invention of artificial light people went to sleep as soon as it became dark and didn't wake up until sunrise. If this were true, it would mean that in the Scandinavian countries, people would sleep solid for two to three weeks during the winter when it's dark the whole day, while those living on the equator would sleep twelve hours out of every twenty-four, since the sun shines there twelve hours a day throughout the year. In fact, before the use of oil and gas lamps in the beginning of the seventeenth century, people alternately slept and awakened during the night. While awake they meditated, chatted with their bedfellows—since before the twentieth century families typically shared the same bed—visited neighbors, or worked by candlelight.[1] This was such a widely established pattern that people commonly referred to their first and second sleep. Thomas A. Wehr of the National Institute of Mental Health did a research study that showed that when subjects were deprived of artificial light they reverted to the preindustrial sleeping mode in which they were asleep and awake in turns during the night. Wehr believes this adaptation occurred because, without artificial light, prolactin hormone levels, which bring about "a state of quiet restfulness," were raised.

Preindustrial peoples viewed wakefulness at night as entirely natural, and even in the twentieth century some medical researchers, like Roger Williams, professor of biochemistry at the University of Texas, believed that waking up at night shouldn't be labeled insomnia if sleep

TWO KINDS OF SLEEP

There are two kinds of sleep: the sleep in which we don't dream, called orthodox sleep, which gets progressively deeper in four successive stages, and a shorter period of sleep when we dream, called rapid eye movement, or REM, because the eyeballs move rapidly during a dream. Some researchers think these two kinds of sleep alternate in cycles throughout the night and that three-quarters of the time we experience orthodox sleep and the other quarter REM sleep. Dreams are most vivid the last two hours of an eight-hour period of sleep.

that is lost at night is made up for during the day. Napping may have gone out of style, but there are still some people who use it to good effect. Rita, the principal of a public high school in New York, is exhausted by the time the school day ends at three o'clock, so as soon as she gets home she takes a half-hour nap. When she wakes up she feels completely refreshed. My great uncle and his family, who lived in Paris before World War II, followed a tradition that was then customary throughout Europe among the professional class. He came home for lunch—which was the big meal of the day—and took an hour's nap afterward.

The practice of indigenous peoples of sleeping in complete darkness makes sense in light of what we now know about the hormone melatonin. Melatonin, which puts us to sleep, is secreted by the pineal gland in the brain and needs complete darkness for normal function. The slightest amount of light reduces melatonin production. Dr. David Blask, an oncologist at Bassett Research Institute in Cooperstown, New York, lowered the melatonin production of rats by exposing them to light while they slept. He then transplanted malignant tumors into the bodies of two groups of rats: one group had been exposed to dim light while asleep and the other group slept in total darkness. The tumors in the rats exposed to faint light grew much faster than those in the rats that slept in total darkness. This is probably because melatonin suppresses estrogen production and estrogen has been linked to cancer.

Studies of blind women in Sweden and Finland support Blask's experiment. Those women who couldn't perceive any light at night had 60 percent less breast cancer. With the increase in the perception of light by some of the blind women, their rate of breast cancer rose. The decrease in cancer in those women who could perceive no light in the darkness proves that the less light perceived while sleeping, the greater the melatonin production (and the lower the level of estrogen). How dark then should we make the rooms in which we sleep? Since tests have shown that the eyes respond to moonlight and light from the street that filters through a window, windows should either be covered with opaque blinds that let no light through or eye masks should be worn.

The quality of sleep, however, depends not only on blocking out all light from the eyes but also on absorbing light through the eyes while we are awake. In fact, strong light works better than any natural supplement or drug medication in putting people to sleep at night. People who develop SAD (seasonal affective disorder) from lack of sunlight during the winter and who use hig-intensity, full-spectrum fluorescent lights to alleviate their symptoms of depression discover that they also sleep better.

How could exposure to intense natural or artificial light improve the quality of sleep when the act of sleeping is triggered by darkness? According to Dr. Dale Edgar, during the day the pressure to sleep builds up. Light then, is not only a wake-up factor, but it also sets in motion the desire to sleep by keeping our internal clock (hypothalamus) wound up.

In addition, when you sleep in complete darkness and are exposed to plenty of light during the day, thyroid function improves. As a result energy levels are raised and more acidic wastes are eliminated.

How Much Sleep Is Enough?

During the day, most men are able to fall asleep at the drop of a hat for a few minutes at a time, something few women can do. Many men can fall asleep anywhere, anytime—on planes, sitting on the sofa in the presence of guests, or at their desks during a coffee break. I know a man who sometimes falls asleep while walking. This aptitude is most likely a biological trait carried over from the physically more demanding way of life led by men during most of the 300,000 years of *Homo sapiens'* existence. It was men who hunted wild animals and, later, harnessed the forces of nature by clearing away brush and felling trees for planting, draining swamps, and cultivating grain fields. To carry out these arduous tasks for long stretches at a time, men needed a quick way to recoup their energy, and cat naps served that purpose. Women, on the other hand, prepared animal skins, foraged for edible plants, cooked, cared for children, and in later times spun, wove, and sewed cloth. They expended energy slowly and steadily, so that the replacement of energy was ongoing, making quick snatches of sleep unnecessary.

The amount of sleep individuals need varies. Some people, mostly men, don't need more than five hours sleep a night. Others need as much as twelve hours to be productive and alert during the day. While in college I read about a research study on sleeping patterns and their effects on longevity in a journal whose name I've long since forgotten. The study made an indelible impression because researchers tracked the sleep habits and life spans of 60,000 subjects. It showed that those who slept seven hours nightly lived the longest. Eight-hour sleepers lived almost as long. However, sleeping even one hour over the standard eight hours sharply curtailed longevity, whereas individuals who slept less than seven hours, even those who slept only four or five hours a night, lived almost as long as those who slept seven hours a night. Seven hours of sleep may very well be most conducive to health and longevity, but if you only feel rested and alert by sleeping longer, curtailing your sleeping hours for the purpose of extending your life span would be counterproductive.

Given the individual variation in the number of hours spent sleeping, it's not surprising that individuals also differ in terms of their sleeping habits. Some people's day begins when they wake up at five in the morning; others wake up long before the alarm goes off; still others take an hour or two to fall asleep at night. How does someone with such an irregular sleeping pattern know if it is a symptom of insomnia? If, despite having trouble going to sleep or waking up too early, you feel full of pep the following day, this is a normal sleeping pattern for you. But if you feel tired (as opposed to sleepy) and need caffeine to wake you up, or if you have to force yourself to work, you have insomnia.

How to Eliminate Insomnia

If you have trouble falling asleep at night, it's most likely because of acid indigestion from food you ate during the day. The most effective remedy is to make sure that what you eat, particularly in the evening, is compatible with your digestive system. Some people who eat the wrong foods for dinner or before they go to bed and are too restless to go to sleep throw up the offending foods and then sleep like a baby. Another cause of wakefulness is stimulants such as caffeine and salt. They activate the adrenal hormones that trigger the liver into converting glycogen into glucose and feeding it into the bloodstream. High levels of blood sugar trigger the release of neurotransmitters that activate the brain cells. This release keeps the brain excited at night when it should be low-keyed.

The individual who goes to sleep easily but wakes up later at night and can't go back to sleep has a different problem. He or she is often addicted to eating large quantities of sugary foods, causing a rush of insulin that lowers the blood sugar too drastically. The result is hypoglycemia (low blood sugar) which brings on dizziness, depression, nervousness, indigestion, muscle pains, worrying, etc.—all of which can cause insomnia. Hypoglycemia can also slow up thyroid function, which can also trigger insomnia. I have a meat-eating metabolism and a slightly underactive thyroid and probably a mild case of hypoglycemia, so when I wake up at five in the morning and can't get back to sleep I eat a few slices of red meat. That causes me to fall asleep immediately. My husband, on the other hand, tended to wake up at five o'clock in the morning because of an underactive thyroid. Once he began taking thyroid supplements, he slept through the night. Still, the most effective antidote for insomnia with the exception of a healthy, metabolically appropriate diet is intense, full-spectrum fluorescent light because it not only synchronizes the biological clock with a twenty-four-hour cycle, but helps normalize thyroid function, enabling the body to dispose of acidic wastes that prevent sleep by irritating the nerves and upsetting the stomach.

SUGGESTIONS FOR INSOMNIA

➤ Ginkgo biloba. It not only helps induce sleep but also improves the quality of sleep. It's especially effective in cases of depression.

➤ Intense light. Designed to prevent SAD (seasonal affective disorder), intense light also promotes sleep (see "Intense light" in Resources). Some people have to use the light device in the morning to avoid altering their biological clocks, which keeps them up at night. In some it induces sleep no matter when they use it.

➤ Diet. Avoid any foods that cause indigestion or stimulate the nervous system.

➤ Thyroid supplements—to correct low thyroid function, which is one cause of sleep disorder (see Chapter 5).

➤ Calcium, magnesium, and vitamin B$_6$. Modest amounts of these nutrients induce sleep by calming the nerves.

➤ Melatonin—less than one milligram.

➤ Inositol—100 milligram daily.

➤ Avoid antidepressants or any other drug medication that prevents dreaming. Many people who take antidepressants don't seem to be bothered by not having dreams. There are no statistics, however, on the many people who quit taking these medications because without being able to dream they experienced feelings of panic or became disoriented.

➤ Complete darkness. Use an eye mask or completely opaque window dressing to normalize melatonin function.

CHAPTER 14

ALCOHOLISM

Robert Dudley, a biologist at the University of Texas, writes that our liking for alcohol was passed on to us from our closest relatives on the evolutionary scale—chimpanzees, gorillas, and orangutans who travel miles through dense forest thickets in search of fermented fruit.[1] Dudley asserts that the purpose is to obtain "precious calories." But why go to such lengths for fuel when fresh fruit that contains plenty of sugar for the production of heat energy is close at hand? I suspect these primates sought fermented fruit for the same reason that the Chinese ferment soybeans and the Eskimos and Hebrides Islanders devised ways to putrefy meat and fish—because eating foods partially broken down by bacteria increases energy, strengthens muscles, and improves digestion. A liking, then, among our primate relatives for the taste and euphoric effect of fermented fruit developed from the health benefits they derived from it.

Among indigenous cultures as well as in more technologically advanced ones, certain forms of alcohol became symbols of religious beliefs. In Christianity, for example, wine taken during communion is regarded as the blood of Christ. In preliterate cultures ceremonial liquor not only expressed the guiding principle of their religion, but was also drunk to improve health in order to ensure the perpetuity of the tribal unit. The liquor in Ghana and elsewhere in West Africa was made from a blend of two contrasting ingredients: bitter roots and sweet fruit (mango, papaya, and pineapple). Being opposite in taste, they expressed the two opposing sides of life. The sweet fruit represented goodness, life, and health, while the bitter roots were a symbol of evil, sickness, and death. Yet both promoted the survival of the tribe, the fruit by increasing fertility and the bitter roots by cleansing the body.

An overpowering compulsion to drink alcohol is an addiction, but the addictive person isn't necessarily an alcoholic. If the heavy drinker doesn't act drunk, remains in good health, and if drinking doesn't interfere with work or family life, he or she is not an alcoholic. Such individuals, however, are rare because only extraordinarily resilient livers and endocrine glands can withstand the toxic effects of alcohol. People who drink too much have at least two of the three following health problems: a deficiency of the liver enzymes needed to detoxify the by-products of alcohol, adrenal glands that are too easily stimulated, and high levels of acidic wastes from the consumption of foods that their digestive enzymes can't break down.

A diet that predisposes an individual to alcoholism is usually one that is not part of the individual's heritage. Thus alcoholic addiction among individuals of Northern European extraction whose ancestors were meat eaters is often caused by the overconsumption of grains, which their digestive systems can't handle. Such individuals usually prefer whiskey that is made out of the grain to which they are allergic—corn, wheat, barley, rye, or potatoes. Eating allergy-causing grains makes some individuals crave the alcoholic form of the grain because the grain allergens make them nervous and jumpy. Alcohol does away with these feelings by relaxing the nerves. Alcoholics are mistaken in thinking they're driven to drink only because they like the way it tastes and the feeling of relaxation and euphoria it gives them. All of this is true, but the root cause of their need to relax and their craving for alcohol is due to acidic wastes that are the by-products of grain and other food allergens. Dr. Theron G. Randolph, author of the four-day rotation diet, found that among forty drinkers, each one was allergic to the food product—corn, wheat, rye, grapes, or potatoes—that was the raw material from which the alcoholic beverage they drank was made.

While meat eaters are more likely to become alcoholics if they eat grains, grain eaters are more vulnerable to alcoholism if they give up their ancestral dietary grain staple for meat and cow's milk. This is because each cultural group has protein-digesting enzymes that have been shaped by the kinds of protein that served as their ancestors' dietary staple. I came across an example of this in a special education course I taught a few years ago. During a class discussion, Isabel, a teacher of handicapped children, talked about parental alcoholism as the cause of learning disabilities in children. She said that most of the parents of her students whom she had met had alcohol on their breath. This reminded her of her own battle with alcoholism, and she stayed after class to tell me her story.

Isabel came from Colombia, South America, and described herself as an indigenous person, a descendent of the ancient Inca Indians. She told me that among Indian families today in Colombia all the family members, even the small children, drink alcoholic beverages, with the result that most Indians become alcoholics at an early age. Isabel, her second husband, and two sons were all alcoholics, but, determined to give up drinking, they moved to the United States to get away from the alcoholic environment in which they were living. This didn't work, so they returned to Colombia and put themselves under the care of a healer, referred to by Isabel as a bio-energetic doctor. This doctor prescribed a number of herbs and outlined a diet designed to heal their body tissues, which the toxic by-products of alcohol had inflamed. Foods that were forbidden because of their inflammatory tendency were cow's milk, meat, fruit, and tomatoes. The first week Isabel and her family were allowed only two foods: potato and pumpkin soup; the second week vegetables and brown rice were added; and the third week goat's milk to reduce inflammation caused by meat and cow's milk. Isabel, her husband, and sons were also given vaccines against parasites, and the doctor swung a pendulum aligned with the liver to increase its flow of energy. Isabel's sons are still fighting alcoholism, but the diet made it possible for her and her husband, an alcoholic schizophrenic, to give up drinking by eliminating their nervousness. Isabel stressed that it was the stabilization of her nervous system that took away her craving for drink—and cigarettes. I was reminded that when I eat a food to which I'm allergic, I become nervous and restless until I go on an eating binge, which has the same relaxing effect on my nerves as a drinking spree has on the nerves of an alcoholic. Isabel's dietary treatment for her alcoholism was successful because it duplicated the grain (rice and quinoa), root vegetable, and goat's milk diet of her ancestors.

How do acidic wastes from undigested food debris set up a craving for alcohol? An individual with the potential to be an alcoholic who eats foods to which he or she is sensitive, may at first suffer no more serious allergic reactions than flushing, sneezing, or hay fever from the histamines triggered by the allergic response. But with the continued consumption of these foods, acidic waste from undigested food debris piles up. This elicits a reaction from the adrenals. They speed up their action when acid levels in the body become high because hyperacidity is taken by the adrenals as a sign that the body's survival is threatened. (That's because anger and fear also raise blood acid levels.) This causes the release of additional quantities of the adrenaline hormone epinephrine, which prepares the individual for extreme physical exertion by elevating the blood sugar, speeding up the heartbeat, raising the blood pressure, etc. The purpose of these physiological changes is to speed up the production and distribution of energy, making it possible for the individual either to run from danger or fight it out. But because in reality there is no necessity to do either, the pent-up energy, rapid heartbeat, etc., has no outlet. This builds tension which sets up a craving for anything—food, alcoholic beverages, caffeinated drinks, or cigarettes—that will relieve the feeling of anxiousness. Which addiction grabs hold of such individuals depends upon where their physical vulnerability lies. The high rate of alcoholism among indigenous peoples, the Irish, and the Russians is attributed by some researchers to a deficiency of the liver enzymes that break down acid aldehyde, the toxic by-product of alcohol. While an alarm reaction, triggered by hyperacidity from undigested food debris, initiates the descent into alcoholism, the craving for alcohol is strengthened whenever the alcoholic takes a drink and the liver can't neutralize and eliminate all the acid aldehyde by-product of the alcohol. Each time the liver becomes overloaded with acid aldehyde the adrenals secrete extra epinephrine. Soon this overexertion exhausts the adrenals and they lose their ability to inhibit the individual's allergic response to food. This means more undigested food debris turns into acidic waste which further exhausts the adrenals and increases the symptoms of a hangover—headaches, dizziness, irritability, trembling, and a lack of coordination. The deeper the hangover, the more intense the craving for alcohol, which explains why alcoholism becomes worse with time.

Alcohol and the Brain

The brain, next to the liver, is most vulnerable to the damaging effects of alcoholism because its energy needs are greater than those of any other organ in the body. In advanced stages of alcoholism, the brain doesn't get the glucose and oxygen needed for the production of energy. The alcoholic liver is not able to supply the brain with these raw materials, and blockages in the small blood vessels prevent them from delivering energy-generating oxygen and glucose to the brain. These blockages occur because when the liver is no longer able to process acidic wastes, they accumulate in the blood and cause the red blood cells to stick together. Acidic waste in the blood also attracts bacteria that feed on it. The result is clumps of agglutinous material that clog the blood vessels throughout the body so that there is very little space in the blood for glucose, oxygen, and other nutrients. Without these raw materials to produce cellular energy and for the repair and regeneration of the cells, brain function breaks down and the neurons drown in their own metabolic waste.

There may be another factor in the brain of the alcoholic that prevents it from generating energy. The brains of hamsters, put on a diet of alcohol for experimental purposes, couldn't use glucose as a fuel, according to the scientist Mary Kay Roach, a coworker of chemist Roger Williams, who conducted the experiment. This indicates that it isn't just a lack of glucose, but also an inability to burn it that prevents the alcoholic brain from meeting its energy needs. However, there is a compound besides glucose that the brain can use for fuel, and that is L-glutamine, which, after it crosses the blood-brain barrier, is converted into glutamic acid. I suspect that the brain can use glutamic acid to manufacture energy because it reduces excess ammonia, a toxic compound (from the breakdown of amino acids) which probably destroys glucose before it has a chance to enter the brain cells and be oxidized. In *Nutrition Against Disease*, Roger Williams writes about several alcoholic individuals in which L-glutamine eliminated the craving for alcohol.[2]

The healing effects of both niacin and L-glutamine, obtained by the removal of toxic waste and alien chemicals, serve as a reminder that acidic wastes are the fundamental cause of alcoholism. But the addiction for alcohol manifests itself only if there is an adrenal weakness that causes wild swings in blood sugar and/or an enzyme deficiency that prevents the liver from breaking down the toxic by-products of alcohol. In many cases, however, these weaknesses cause alcohol addiction only when the diet is not compatible with the metabolism. An unhealthy diet triggers the actions of adrenal hormones that disrupt the concentration and normal distribution of sugar—one of the most important factors in metabolic function. The first step, then, in a program designed to overcome alcoholism is a change in diet.

Cirrhosis

Not only does putting the body on emergency alert (adrenal overstimulation) create anxiety and tension that drives some people to alcoholism, it also starts a cycle of reactions that ultimately destroy the liver. The liver, responding to the alert from the adrenals to raise blood sugar levels, takes an excessive amount of glucose out of storage and releases it into the bloodstream. Because there is really no need for this sudden rise in blood sugar, the insulin hormone, released from the islet of Langerhans in the pancreas, drastically lowers blood sugar levels, causing hypoglycemia (low blood sugar). Low blood sugar means sluggish energy production, which interferes with liver function. It can also cause fatigue and depression, symptoms that, like anxiety, increase the craving for alcohol. As long as the individual continues drinking and acid levels in the body remain high, the adrenals will direct the liver to raise blood sugar excessively and insulin will respond by reducing it precipitously.

Eventually the liver can't comply with the adrenal hormones' "request" for more glucose because it no longer has any. (The liver stores glucose in the form of glycogen.) One reason for this is that the drinker, preferring alcohol to food, doesn't supply the liver with the carbohydrates, protein, and fat it needs to make glucose. Another is the presence of fat, which should pass out of the liver into general circulation but can't because of alcohol's destruction of the B vitamin choline. (The absence of choline prevents fat from being converted by the liver into phospholipids which would enable it to pass through phospholipid molecules in the cellular membrane.) So fat molecules, remaining in the liver and needing a place to park themselves, fill up the spaces in the liver that are designed to store glucose. Fatty deposits also replace liver cells that have been destroyed by the alcoholic by-product, acid aldehyde. As if that weren't enough, metabolic wastes and acid aldehyde inflame the liver by destroying oxygen. Inflamed tissue develops scars, just like a wound or incision does. But scar tissue on the surface of the skin is harmless, whereas scar tissue in the liver destroys its ability to function by impeding circulation. This turns the liver tissue into hard fibers, a sign that the liver has developed cirrhosis, a disease that, without early nutritional intervention, is fatal.

SUGGESTIONS FOR ALCOHOLISM AND CIRRHOSIS

➤ Thyroid supplements. Normalizing energy levels improves the liver's ability to detoxify and rebuild its tissues.
➤ Vitamin E. Take 800 to 1,000 units daily to assist the thyroid supplements in improving thyroid function.
➤ Appropriate changes in diet.
➤ Far infrared heating pad or magnetic mattress pad and pillow to reduce acidic waste in the body; also magnetic pads placed directly on the liver. (See Resources.)

When symptoms have lessened, the following nutritional supplements can be gradually added:

➤ Magnesium—400 to 800 milligrams to help neutralize acids.
➤ Choline—250 milligrams four times daily.
➤ B complex capsule—three times daily.

> Vitamin C—1,000 milligrams a day.
> L-glutamine—one to four grains a day. L-glutamine picks up excess ammonia and converts it into glutamine. It is also used by the brain for energy.
> Niacin—three to ten grams. Most alcoholics respond best to six grams.
> Acupuncture—as often as needed. A Korean woman with cirrhosis of the liver, given only six months to live, was treated by my acupuncturist, Dr. Yuet Soong. I met her at Dr. Soong's office ten years after her first treatment and she was still in good health. The treatments, which at first she had five times a week and later twice weekly, stopped the progression of the disease.

CHAPTER 15

PROSTATE ENLARGEMENT

Sometime in his late forties Tony began having difficulty urinating, and for the first time in his life had to get up at night to go to the bathroom: first once a night, then two times, until finally he was getting up five times. The doctor confirmed that he had an enlarged prostate. Because his prostate specific antigen (PSA) was zero, bacterial inflammation and cancer could be eliminated as possible causes of his prostate enlargement. This left excess prostate tissue, referred to as benign prostate hypertrophy (BPH). A combination of herbs that includes red clover, pygeum, saw palmetto, stinging nettles, and goldenseal is often the most effective treatment for BPH so Tony took two capsules of this herbal combination each day along with a zinc supplement, since more zinc is used by the prostate than by any other organ and men with prostate enlargements usually have a zinc deficiency. (There is eight times more zinc in the prostate than in any other organ.[1]) Tony also took vitamin B_6, which converts zinc into a form that can be absorbed by the prostate cells. Although nutritional supplements are less likely to shrink a prostate that is enlarged because of excessive tissue growth rather than inflammation, Tony's prostate shrank after he had been taking supplements for a few months. He now only had to get up twice a night to urinate. Tony's remaining problem was to find a way to get back to sleep after he got up at night. The solution turned out to be melatonin, a hormone secreted by the pineal gland in the brain that not only induces sleep but also helps maintain the health of the prostate by transporting zinc and facilitating its absorption.

Two stress hormones, dihydrotestosterone (DHT) and estrogen, are responsible for the abnormal growth of the prostate. It's only in middle and older age, however, that these two hormones become injurious to the health of the prostate. During puberty they perform an essential function, stimulating the growth of cells that bring the penis, testicles, and prostate and the secondary sexual characteristics to maturity. Once puberty is over and their usefulness declines, testosterone is no longer converted to DHT and estrogen levels drop. But then as men grow older and their testosterone diminishes, an enzyme in the prostate, 5 alpha reductase, converts the remaining testosterone into DHT, and estrogen levels increase.[2] These two hormones not only trigger the excessive growth of prostate tissue, but also diminish the sex drive and cause fewer and less viable sperm to be produced.[3]

Testosterone's influence extends far beyond the prostate. When the body is placed on emergency alert because lowered testosterone levels have enabled the adrenal hormones to become permanently elevated, imbalance in organ function becomes permanent. The muscles, nerves, heart, and lungs become chronically overactive, while the digestive, excretory, and regenerating systems slow up and so are unable to dispose of all the acidic waste from metabolic function and partially digested food. The increasing aggregation of wastes clog the blood vessels and poison the cells and the extracellular fluids, causing the organ systems to degenerate. The elevation of the stress-promoting estrogen is particularly lethal because it destroys oxygen, causes the blood to clot, lowers thyroid function, alters fats and oils, and increases histamine levels. The elevation of these stress hormones explains why so many men develop arthritis and low-grade infections, and lose vitality and sharpness of intellect after their prostate becomes enlarged.

Reasons for the Epidemic of Prostatitis

According to a paper published in *Grana Palynologica* in 1960 by Erik Ask-Upmark, M.D., of the University of Upsala in Sweden, an enlarged prostate was at that time considered a new pathological condition.[4] Curiously, the processing of flour, widespread by 1900, which removed from grains nutrients vital to the prostate such as zinc, magnesium, and vitamin E, didn't cause an epidemic of prostatitis and/or benign prostate hypertrophy in the early part of the twentieth century as it did coronary heart disease. This is an indication that enlargement of the prostate had a different cause. When enlarged prostate glands were first noted in 1960, insecticides such as DDT and chemical food additives had only been in widespread use for about ten years because the chemical industry didn't go into high gear until a few years after World War II had ended. By 1976, when 60 percent of the men over sixty in North America were found to have some prostate enlargement, insecticides and chemical food additives had been in use for about twenty-five years, enough time for these chemicals to have caused prostate disease in older men to have become commonplace.

Medical researchers suspect that an increase in the enzyme 5 alpha reductase, which converts testosterone to DHT, causing excess growth of prostate tissue, is caused by pesticides and industrial solvents. The problem with these manufactured chemicals is that they can't be broken down in the digestive tract, deactivated by the liver, or excreted by the kidneys or lungs, so they're either stored in the liver or go back into general circulation. Along with acidic waste from undigested junk food, they are deposited by the circulating blood in the tiniest capillaries, the ones that carry oxygen and nutrients to the organs. Some of this toxic waste seeps out of these capillaries into the extracellular fluid surrounding the prostate and inflames it. The rest of it clogs the capillaries, which prevents the prostate from getting sufficient nutrients and oxygen. This partial cutoff of nutrients and oxygen is especially harmful to the prostate gland because of its poor blood supply. (This could explain why alanine, glycine, and gluatmic supplements, three amino acids that have been found to be deficient in enlarged prostates, are effective in reducing prostate enlargement, as Doctors H. M. Feinblatt and J. C. Gant found in their crossover study of patients with enlarged prostates.[5]) This connection between manufactured chemicals and the deterioration of the prostate gland in the majority of men over sixty over the last forty years highlights the importance of avoiding food with chemical additives and of drinking only purified water.

The fact that estrogen and dihydrotestosterone (DHT) are responsible for the enlargement of the prostate gland makes those herbs that contain tiny but potent amounts of sex hormones, such as saw palmetto, pygeum, and pollen seed, effective in treating BPH. The hormones in these herbs either prevent the conversion of testosterone to DHT or prevent DHT and estrogen from binding to the receptors (openings) of the prostate cells. Zinc, if taken with vitamin B_6, also prevents the enzyme 5 alpha reductase from converting testosterone to DHT. The resulting shrinkage of the prostate helps normalize urine flow and heal possible kidney damage caused by the pressure of the prostate gland.

SUGGESTIONS FOR PROSTATE ENLARGEMENT

➤ Thyroid—to speed up the disposal of acidic wastes.
➤ Pregnenolone—two pinches of this white powder daily (see Resources).
➤ One raw carrot daily—to reduce inflammation.
➤ Zinc arginate—forty-five to sixty milligrams daily.
➤ Vitamin B_6—sixty milligrams. Must be taken with zinc to facilitate its absorption.
➤ Saw palmetto—320 milligrams daily.
➤ Red clover extract—fifty milligrams daily.
➤ Stinging nettle—600 milligrams daily.
➤ Pygeum—200 milligrams daily.
➤ Pollen seed extract—300 to 500 milligrams daily.
➤ Vitamin E—800 to 1,600 units daily. Vitamin E is a prostate cancer preventive, according to a controlled study done in Finland which was coauthored by Dr. Demetrius Albanes of the National Cancer Institute.[6]
➤ Caprylic acid—400 to 1,000 milligrams daily, in buffered form. Effective for prostate infections caused by yeast cells.

CHAPTER 16

FEMALE REPRODUCTIVE DISORDERS

There is an ongoing struggle in the body between the stress-promoting hormones that endanger life and the life-supporting hormones that enhance it. A hormone is life-supporting as long as it exists in normal quantities; but when it becomes elevated it causes stress. It does so by suppressing the life-promoting hormones that have a moderating influence, and then triggering the overproduction of chemicals.

Nowhere is this battle between life-promoting and stress-promoting hormones more evident than in the female reproductive system. The antagonists are estrogen and progesterone, the two principal regulating hormones. Both hormones are generated by the cuplike follicle in which egg cells are encapsulated in the ovaries, but they function in opposite ways. Estrogen engineers the release of the egg into the fallopian tube (ovulation), triggers the growth of tissues in the uterus for the support of the embryo, and initiates the menstrual cycle. Progesterone, referred to as the pregnancy hormone, maintains the nutritional needs of the embryo and the uterine tissues to which it is attached. When these two hormones are in balance, reproductive function is normal, but estrogen levels have a tendency to rise, and when they do they lower progesterone levels.

When estrogen and progesterone levels are normal, they act as a brake on each other to ensure balanced function. If progesterone, in an effort to ensure adequate nourishment of the fetus, raises blood sugar too high, estrogen triggers the production of additional insulin to take the excess glucose out of circulation. (The excess glucose is converted to fat and stored in the adipose tissues.) Or if progesterone causes the metabolism of too much fatty acid, estrogen reduces the level of fatty acid. Estrogen also lowers exorbitant accretions of abdominal fat in the expectant mother (thus lessening the risk of heart disease). On the other hand, when estrogen spurs an overgrowth of tissue and blood in the reproductive organs, progesterone lowers it.

While hormone replacement therapy and the growth hormone stimulants in meat are certainly factors in estrogen excess, the greatest single cause is elevated blood acid levels. Hyperacidity can be caused by several different factors. Strenuous exercise is one. When I went on a walking tour in Italy, I averaged twelve miles a day, ten more miles than I usually walk each day. After my return to New York, I discovered a hard, ridgelike area in my breast. While I was initially alarmed, after some reflection I realized what had happened. By walking twelve hours straight every day, my muscles eventually used up all the available oxygen for energy and had to produce energy anaerobically (without oxygen). The waste by-product of anaerobic respiration is lactic acid. The elevated lactic acid levels in my blood raised estrogen levels, and the estrogen triggered the growth of fibrous tissue. Going back to walking about two miles a day after my return to New York, I wasn't surprised that in one week the fibroid mass in my breast had disappeared.

For most of human existence, fear and excitement in the face of physical danger was the principal cause of heightened blood acid levels. Hyperacidity serves as an alarm signal, alerting the adrenals to a possible threat to survival. The adrenals respond by stimulating the production of additional estrogen, as well as adrenaline and cortisone. Estrogen, when in excess, diverts oxygen away from the digestive and excretory organs so that it flows to the muscles and general circulatory system, thereby empowering the body to act quickly. Because fear and anxiety go away when danger passes, these emotions cause only temporary increases in blood acidity, so adrenal secretions and estrogen are elevated for only a short time and the organ systems are not injured.

In the present era, however, danger comes in a different form: processed foods, which, only partially digested, turn into acidic waste. When the individual's diet is consistently poor, hyperacidity in the blood becomes chronic, and, in response, estrogen levels become permanently elevated. The organs, including the uterus, cervix, ovaries, or breasts, suffer the consequences. Chronically subjected to inadequate levels of oxygen by excess estrogen, they become inflamed and degenerate.

Excess Estrogen and Cancer

When conception occurs, the newly fertilized egg, the size of a speck of dust, must be attached almost instantly to the uterine wall before it falls out of the uterus through the cervix. Once attached, the nutritional needs of the embryo must be met almost as fast. Trophoblastic cells in the embryo, triggered into action by estrogen, serve that purpose. Multiplying at a tremendously fast rate, they hook the embryo into the wall of the uterus, create half the placenta (the uterus creates the other half), and then the umbilical cord, which attaches the embryo to the placenta, the source of its food supply. Trophoblastic cells are able to grow wildly in the uterus because they can generate energy by fermentation, that is, without oxygen. Estrogen makes this possible by lowering oxygen levels in the uterus. When the embryo has been in the uterus for seven or eight weeks, the work of the trophoblastic cells comes to an end and they migrate to the embryo's ovaries or testicles, where they are converted by enzymes into germ cells (egg or sperm cells).

This is not necessarily the end of the trophoblastic cells, however. The germ cells can be converted back into trophoblastic cells any time estrogen levels become excessive. What is frightening about this is that trophoblastic cells multiply as fast as cancer cells. In fact, according to biochemist Dr. Ernst F. Krebs Jr., who studied 17,000 research experiments on the subject, trophopblastic cells are identical in all respects to cancer cells.[1] Two obvious similarities are the way in which the fingerlike projections of trophoblastic cells invade the uterine wall in order to implant the fetus, and the fact that trophopoblastic cells, like cancer cells, generate energy without oxygen.

When estrogen is elevated, like all other chemicals in the body that are in excess, it no longer reacts according to the body's needs. It can create an oxygen-poor environment anywhere in the body and at any time. If oxygen deprivation is severe enough, it causes cancer, because without oxygen, normal cells cannot generate energy. In order to survive, they convert into trophoblastic or cancer cells so they can generate energy anaerobically (without oxygen). If estrogen levels in the blood aren't reduced (mainly by reducing dietary acidic waste), the number of cancerlike cells keeps growing and a malignant tumor in the breast, uterus, cervix, or ovaries forms.

Many studies confirm the role of estrogen in causing cancer. Dr. Ross Trattler, in *Better Health Through Natural Healing*, writes about a study linking estrogen therapy to a five- to twelvefold increase in uterus and breast cancer. Another study found that estrogen therapy without progestin causes a fourteen-fold increase in endometrial cancer.[2] Especially significant because it tracked 46,355 women is a recent study published in the *Journal of the American Medical Association*, January 26, 2000. The study found that those who took hormone replacement therapy (HRT) for five years were 40 percent more likely to develop breast cancer than women who were not on HRT.

Doctors prescribe HRT not only to ease menopausal symptoms but also to prevent osteoporosis in menopausal and postmenopausal women. This is ironic since any organ deprived of oxygen absorbs calcium, which hardens it. While this may work to the advantage of the bones, when estrogen-induced oxygen removal causes degeneration in soft tissue and then triggers its retention of calcium, the result is a hardening or degeneration of the tissue. Thus the logical consequences of long-time use of HRT are stronger bones and degeneration of the soft tissue organs.

Health Problems Associated with Estrogen Imbalance

Infertility and Heavy Periods

When estrogen lowers energy levels by destroying oxygen, the pituitary can't produce the follicle-stimulating hormone and as a result, follicles are not produced. When not encased in a follicle, egg cells cannot be released. Not only does that make pregnancy impossible, when ovulation fails to occur there is a buildup of the uterine lining that causes heavier and more frequent periods.

Endometriosis

The lowering of oxygen levels by excess estrogen in the uterus increases acidity. The sharp acid crystals irritate and inflame the lining of the uterus. If oxygen deprivation is sustained, it results in endometriosis, inflammation of the uterine lining. When inflammation is chronic, the lining disintegrates, and the fragments are carried by fluids to the ovaries, where they cause adhesions and cysts to form. Intercourse during menstruation can exacerbate endometriosis because it pushes mucus and blood up the uterus and fallopian tubes into the ovaries.

Heavy Periods and Menstrual Cramps

Estrogen causes an increase in the amount of blood in the uterus for the purpose of menstruation, so when estrogen builds up, it causes excessive menstrual bleeding. Heavy bleeding is often accompanied by menstrual cramps because the overflow of blood in the uterine blood vessels dilates the vessel walls, causing them to go into a spasm.

Premenstrual Syndrome

Premenstrual syndrome (PMS) is related to excessive estrogen. The bloating, irritability, depression, migraine, acne, and so forth that occur anywhere from four to ten days before menses suggests that when estrogen is excessive, it tries to trigger the onset of menstruation before it is due.

SUGGESTIONS FOR PMS AND ENDOMETRIOSIS

➤ Fatty acid blood profile. This profile indicates possible deficiencies in GLA, ALA, DHA, and AA. Primrose oil, which contains GLA fatty acid, has relieved PMS symptoms. Michael

Schmidt in *Smart Fats* states that British studies show that GLA relieves menstrual tension in 90 to 95 percent of the cases. (See Resources.)

➤ Avoid milk. Milk is linked to a variety of reproductive disorders because the mucus it generates blocks the fallopian tubes.

➤ Thyroid supplements. A slightly above normal thyroid function (as indicated by a temperature slightly higher than 98.6 degrees) helps PMS and endometriosis by getting rid of acidic wastes.

➤ Avoid caffeine in coffee, tea, chocolate, and cola soft drinks.

➤ Black cohosh, valerian, and wild yam roots contain hormones that normalize estrogen levels.

Miscarriages

High estrogen levels also trigger miscarriages by causing excessive bleeding in the uterus during pregnancy. (Estrogen has also been implicated in dilating the walls of the veins carrying blood back to the heart, thus delaying the return of the blood to the heart and slowing the heartbeat.)

Excessive Clotting

The excessive clotting of menstrual blood caused by estrogen has its antecedent in estrogen's blood clotting function during childbirth to prevent excessive blood loss.

Fibroid Uterine Tumors and Cystic Breasts

When estrogen levels are normal, after the menstrual period has ended, estrogen causes the uterine wall to rebuild its tissue in preparation for the possibility that the next egg released in the fallopian tube will be fertilized. Excess estrogen, however, overstimulates the growth of tissue in the uterus, making such a thick uterine lining that it fails to disintegrate when the egg is not fertilized. As one layer of tissue is laid over another, the hard, fibrous tissue thickens and forms a tumor. It seems probable, since excess estrogen causes the growth of excessive tissue in the uterus, that hormone replacement therapy has increased the number of women with uterine fibroid tumors. Of the six women I know who are on HRT, four have developed fibroid uterine tumors. Excessive estrogen also spurs the growth of breast tissue when it is not needed for lactating purposes, causing cysts to develop in the breasts.

Immune System Depression

Estrogen, which lowers the expectant mother's immune system during pregnancy to prevent it from rejecting the fetus, when excessive, lowers immune function at other times.

Low Blood Sugar

Another of estrogen's functions during pregnancy is to lower excessive blood sugar. When levels of estrogen become elevated, however, it depresses blood sugar even when blood sugar levels are normal. If this happens during pregnancy, the fetus is deprived of the glucose necessary for normal development. Estrogen-induced low blood sugar may also be one reason why far more women than men suffer from depression and insomnia.

The most important factor in normalizing estrogen levels is to improve liver function since it disposes of excess estrogen. This can be done, first, by working out a diet that produces the least amount of acidic toxic waste to reduce the liver's workload. The ability of the liver to get rid of estrogen, however, is also dependent upon protein;[3] so those nutrients that metabolize protein should be taken: the amino acid methionine, vitamins B_1, B_2, E, and C. Vitamin A and thyroid extract also aid in protein metabolism, and in addition are the raw materials that convert cholesterol molecules into progesterone. An increase in progesterone lowers estrogen levels. Vitamin E counteracts estrogen's destruction of oxygen molecules because of its oxygenating effects and also lowers estrogen levels by reducing raised adrenal secretions.

Another way to balance estrogen and progesterone levels is to stimulate the function of the pineal gland. The pineal, located in the brain, delays puberty by lowering estrogen levels. It also wakes us up in the morning by absorbing sunlight, and brings on sleep when darkness triggers its secretion of melatonin. By strengthening this function, the pineal gland's ability to reduce estrogen becomes permanent. This can be done by exposing the eyes to sunlight during the day and, when overcast, sitting in front of a high-intensity light (see Resources). To increase exposure to darkness during sleep, wear an eye mask, preferably padded, to keep out as much light as possible.

Fertility and Enhanced Sex Drive

Timothy and Maureen badly wanted children, but the chances of Maureen becoming pregnant were dim. Tim and Maureen married when both were thirty-five. It is well known that from the age of thirty on, there is a slight drop each year in fertility. By age thirty-five, however, the chances of becoming pregnant plummet. Not only might Maureen's age make it hard for her to become pregnant, a more serious liability was the fact that she ovulated only twice a year, so there were only two short periods during the year when she could get pregnant. These two difficulties were compounded by the fact that neither Maureen nor Timothy had much of a sex drive.

Testosterone, although the principal male hormone, is also present in females and is responsible for the sex drive in both sexes. Supplements or injections of pure testosterone invariably boost the libido of men (and have a general revitalizing effect) and presumably would do the same for women. Testosterone levels, however, can also be boosted by taking a precurser hormone called pregnenolone that is converted in the cells into testosterone. Maureen and Tim took a natural form of pregnenolone, extracted from the yam. They also tried to stimulate the synthesis of pregnenolone in their own bodies by taking vitamins E and A, thyroid extract, and copper, and sitting in front of a high-intensity light for one-half hour each day. Both experienced an increase in their libido. Based on the experiences of those who have consulted with me, the likelihood is that vitamin E improved Tim's sex drive, while pregnenolone increased Maureen's.

Four months after they went on this regimen, Maureen became pregnant. To avoid miscarriage and to make sure that her blood nutrient levels were maintained, she took a natural form of progesterone, an oil which she used topically (see Resources). (The previously mentioned study of 46,355 women found that women who took a combination of estrogen and progestin had an 8 percent higher rate of breast cancer than those who took estrogen alone. Progestin made in the lab, however, is chemically different from the progesterone extracted from yams that Maureen took.) Nine months and two weeks after she became pregnant, Maureen gave birth to a beautiful, healthy, and intelligent baby girl.

Nutritional Requirements Before Conception, During Pregnancy, and After Birth

Three to six months before conception women should begin following a diet compatible with their individual digestive system in order to keep toxic acidic waste products to a minimum (see Chapters 1 and 2). The next step is to eat an abundance of those foods that are needed to satisfy the nutritional requirements of the fetus. Of primary importance is extra sugar because higher than average blood sugar levels are necessary for the production of sufficient energy to sustain the growth of the fetus. Vitamins E and A as well as magnesium help maintain normal blood sugar, as does the appestat mechanism—by causing the expectant mother to crave sweets.

Since the quality of the sugar consumed is as important as the quantity, the craving for sweets should be satisfied by eating fruit. Not only is the fructose in fruit healthier than refined white sugar, all fruits are rich in potassium. Potassium in the blood acts like insulin, facilitating the entry of sugar molecules into cells for their use in making energy. Potassium also removes sugar from the blood without causing blood sugar levels to drop precipitously the way elevated insulin does. High insulin (caused by the overconsumption of white sugar and refined carbohydrates) also lowers blood levels of calcium and phosphorus, which are needed to build the bones of the developing fetus. The old adage, "a tooth lost for every child," acknowledges the draining of calcium reserves from the maternal blood supply. A study done in Norway confirms that in the later months of pregnancy blood calcium levels become deficient.[4] A highly mineralized water helps make up for the loss of alkaline minerals during pregnancy and also maintains the alkaline pH of the blood.

Another important dietary measure during pregnancy is an increase in fats. The expectant mother's body relies increasingly on fat for its energy needs since the fetus uses up her supply of blood sugar and also because fatty acids in the maternal blood are used in the generation of the fetus's cellular membranes. What kind of fats should the gestating woman eat?

The commonly held belief that most people are deficient in omega-3 fish oil is being shattered by the latest fatty acid research, which, according to Dr. Patricia Kane, a researcher at the Body-Bio Corporation, shows that there is a growing deficiency of omega-6 fats in many people due to the avoidance of meat fat, butter, and eggs in an effort to lower cholesterol. While omega-6 polyunsaturated oils such as corn, cottonseed, sesame, sunflower, and canola should not be consumed during pregnancy because they lower blood sugar, organic meat fat, organic raw egg yolk, and butter are good for building healthy fetuses. The supersaturated coconut oil is also good for the fetus because it normalizes energy production and is itself a good source of energy. Green leafy vegetables are important as a source of omega-3 oil.

Although saltwater fish is the best source of the docosahexaenoic acid (DHA), an omega-3 fatty acid, the Food and Drug Administration warns that women who are pregnant or planning to become pregnant should avoid shark, swordfish, king mackerel, and tilefish because they contain enough mercury to harm the developing fetus's brain. Salmon, mackerel, sardines, and anchovies are not on this list and are even better sources of DHA oil.

High fat consumption during pregnancy, while vital to the fetus, has one drawback: it destroys vitamin B_6. This is one of many reasons it is necessary to consume plenty of quality protein with its whole range of B vitamins. Besides the use of protein as a building block of the body, its supply of B_6 replaces what is destroyed by high fat levels. Choline, another B vitamin, which is plentiful in meat, enhances the fetus's memory by altering the hippocampus, the memory center of the brain, according to researchers at the University of North Carolina at Chapel Hill.[5]

The B vitamins also play a key role in normalizing excessive hormonal levels. For example, pantothenic acid destroys excess insulin, and all the B vitamins are involved in keeping estrogen levels from becoming elevated. The normalization of estrogen and insulin may prevent cancer after birth. If high levels of insulin and estrogen in the maternal blood are absorbed into the fetal blood system, "they may alter mammary tissue in such a way that it responds to estrogen during puberty by becoming malignant."[6] Further, a study conducted by Pamela J. Goodwin, M.D., found that women with breast cancer and high insulin levels were eight times more likely to die of breast cancer than those with breast cancer who had low insulin levels.[7] One way of preventing breast cancer and at the same time building the intelligence and immune system of your baby is to breast-feed for two years or longer. According to a Yale University study of women in rural China, this reduces the chance of developing breast cancer by 50 percent.[8]

Besides the right diet, nutritional supplements are needed in most cases to make up for any deficiency in the diet. A prenatal vitamin, although too low in all the B vitamins except folic acid, is a good idea, but choose one that contains no iron. For many reasons iron should be avoided. The liver has no way of excreting excess iron and it destroys vitamin E, the single most crucial vitamin for conception. Additional vitamin E should be taken since the amount of E in prenatal supplements is minuscule. Also, a woman whose thyroid tests underactive should take thyroid supplements. It's also a good idea to have blood levels of progesterone tested and if they are too low to take progesterone supplements (see Resources). Avoid caffeine during pregnancy. One to three cups of coffee a day increases the risk of miscarriages by 30 percent, according to a study conducted jointly by Sweden and the United States of 562 women who had miscarriages after six to twelve weeks of pregnancy.[9]

SUGGESTIONS FOR FEMALE REPRODUCTIVE HEALTH

As individual needs vary, how much you should take of any supplement is largely determined by your reactions to it. These suggestions are for women who are not pregnant.

➤ Progesterone—five to fifteen drops a day depending on need when symptoms or test results indicate estrogen is elevated and/or progesterone levels depressed.

➤ Vitamin E—400 to 1,200 units daily.

➤ Vitamin A—10,000 to 25,000 units daily.

➤ Vitamin D—400 to 1,000 units daily.

➤ Vitamin B_6—250 to 500 milligrams daily.

➤ Magnesium—400 to 1,200 milligrams daily.

➤ Zinc—fifty milligrams daily.

➤ Vitamin C—500 milligrams five times a week.

➤ Calcium lactate—400 to 800 milligrams daily.

CONCLUSION

Scientists have led us to believe that good health and longevity are largely a matter of luck, that we are hostages to the genes handed down to us by our parents and also to genetic recombination, the crossover of genes between chromosomes. The discovery of genes that predispose people to such serious illnesses as breast cancer, heart disease, and Type I diabetes would appear to confirm this belief. What is omitted from this cause-and-effect equation is the fact that genes that increase susceptibility to disease (as opposed to genetic abnormalities that prevent the production of a vital enzyme or an extra chromosome that stimulates the production of too many metabolites) need a trigger before they can do any harm. That trigger is acidic waste.

Describing health as the balance between two opposites—the way every healing system except the modern Western medical establishment has defined it—we would have to say that a state of health exists in anyone whose acid and alkaline balance is normal. Yet the relationship between the latter and acidic waste levels in the body is not easy to establish. First, acid-forming foods such as grain don't acidify the alkaline pH of the blood. Nor necessarily does elevated acidic waste that causes hardening of the arteries, cancer, and other degenerative disease. Acid waste triggers the imbalance of acid and alkaline in a more circuitous way: by stimulating the overproduction of the stress-related hormones. This upsets the equilibrium between the two halves of the autonomic nervous system, which controls the speed at which organs function—the predominantly acidic sympathetic and the predominantly alkaline parasympathetic. The result is that some organ systems function at too rapid a rate, while others become sluggish.

Balancing organ function then depends upon eating foods that generate as little acidic waste as possible. To do so, the first priority is to avoid misconceptions as to what constitutes a healthy diet. Planning a diet around a "balanced" meal, that is, protein, carbohydrates, and fat, the gospel of the medical profession until the 1960s, is fine in principle. In practice it was a failure. It not only encouraged belief in a standardized diet, but also a belief that refining flour and sugar and overcooking did not reduce the nutrient values of food. In the 1970s, the medical profession forgot about the importance of the balanced meal and embraced a low-cholesterol diet instead. This diet has increased the incidence of gallstones and strokes.

The diet of the hunter-forager, a way of life now almost extinct, was the ideal. Eating animals and plants untouched by humans, much of it raw or, in the case of meat and fish, barely singed by the cooking fire, provided enough enzymes to convert the exact amount of raw materials needed to repair and rebuild the body. Plentiful food-digesting enzymes also meant that there was very little acidic waste left over after digestion had taken place. Such food guaranteed a slim and healthy body.

But emulating the diet of the hunter to the extent that it is possible is only part of the answer. The other part is finding foods that your body can handle. Testing yourself for allergies and your metabolic type is a good start, but awareness of how your body reacts to the foods you eat is even more important. The key to good health is to keep track of the foods you ate before you began to feel unwell and avoid them in the future. Only then can you be sure that your body is not producing too much acidic waste, the cause of all degenerative disease.

RESOURCES

Air cleaner. Alpine Industries, Robert T. Leary Jr., 631-368-5410.

Alkaline water. Sang Whang, 888-261-0870.

Castor oil therapy. Edgar Cayce products, 800-862-2923; The Heritage, Dept. C, PO Box 444, Virginia Beach, VA 23458-0444.

Celastyn (cetyl myristate). For arthritis and high blood pressure. STAT, Apartado Postal No. 2392, Tijuana, B.C.N., 22000, Mexico; 011-5266-801-103.

ChitoPlex. For obesity. The gel in this resin absorbs fat. Gero Vita, 800-232-3344.

Cynoplus. For treatment of low thyroid. 011-5266-801-103.

Far infrared. Far infrared and magnetic sleeping system and body straps. Nikken, Penny Olsen, 845-986-8600. Far infrared sleeping system. New Nissin Company, 213-383-1204 3850; Wilshire Blvd., Suite 333, Los Angeles, CA 90010.

Fatty acid blood profile. Dr. Patricia Kane, 856-8258-338.

Gelatin (made from beef). For digestion problems and diabetes. Bernard Jensen, 800-755-4027.

Intense light. For treatement of insomnia. Living Sunshine, 631-368-5410.

Ketogenic diet. For treatment of epilepsy. 800-FOR-KETO.

Lotus Health Food Store. Nutritional supplements. Mail order: 212-423-0345; Fax: 212-828-1092. Narain Chandra, the owner, has a background in biology and chemistry and is knowledgeable about the nutritional supplements he sells.

Magnetic pads. Dr. William Philpott, Institute for Bio-Eco Medicine, Oklahoma City, OK 73154; 405-390-3009.

Mattresses and box springs. Natural latex/organic cotton. Samina, 1-516-869-6004; Sleeptek, 1-613-727-5337.

Oils. Including grape seed oil mayonnaise. Omega Nutrition, 800-661-3529.

Ox bile. 011-5266-801-103.

Pregnenolone (natural). Dr. Ray Peat, Kenogen, PO Box 5764, Eugene, OR 97405; 541-345-9855.

Progesterone (natural). See Pregnenolone for contact information.

NOTES

Introduction

1. Heather Pringle. *The Mummy Congress: Science Obsession and the Everlasting Dead*. New York: Hyperion, 2001.

Chapter 1

1. Ray Peat. *Generative Energy*. Eugene, OR: self-published, 1994.
2. Keichi Morishita. *The Hidden Truth of Cancer*. Oroville, GOMF, 1976.
3. Sang Whang. *Reverse Aging*. Miami, FL: JSP Publishing, 1990.
4. Malachy McCourt. *A Monk Swimming: A Memoir*. New York: Hyperion, 1998.

Chapter 2

1. R. A. Wiley. *Bio Balance*. Hurricane, UT: Essential Science Publishing, 1998.
2. Dr. Weston Price. "Parental Malnutrition and Physical Degeneration," *Price-Pottenger Nutrition Foundation Journal*, 2000.
3. Dr. Gary Paul Nabhan. "Interview," *Omni*, July 1994.

4. *New York Times*, June 21, 1997.

5. Ray Peat. *Nutrition for Women*, fifth edition. Eugene, Oregon: self-published, 1993.

6. Roger Williams, M.D. *Nutrition Against Disease*. New York: Bantam Books, 1978.

7. Max Gerson, M.D. *A Cancer Therapy*. Bonita, CA: Gerson Institute, 1999.

8. Arthur F. Coca, M.D. *The Pulse Test*. New York: St. Martin's Press, 1994.

9. *New Life*, March–April 2000.

10. Thomas Cowan. "Raw Milk," *Price Pottenger Nutrition Foundation Journal* 21, No. 2.

11. *New York Times*, May 12, 2000.

12. Sally Fallon. "PPNF at World Med 1996," *Price-Pottenger Nutrition Foundation Journal*, Summer 1996.

13. Udo Erasmus. *Fats That Heal, Fats That Kill*. Burnaby, Canada: Alive Books, 1993.

14. *New York Times*, November 17, 1991.

15. Karjalainen, J. A. "A Bovine Albumin Peptide as a Possible Trigger of Insulin-Dependent Diabetes Mellitus," *New England Journal of Medicine*, May 2000.

16. R. W. Apple Jr. "An Iowa Heirloom: Pork with Real Flavor," *New York Times*, March, 29, 2000.

17. R. W. Apple Jr. "A Springtime Rite Worth the Year's Wait," *New York Times*, April 19, 2000.

18. Max Gerson, M.D. *A Cancer Therapy*. Bonita, CA: Gerson Institute, 1999.

19. Sang Whang. *Reverse Aging*. Miami, FL: JSP Publishing, 1990.

Chapter 3

1. Frances M. Pottenger Jr. "Hydrophilic Colloidal Diet," *Price-Pottenger Nutrition Foundation Journal* 21, No. 1.

2. Bernard Jensen. *Foods That Heal*. Wayne, NJ: Avery Publishing Group, 1993.

4. The staff of *Prevention* magazine. *The Encyclopedia of Common Diseases*. Emmaus, PA: Rodale Press, 1976.

5. Jean Carper. *Food—Your Miracle Medicine*. New York: HarperCollins, 1993.

6. Garnett Cheney. "Anti-Peptic Ulcer Dietary Factor," *Journal of the Amercian Dietetic Association*, 1950.

7. The staff of *Prevention* magazine. *The Encyclopedia of Common Diseases*. Emmaus, PA: Rodale Press, 1976.

8. Jon A. Kangas, Ph.D., K. Michael Schmidt, Ph.D., and George F. Solomon, M.D. "The Effects of Vitamin E on Rats with Ulcers," *American Journal of Clinical Nutrition*, September 1972.

9. T. L. Harris. *Society for Experimental Biology and Medicine*, March 1947.

10. Jean Carper. *Food—Your Miracle Medicine*. New York: HarperCollins, 1993.

11. Lynn Payer. *Medicine and Culture*. New York: Henry Holt and Company, 1988.

12. The staff of *Prevention* magazine. *The Encyclopedia of Common Diseases*. Emmaus, PA: Rodale Press, 1976.

13. The staff of *Prevention* magazine. *The Encyclopedia of Common Diseases*. Emmaus, PA: Rodale Press, 1976.

14. Michael Crichton, M.D. *Five Patients*. New York: Ballantine Books, 1989.

15. Ronald L. Hoffman. *Newlife*, January/February 1997.

16. Ronald L. Hoffman. *Newlife*, January/February 1997.

17. Jean Carper. *Food—Your Miracle Medicine*. New York: HarperCollins, 1993.

Chapter 4

1. Edward Howell, M.D. *Enzyme Nutrition*. Wayne, NJ: Avery Publishing Group, 1985.

2. Eddy Kohman, et al. *Nutrition*, April 1977.

3. "The review of an article 'Diabetes Danger in a Taste of Chinese,'" *The London Times*, April 8, 1992.

Chapter 5

1. Stephen E. Langer, M.D., and James F. Scheer. *Solved: The Riddle of Illness*. New Canaan, CT: Keats Publishing, 1995.
2. Stephen E. Langer, M.D., and James F. Scheer. *Solved: The Riddle of Illness*. New Canaan, CT: Keats Publishing, 1995.
3. Ray Peat, Ph.D. *Progesterone in Orthomolecular Medicine*. Eugene, OR: self-published, 1993.

Chapter 6

1. Mark Herzberg and Maurice Meyer. Presentation at a meeting of the American Association for the Advancement of Science in Philadelphia, reported in the *New York Times*, February 17, 1998.
2. Publisher's foreword, in *Health Research*. Mokelumne Hill, California, 1990.
3. *New England Journal of Medicine*, April 1999.
4. *Price-Pottenger Nutrition Foundation Journal*, 20, No. 2, 1976.
5. Lawrence K. Altman. "Study Finds Heart Regenerates Cells," *New York Times*, June 7, 2001.
6. Kilmer McCully, *The Homocysteine Revolution*. New Canaan, CT: Keats Publishing, 1997.
7. Karen Springen, Mary Hager, and Anne Underwood. "Attackers," *Newsweek*, August 11, 1997.
8. Peggy van der Hoogen, *National Institute of Public Health*, January 2000.

Chapter 7

1. Jane E. Brody. "Personal Health," *New York Times*, March 5, 1999.
2. Karen Wright, "Postmortem with Strings," *Discover*, June 2000.
3. M. Iguchi. "Clinical Effects of Prophylactic Dietary Treatment on Renal Stones," *Journal of Urology*, 1990.

Chapter 8

1. Sandra Blakeslee. "New Way of Looking at Diseases of the Brain," *New York Times*, November 10, 1999.
2. Dana Mackenzie. "The Shape of Madness," *Discover*, January 2000.
3. The staff of *Prevention* magazine. *The Encyclopedia of Common Diseases*. Emmaus, PA: Rodale Press, 1976.
4. The staff of *Prevention* magazine. *The Encyclopedia of Common Diseases*. Emmaus, PA: Rodale Press, 1976.
5. Study cited by Daniel Goleman. "Forget Money; Nothing Can Buy Happiness, Some Researchers Say," *New York Times*, July 16, 1996.
6. Curt Rist. "The Pain is in the Brain," *Discover*, March 2000.
7. Atkinson, Miles. *Archives of Otolaryngology* 175 (1962): 220. Cited in *The Encyclopedia of Common Diseases*.
8. "A Gene Detective on the Trail of Alzheimer's," *New York Times*, December 5, 2000.
9. *The New England Journal of Medicine*, April 1999. Cited in Jane E. Brody. "Vitamin E May Slow Age Damage," *New York Times*, May 28, 1996.
10. Hal Huggins, D.D.S. *It's All in Your Head: The Link Between Mercury Amalgams and Illness*. Wayne, NJ: Avery Publications, 1993.
11. Conversation with Ray Peat, June 5, 2001.

Chapter 9

1. *New York Times Magazine*, March 28, 1993.
2. Harry N. Holmen. *Southern Medicine and Surgery*, CX111, 1951.
3. *American Journal of Respiratory Molecular Biology*, cited in staff of *Prevention* magazine, *The Encyclopedia of Common Diseases*. Emmaus, PA: Rodale Press, 1976.
4. Ellen Ruppel Shell. "Does Civilization Cause Asthma," *The Atlantic Monthly*, May 2000.

5. C. Edward Burtis. *Nature's Miracle Medicine Chest*. New York: Arco Publishing, 1974.

6. *The Atlantic Monthly*, May 2000.

7. *Lung Health* 5, No. 3. Cited in Jane E. Brody. "Study Finds Stunted Lungs in Young Smokers," *New York Times*, September 26, 1996.

8. Staff of *Prevention* magazine. *Encyclopedia of Common Disease*. Emmaus, PA: Rodale Press, 1976.

9. Pete Billac. *The Silent Killer*. Alvin, TX: Swan Publishing, 2000.

10. Carl Stough and Reece Stough. *Dr. Breath: the Story of Breathing Coordination*. The Stough Institute, 1981.

Chapter 10

1. Michael A. Weiner. *Maximum Immunity*. New York: Pocket Books, 1987.

2. Dale Alexander. "A Commonsense Approach to Arthritis," *Price-Pottenger Nutrition Foundation Journal* 17, Nos. 3 and 4, December 1993.

3. *Texas Report on Biology and Medicine* 8, No. 3 (Fall 1950). Cited in *Encyclopedia of Common Diseases*.

4. J. P. Seegmitten. *Gout*. Grine and Statton, 1967.

5. The staff of *Prevention* magazine. *Encyclopedia of Common Diseases*. Emmaus, PA: Rodale Press, 1976.

6. I. S. Klemes, M.D. *Industrial Medicine and Surgery*, June 1957. Cited in *Encyclopedia of Common Diseases*.

7. A. F. Coburn, et al. "Effects of Egg Yolk in Diets on Anaishulatic Arthritis in the Guinea Pig," *Journal of Experimental Medicine*, 1954.

Chapter 11

1. Walter Pierpaoli, Ph.D., and William Regelson, M.D. *The Melatonin Miracle*. New York: Pocket Books, 1995.

2. The staff of *Prevention* magazine. *Encyclopedia of Common Diseases*. Emmaus, PA: Rodale Press, 1976.

3. Ray Peat, "The Transparency of Life: Cataracts as a Model of Age-Related Disease," in *Ray Peat's Newsletter*, 1996.

4. Symposium of the Biological Effects and Health Implications of Microwave Radiation, September 1969. Cited in *Encyclopedia of Common Diseases*.

5. Dr. Michele Virno. *Eye, Ear, Nose, and Throat*. Cited in *Encyclopedia of Common Diseases*.

6. *New York Times*, March 10, 1988.

7. Ross Trattler, M.D. *Better Health Through Natural Healing*. New York: McGraw-Hill Company, 1985.

Chapter 12

1. *New York Times*, December 1976.

2. Denise Grady. "Cell Transplants Offer Hope for Severe Cases of Diabetes," *New York Times*, December 1999.

3. Denise Grady. "Diabetes Rises: Doctors Foresee a Harsh Impact," *New York Times*, August 24, 2000.

4. John Ellis, M.D. "Diabetes New Therapies," *Price-Pottenger Nutrition Foundation Health Journal*, Fall 1995.

Chapter 13

1. Joyce and Richard Wolkomir. "When Bandogs Howle and Spirits Walk," *Smithsonian*, January 2000.

Chapter 14

1. Robert Dudley, *Discover*, June 2000. Cited in Josie Glausiusz. "Homo Intoxicatus," *R&D News of Science, Medicine, and Technology*.

2. Roger Williams, M.D. *Nutrition Against Disease*. New York: Bantam Books, 1978.

Chapter 15

1. Reported by Bertrand and Vladesco to the French Academy of Science in 1921. Cited in *Encyclopedia of Common Diseases.*

2. K. M. Pirke and P. Doerr. "Age-Related Changes in Free Plasma Testosterone, Dihydrotestosterone, and Oestradiol," *Acta Endocrine* (Copenhagen) 89 (1975): 171–178.

3. J. M. Holland and C. Lee. "Effects of Pituitary Grafts on Testosterone-Stimulated Growth of Rat Prostate," *Biology Reproduction* 22 (1980): 351–357.

4. Erik Ask-Upmark, M.D. "On New Treatment of Prostatitis," *Grana Palynologica*. Cited in *Encyclopedia of Common Diseases.*

5. H. M. Feinblatt, M.D., and J. C. Gant, M.D. *Journal of the Maine Medical Association.*

6. *New York Times*, March 17, 1995.

Chapter 16

1. "Interview with Dr. William Donald Kelley." *Healthview Newsletter* 1, No. 5, 1977.

2. Jane E. Brody. "Hormone Replacement Therapy: Weighing Risks and Benefits," *New York Times*, July 7, 1998.

3. Lippschuts, *Steroids and Tumors*, 1950. Cited in Ray Peat, Ph.D., *Nutrition for Women*. Eugene, OR: self-published, 1993.

4. K. U. Toverud. "Studies of the Mineral Metabolism During Pregnancy and Lactation," Norsk Mag. *Laegevidenskap* 91 (1930): 53, 286.

5. "Boost Infants' Memory with Choline," *Greatlife*, February 2001. (Study author, Steven H. Zeisel, M.D.)

6. Sharon Begley. "Shaped by Life in the Womb," *Newsweek*, September 27, 1999.

7. Lawrence K. Altman. "High Level of Insulin Linked to Breast Cancer Advance," *New York Times*, May 24, 2000. (The study was carried out at Mount Sinai hospital of the University of Toronto and the findings were presented to the American Society of Clinical Oncology.)

8. "Prevent Breast Cancer by Breast-Feeding," *New York Post*, January 31, 2001.

9. Associated Press. "Study Links Use of Caffeine to Higher Risk of Miscarriage," *New England Journal of Medicine*, December 21, 2000.

BIBLIOGRAPHY

Aceves, J., and H. King. 1978. *Cultural Anthropology*. Morristown, NJ: General Learning Press.

Aihara, Herman. 1986. *Acid and Alkaline*. Oroville, CA: George Ohsawa Macrobiotic Foundation.

Anglesey, Debby. 1997. *Battling the MSG Myth*. Kennewick, WA: Front Porch Productions.

Bechamp, E. 1912. *The Blood and Its Third Anatomical Element*. London: John Ouseley Limited.

Billac, Pete. 1999. *The Silent Killer*. Alvin, TX: Swan Publishing.

Braverman, E., M.D,. and C. Pfeiffer, M.D. 1987. *The Healing Nutrients Within*. New Canaan, CT: Keats Publishing Inc.

Carper, Jean. 1993. *Food—Your Miracle Medicine*. New York: Harper-Collins Publishers.

Cawod, Frank. 1986. *Vitamin Side Effects Revealed*. Peachtree City, GA: Banta Company.

Coca, Arthur. 1994. *The Pulse Test*. New York: St. Martin's Press.

Colbin, Annemarie. 1996. *Food and Healing*. New York: Ballantine Books.

Crichton, Michael, M.D. 1989. *Five Patients*. New York: Ballantine Books.

D'Adamo, Peter, N.D. 1996. *Eat Right For Your Type*. New York: G. P. Putnam's Sons.

Erasmus, Udo. 1993. *Fats That Heal, Fats That Kill*. Burnaby, BC, Canada: Alive Books.

Fredericks, Carlton, Ph.D. 1988. *Psycho-Nutrition*. New York: Berkley Books.

"Phillipus Paracelsus." 1967. *Funk & Wagnalls*. New York: Standard Reference Works.

Gerson, Max, M.D. 1999. *A Cancer Therapy*. Bonita, CA: Gerson Institute.

Hagglund, Howard, M.D. 1989. *BioBalance*. Hurricane, Utah: Essential Science Publishing.

Hallman, Rick. 2000. *The Living Environment Biology*. New York: Amsco School Publications.

Howell, Edward, M.D. 1985. *Enzyme Nutrition*. Wayne, NJ: Avery Publishing Group.

Kraus, David. 1995. *Modern Biology*. New York: Globe Book Company.

Langer, Stephen E., M.D., and James F. Scheer. 1984. *Solved: The Riddle of Illness*. New Canaan, CT: Keats Publishing.

Matsen, John, N.D. 1987. *The Mysterious Cause of Illness*. Canfield, OH: Fischer Publishing Corporation.

McGarey, William A. 1981. *Edgar Cayce and the Palma Christi*. Virginia Beach, VA: Edgar Cayce Foundation.

Morrison, Marsh. 1978. *Research Report*. Cottage Grove, OR: Ecology Improvement Press, Inc.

Newbold. 1991. *Dr. Newbold's A Type B Type Weight Loss Book*. New Canaan, CT: Keats Publishing Inc.

Payer, Lynn. 1988. *Medicine and Culture*. New York: Henry Holt and Company.

Peat, Ray, Ph.D. 1993. *Nutrition for Women*. Eugene, OR: self-published.

———. 1993. *Progesterone in Orthomolecular Medicine*. Eugene, OR: self-published.

———. 1994. *Generative Energy*. Eugene, OR: self-published.

———. 1994. *Mind and Tissue*. Eugene, OR: self-published.

Philpott, William H., M.D. 1998. *Magnetic Health Enhancement*. Midwest City, OK: self-published.

Pierpaoli, Walter, M.D., and William Regelson, M.D. 1995. *The Melatonin Miracle*. New York: Pocket Books.

Sahelian, Ray, M.D. 1995. *Melatonin*. Marina Del Ray, CA: Be Happier Press.

Schmidt, Michael A. 1997. *Smart Fats*. Berkeley, CA: Frog, Ltd. C/o North Atlantic Books.

Shute, Wilfrid E. 1974. *Vitamin E for Ailing and Healthy Hearts*. New York: Pyramid Books.

The staff of *Prevention* magazine. 1976. *The Encyclopedia of Common Diseases*. Emmaus, PA: Rodale Press.

Tips, Jack, Ph.D. 1998. *Your Liver . . . Your Lifeline*. Austin, TX: Apple-A-Day Press.

Trattler, Ross, M.D. 1985. *Better Health Through Natural Healing*. New York: McGraw-Hill Company.

Twentyman, Ralph. 1992. *The Science and Art of Healing*. Edinburgh: Floris Books.

Walker, N., D.Sc. 1978. *Become Younger*. Prescott, AZ: Norwalk Press.

Walker, N., D.Sc. 1978. *Fresh Vegetable and Fruit Juices*. Prescott, AZ: Norwalk Press.

Whang, Sang. 1990. *Reverse Aging*. Miami, FL: JSP Publishing.

Weiner, Michael. 1987. *Maximum Immunity*. New York: Pocket Books.

Williams, Roger, M.D. 1978. *Nutrition Against Disease*. New York: Bantam Books.

Wilson, Denis, M.D. 1996. *Wilson's Syndrome*. Orlando, FL: Cornerstone Publishing Company.

Wolcott, William. 2000. *The Metabolic Typing Diet*. New York: Doubleday.

INDEX

ABOUT THE AUTHOR

Starting out as a teacher in the inner city, Felicia Kliment was determined to find out what caused the learning disabilities and behavioral disorders in the children she taught. She found the answer when, as a faculty member at City College, she and a colleague conducted a research study that documented the adverse effect of processed food on schoolchildren.

This study, along with her own personal experience, consultations, and study of Chinese medicine and modern chemistry, caused her to come to the startling conclusion on which this book is based. Kliment's numerous articles on alternative medicine have been published in academic journals and popular magazines.